BARBAROUS SOULS

DAVID L. STRAUSS

AFTERWORD BY STEVEN A. DRIZIN

D0093990

NORTHWESTERN UNIVERSITY PRESS
EVANSTON, ILLINOIS

Northwestern University Press
www.nupress.northwestern.edu

Copyright © 2010 by David L. Strauss. Afterword copyright © 2010 by Steven A. Drizin. Published 2010 by Northwestern University Press. All rights reserved.

Printed in the United States of America

10 9 8 7 6 5 4 3 2 1

Library of Congress Cataloging-in-Publication Data

Strauss, David L.
    Barbarous souls / David L. Strauss ; afterword by Steven A. Drizin.
      p. cm.
    ISBN 978-0-8101-2671-8 (pbk. : alk. paper)
    1. Parker, Darrel F.—Trials, litigation, etc. 2. Trials (Murder)—Nebraska—
Lancaster County. 3. Judicial error—Nebraska—Lancaster County. 4. Confession
(Law)—Psychological aspects. I. Drizin, Steven A. II. Title.
KF224.P36S77 2010
364.152'3092—dc22
                               2010010409

CONTENTS

AUTHOR'S NOTE

Barbarous Souls is written in a style that is popularly described as a nonfiction novel. My sources are the trial transcript, newspaper accounts of the day, and oral histories from Darrel Parker, Judge Thomas McManus, Virgil Falloon, and the late Stanley Cohen. All of the incidents actually occurred, although some of the conversations are conjectural and were added for the sake of the narrative.

BARBAROUS SOULS

CHAPTER ONE

At the very edge of the broad and fertile great plains in the southeastern corner of Nebraska stands Lincoln, the sedate, red-bricked, and rigidly straitlaced state capital. Founded in 1867, Lincoln lies a little more than fifty miles from Omaha at a point south of the Platte River where the flat agricultural lands to the west have gradually turned into rolling hills that carry eastward, all the way to the Iowa border and the rugged bluffs of the Missouri River valley. Sprawled haphazardly in a large shallow bowl, the few whitewashed frame buildings that made up Lincoln at its inception once stood in stark contrast to the imposing horizontal landscape and were clearly visible for miles around. At a time when lush prairie grasses were the dominant feature in an otherwise barren tableau, the expansive and unimpeded vistas that spread beneath the dome of a broad and seemingly endless sky made the tiny city's existence seem even more tenuous than it really was. Trees were a rarity and existed almost entirely along creek banks and rivers in the form of cottonwoods, willows, and locusts. As testament to the scarcity of trees in Lincoln's early days, a giant lone elm stood sentinel near what would later become known as Haymarket Square. It was such a novelty that it served as the landmark and focal point for the early merchants and barterers who gathered to trade beneath its soothing shade. As settlers slowly populated the area, they began an arboreal tradition that became virtually self-perpetuating—planting a magnificent array of trees along their streets and alleyways and in their parks.

After the turn of the century, the city watched with eager anticipation as the ten-year construction of the new state capitol building progressed—a structure that would come to dominate the skyline and eventually overshadow what had previously been the town's tallest structures, the towering white grain elevators that skirted the city's perimeter. When the mighty building was at last complete and people could ascend to the dizzying heights of its forty-story observation level, they were immediately struck by the ocean of trees that undulated outward in windswept waves to the horizon in all directions—oak, ash, walnut, elm, maple, poplar, mulberry, spruce, locust, cedar, white pine, Scotch pine, birch, Austrian pine, and on and on. The soil was superb. Moisture was excellent. Lincoln and Lancaster County enjoyed the perfect climate to grow not only a host of crops but also an ever expanding plenitude of trees.

After World War II, Lincoln's population swelled to more than one hundred thousand people as soldiers returned in droves to enroll at the university, buy new automobiles, and purchase homes, all on the G.I. Bill. Many thought the times were golden. As Lincoln's first mass-produced suburbs expanded outward, mostly to the south and east, so did the attendant profusion of trees. It only followed that in 1954 the city's park department finally saw the need to hire its first full-time city forester.

A shy, studious, and athletic twenty-three-year-old Iowan, Darrel Parker was hired for the position of Lincoln city forester right out of college. He had been highly recommended for the job by Harold McNabb, his favorite professor at the widely acclaimed School of Forestry at Iowa State University. Raised in Lincoln himself, McNabb still had many connections there, enough that his glowing recommendation of Parker carried considerable weight.

Darrel had tenaciously worked his way to the very top of his class, and by the time he graduated he knew that the decision he'd made as a high school senior to go into forestry had been the right one. McNabb, for his part, knew that Darrel's diligence, self-discipline, and healthy work ethic would see him through any challenge. Of all his students, Parker was the man McNabb felt was best suited for the job in Lincoln. Yet, despite the attraction of the job, despite it being what he termed "just the right thing at just the right time," if Darrel could somehow have known what lay in store for him in Lincoln, he would have never left Iowa. But then one can never know such things.

Anchored solidly in the soil, like the trees he studied, Darrel had grown up on the family farm in the rich Corn Belt of western Iowa near Henderson, a small rural town of 207 staunchly resolute residents. About equidistant from Shenandoah and Council Bluffs, Henderson was, in a direct line, not much more than twenty miles east of the Missouri River. Darrel's family had lived on the same farm his entire life. He knew nothing other than rock-ribbed midwestern country life, and as a boy he didn't want to know anything else. The bounty of nature. The change of seasons—planting, harvesting. He was steeped in the tradition of farming and was boundlessly happy in his world.

His father, Lynn Parker, had maintained the hope that his boys—Darrel had an older brother, Dwight—would one day take over the farming duties. He'd even purchased a second farm with the idea that one day each son would have his own place. His dream was for naught. Dwight would never farm. For him the only anchor of rural life was around his leg. He felt that country life was much too circumscribed, too isolated from the rest of the world. Shortly after graduating from high school he moved to Wichita, Kansas, to work at the thriving Boeing airplane plant, where the primary aircraft being built was the B-47, the country's first mass-produced jet-powered strategic bomber.

That left Darrel as the sole heir to carry on the family tradition, and he accepted the role willingly. As a child he eagerly shadowed his father around the farm. In the spring at planting time, he proudly rode on the tractor beside his father and marveled at the huge flock of gulls that always seemed to appear from nowhere to follow along behind the planter, rising and falling in the air like the raging white water of a mountain river as they gorged themselves on upturned insects and worms. At harvest time in the fall, the gulls mysteriously disappeared only to be replaced by dozens of red-tailed hawks that wheeled gracefully in tight circles high in the air, waiting to drop unseen onto the rabbits and mice that scurried up and down the rows in the corn picker's wake.

Like any young boy, Darrel wanted to be just like his father. In his mind, as well as his father's, moving into his father's shoes was the natural order of things—a farm was gradually built up for the younger generation, who would then take over and repeat the cycle.

At the age of fifteen, Darrel took his first and only trip away from home, to the rugged mountains of Wyoming with the local 4-H youth group. It was his first experience of being "out there," of coming up against the great American expanse that existed in all directions beyond Mills County, Iowa.

His dreams of farming, of an inherited life in agriculture, however, came long before his childhood asthma had developed to the point that it was aggravated by virtually all of the dusts and pollens, flora and fauna, that were omnipresent on the farm. By the time he'd reached high school he was made painfully aware of the fact, as much to the disappointment of his father as to himself, that his lifelong imaginings of continued life on the farm had vanished.

At the same time he had to divest himself of his childhood dreams, his life apart from the family farm had become ever more active and gave anyone who observed him an inkling of a life about to bloom and move in a new direction. He was an established fixture at church—at one point having gone for three years without missing a service. A recognized voice in the choir, he was often called upon to solo and also, aware of the considerable responsibility placed in his hands, solemnly taught Sunday school. His many years of activity in 4-H had prepared him for life at Henderson High School, where he excelled at basketball, participated in student government, and was the valedictorian of his senior class. Reverend Peter Trucano, pastor of Wesley Chapel Church, the Parkers' church, remembered Darrel as the most responsible member of his class: "He worked hard, was always on the fair side, avoided conflict, and was honest to a fault. He respected authority, and he respected his elders. He was a good boy, a model boy."

By the time he graduated from high school Darrel had traveled out of the state only one time. With the prodding of his older brother, however, Darrel had become a young man ready to leave the security of the rural island he'd known all his life. Based on his love of the outdoors and with the help and advice of his senior class teacher, he chose forestry as his vocation. They both thought it would allow him to continue working outside and at the same time nurture things as they grew. Iowa State University in Ames, a little more than a hundred miles away and renowned for its forestry program, was the logical choice.

When he first arrived on campus, Darrel was struck by the intimidating enormity of the university but calmed himself with the knowledge that his ethic of hard work and perseverance would carry him through. Along with one of his high school classmates he joined a fraternity, where he gradually overcame his innate shyness and became an officer—subsequently "meeting more people in my first year than I had known in my entire life in Henderson."

When his fraternity brothers discovered that Darrel's major was forestry, he was constantly harassed and made the butt of jokes because of his middle name—Forest, not with two r's but one. "You can't see the Forest for the trees . . . If a tree falls in the Forest . . ." He didn't mind the ribbing; it made him feel accepted, made him feel like one of the guys. He had reached out and found his place, knew that in spite of his homespun rural childhood he'd found his niche, had made the right choice and would surely succeed.

Along with his academic accomplishments Darrel's social life likewise sparkled. Early in his second year he accepted his first blind date, arranged on the spur of the moment by one of his older fraternity brothers. The evening of the date Darrel was nervous and unexpectedly anxious, exhibiting all the attendant predate jitters. Any apprehension he had quickly melted away when he was introduced to his date, Nancy Ellen Morrison of Des Moines. Enamored from the outset, Darrel uncharacteristically spoke up and asked for another date that very evening. And then another and another. Nancy's buoyant, outgoing personality, he felt, was the perfect antidote for his sober and retiring ways. Nancy was equally taken by Darrel, with his sharply hewn features, short brown hair, high forehead, and serene, yet deeply brilliant blue eyes. To her friends Nancy described Darrel's shyness and restrained demeanor as reflective of "a very mature personality."

She was a year behind Darrel, but that made no difference to either of them. From their first date forward, they had become a pair. Neither of them dated anyone else. By his senior year, ready to take the next step out in the world, Darrel proposed marriage and Nancy readily accepted. They were married in Des Moines on March 20, 1954, by Reverend Duane Ferris—the newspaper quoted him as saying, "I've never wed a happier couple. They are deeply in love, and I'm sure their love will be just as strong in twenty years as it is today."

Their delayed honeymoon came the following summer when they took a fun-filled one-week excursion to Nancy's beloved Black Hills of South Dakota, a place where she'd worked the summer after her freshman year. Her souvenir of the trip was a foot-high ceramic doll of Smokey the Bear that Darrel purchased in the gift shop at Sylvan Lake Lodge. Upon her return she displayed the figure with girlish pride on her dresser, never for a moment considering that it might be too childish.

After graduation Darrel took a short-term summer job as an assistant with the School of Forestry as part of a student team conducting a tree survey throughout the state of Iowa, mapping the location, species, and phylum of the trees that populated the state from east to west and north to south.

When that job was complete, Professor McNabb informed Darrel of the opening for a forester in Lincoln, Nebraska. His application was promptly submitted, along with McNabb's glowing recommendation, and he was quickly accepted to begin work on November 15, 1954. In Lincoln, Darrel rented a small, sparsely furnished basement apartment while Nancy finished school at Iowa State. They saw each other whenever possible on weekends and talked long and often on the telephone about how exciting it was going to be to set up house in Lincoln and be together again once Nancy graduated.

Darrel was enamored of his new position, and after his experiences at Iowa State he quickly learned to fit in with his new workmates. He was originally unsure of how he would be accepted as a young supervisor, but those under him liked him to a man, even though most of them were twenty or thirty years his senior. His likable demeanor, equanimity, and willingness to roll up his sleeves and take part alongside his men in whatever job was undertaken made him an immediate success.

With Nancy still in Ames, Darrel made it a point to fill his spare time with innumerable activities outside of work. He was asked to join the junior chamber of commerce, where he resumed his musical interests as a member of the choir; he put on regular after-hours informational meetings for his men, covering every aspect of the care and maintenance of the city's trees; he traveled occasionally to forestry seminars held throughout the Midwest; and he began selectively shopping for inexpensive household items for their future residence. In his work he felt fulfilled. In fact, for the first time in his life he felt that he was truly master of his own ship.

When Nancy excitedly arrived from Iowa in the early summer of 1955, Darrel could no longer keep his secret from her. She expected that they would continue to live in the dank basement apartment, but Darrel surprised her with the news that they were going to get their own house in Antelope Park, a fringe benefit of Darrel's job. James Ager, head of the park department, was going to move an older frame house that dated from the 1930s out of a low-lying area in the park and onto a site near the city's dance pavilion and have it renovated for Darrel and Nancy. He told Darrel it would be just like Europe, where public park superintendents lived in keepers' lodges in the same parks they took care of. Darrel didn't know about that, but nonetheless he was excited about the prospect of having their own home and one that would be a convenient half mile from park headquarters.

The two were giddy at their prospects. They were so happy that at times they felt things were going almost too well, that something had to go wrong just to balance things out. But those feelings did not linger. Nearly every evening after work they would drive by the homesite to check on the latest progress. Their house would be the first and only home in Antelope Park. The only thing comparable was James Ager's house that sat near park headquarters, the zoo, and the garages in the administrative part of the park on the north side of A Street. Darrel liked the fact that their house would be isolated and said it would be as close as you could get in the city to living on a farm—"where your nearest neighbor was a mile or more away and you're right next to nature." Only in this case nature would be the park rather than the green pastures, tree-lined windbreaks, and rolling cornfields of Iowa.

The largest part of Antelope Park, more than a hundred acres, spread out on the south side of A Street and ran between the Rock Island railroad tracks that bounded it on the west and Normal Boulevard and Antelope Creek to the east. Their home would sit on a slight rise two blocks east of the tracks and at the southeast corner of the dance pavilion parking lot. The pavilion, a large white framed affair, had tall arched windows on three sides and saw spotty use by various groups—the square dance and polka crowd used it in the fall and winter, and in the spring and summer the teenagers took it over with the latest craze, rock-and-roll music, and their weekend Keen Time dances. The homesite was bounded on three sides with a cluster of honey locusts that continued down the slope in the backyard to the creek. On the south side of the lot stood a tall, thick hedge that paralleled Sumner Street and ran east from the concrete wall of the massive pavilion entrance pylon to a point even with the back of the house.

After ground was broken, every step of the progress was noted by Nancy and hastily recorded on a calendar in their kitchen. The work never seemed to proceed fast enough to suit Darrel and Nancy, even though it never varied more than a few days from Ager's closely monitored construction schedule. On weekends they continued Darrel's habit of going to sales, where they carefully and frugally selected an eclectic assortment of furniture and appliances. They purchased an oak coffee table with only one small scratch on it, a corner chair for the living room with a matching footstool, and a pair of card tables for impromptu entertaining. A "like new" brown couch, upholstered with the glittery metallic looped fabric of the day, completed their living room ensemble. Finalizing their furnishings was another surprise presentation by Darrel—a bookcase and dining table that he built while Nancy was in Ames, constructing them bit by painstaking bit during his off hours in the shop at park headquarters.

The day they'd been anxiously awaiting came in late July, when the house was moved all at once onto the foundation and the final phase of remodeling began in earnest. The modest house was a twenty-four by thirty-two, one of a myriad of standardized houses built across the country for decades. When you walked in the front door there was a living room to the right, a kitchen and dining room behind that, and to the left two bedrooms—one slightly larger than the other—and a bathroom. The exterior of the house was painted white, the storm window frames were painted black, and, in its only departure from the standard design, the attic had been enlarged with the addition of dormers built on either side of the gable roof, each with two double-hung windows. Seen from the front—the side that faced the pavilion parking lot, the house was perfectly symmetrical—three double-hung windows on the north side of the front door in their bedroom and three more to the south in the living room. The dormers were centered on the roof and the front door perfectly centered between them all. When the house was nearly complete at the end of September, Nancy purchased sheer white lace drapery material and made drapes to cover the pull-down shades in every room.

They glowed in their achievements. Darrel had a job that was beyond anything he'd ever imagined, and Nancy had just begun working as a dietician for Gooch's Flour Mills, where she and another lady, Opal Closner, created a diversity of recipes that always used Gooch's flour and noodles. After the recipes were successfully tested, they would be printed on the bags of Gooch's flour and noodles and sold throughout the Midwest. She had also begun demonstrating her cooking skills on the city's first televised cooking show presented live on KOLN-TV, Channel 10.

They felt independently wealthy with the house, two incomes, and two cars—Darrel's tan and white 1953 Chevy and Nancy's new white Chevy station wagon, given to her by Gooch's. "Not bad for two kids," said Darrel. That's how they felt about each other, like they were still in college, still kids. The things they had achieved in the adult world in such a short time had come so fast that they were still being digested, still had a bit of the unreal about them.

The house was ready as scheduled by early October, and on the thirteenth they moved in. Darrel borrowed one of the park's pickup trucks, and he and Warren Andrews, his cohort from work, moved the few pieces of furniture they had stored in the park garage. By evening all of the drapes were mounted, all of the appliances moved in, all of the clothes hung in the closets. For their first night in the house Nancy cooked a full-course steak dinner, which they ate by candlelight and finished off with lemon meringue pie. When supper was over they washed the dishes together, laughingly toasted each other with glasses of 7-Up, and toured the house—each carrying a candle—in celebration of their youthful good fortune.

Once she'd settled in, Nancy eagerly began crafting decorations for Halloween, what she looked at as her first chance to entertain. When the day finally arrived, Nancy had stocked a huge supply of candy. Darrel observed, "We're so far from the other houses in the neighborhood, we'll be lucky if any kids come." The nearest house, the Seacrest mansion, was a block away on the south side of Sumner. Sitting on more than two acres of land, the big house dominated the other homes in the area and reminded Darrel of pictures he'd seen of Mount Vernon with its tall white entrance columns going straight up two stories, right to the overhanging porch roof. Behind the columns a huge black entrance light was suspended above the portico and anchored from blowing in the wind by long swooping chains. The Seacrest family owned one of the two Lincoln newspapers, the *Lincoln Evening Journal*. Their house, however, would not be open to trick-or-treaters this year. It would be dark and empty for Halloween due to a lengthy remodeling job that had been going on since late summer.

On Halloween, Darrel came home early to help Nancy prepare for the evening. After lighting the candle in the pumpkin he'd carved, he placed it on the front porch step next to the black wrought iron railing. He turned on the outside lights and all the lights in the kitchen and living room. The brilliant illumination, he thought, would surely compensate for the isolation of their house and the ghostly effect it might otherwise impart if it was left unlit. As a result of their joint efforts they were visited by nine little tricksters who came to the door in a colorful if not very frightening array of homemade costumes. In their hands they clutched brown grocery sacks that were nearly as big as they were. Nancy laughed uncontrollably while generously dishing out the candy. Darrel sat on the couch wistfully musing over who was having more fun, Nancy or the children. She loved kids; they both did. In fact they'd talked repeatedly about when would be the right time to have children of their own. They decided, since they had the stability of Darrel's job and their new home, to start trying immediately. Their newfound sense of permanence and confidence in the future had spurred them to begin making long-term plans. Nancy's homemaking instincts would now be turned to the northeast bedroom, the baby's room. Darrel, in idle moments, began sketching a set of dresser drawers that, once complete, he would translate into stained and varnished pine capable of accommodating all of the baby's clothes.

The first opportunity to show off the new residence to their friends was belatedly scheduled for Sunday, November 13. They invited Darrel's coworkers and their wives along with Mr. and Mrs. Ager to a good old-fashioned housewarming. Nancy made a huge batch of fried chicken, coated, of course, with Gooch's flour, and completed the other end of the meal with a top-laced cherry cobbler. Each couple brought their own contribution, assigned by Nancy to round out the menu. The kitchen table was turned into a buffet for the bounty, with everyone, once served, seated in the living room at the two card tables. Everything worked out according to plan. In Nancy's eyes it couldn't have been more perfect. The dinner started a little before 5:00 and ended at 7:00. The visitors extolled Nancy's cooking prowess and praised the couple for turning the "old house" into a comfortable and inviting new home.

When the meal was over, Warren Andrews and his wife remained behind after the others left and helped straighten the house. When the kitchen was cleared, Warren asked Darrel if he and Nancy would like to go to his house and watch television. They quickly agreed, happy to end the evening with their new friends. They went to the Andrews', watched *Playhouse 90,* and returned to the park a little after 10:00.

When they arrived home and entered the kitchen, they were shocked to see broken glass scattered on the dining room floor. The drapes were blowing in the wind from the broken window, and the dining table had been shoved aside by whoever had climbed in. As they walked through the house they found neatly piled mounds of items laid out on their bed, dresser, and kitchen counter—a shaver, a pair of ear muffs, books of green stamps, and a few sweaters. Not much because they didn't have much to steal. In addition to the items left out, Darrel noticed that one of the shades facing the parking lot in their bedroom had been raised six inches, cracked enough for someone to see the driveway and overlooking the pavilion parking lot.

Darrel immediately called the police. When they arrived, one of the officers walked around the outside of the house shining his flashlight onto the ground and into the trees that surrounded the backyard, while the other officer talked to Darrel and Nancy. After inspecting the house he concluded that the prowler had been surprised by their arrival home. "He climbed in the dining room window," said the officer, stating the obvious, "and exited out the window in the northeast bedroom," leaving his almost stolen goods and his black boot marks on the wall behind. After spending a few more minutes circling the house, the policemen left. The Parkers would never hear from the police again regarding the attempted burglary.

The next night Darrel had his weekly choir practice. Concerned for Nancy, he asked if she would like to be dropped off at the Agers' while he sang, rather than stay home alone. Nancy told Darrel that she didn't mind staying home, she'd "be all right." She wanted to get used to being there, she insisted, while Darrel was gone. Upon his arrival home Darrel found the Agers sitting with Nancy in the living room. Nancy had heard noises and called Jim. Jim told Darrel that he had been meaning to put up a security fence around the house and he wouldn't delay any longer. He would have some of the men start on it first thing in the morning.

Tuesday morning, true to his word, Ager had a crew putting in six-foot metal fence posts around the backyard. Nancy had gone out early to thank the men for their work, and by the middle of the morning she reappeared with a batch of freshly made chocolate chip cookies at break time. As the men hastily devoured the plateful of cookies, one of them stood back at the outer edge of the group. He said nothing, did not thank her, did not talk with any of the other men, but watched the unfolding scene with vacant eyes.

And so it was that the man who had broken into the Parker house just two days before was working on the crew that put in the security fence. The fence that would secure nothing.

CHAPTER TWO

A dark undercurrent now shaded the lives of Darrel and Nancy Parker. They continued to call the police department to see if any progress had been made toward finding the burglar—surely there weren't that many burglars in a town the size of Lincoln. They second-guessed their decision to move into the isolated house. Nancy wanted to suggest that they move into another home in the area where they'd have plenty of neighbors, but she didn't mention it to Darrel. Where else could they find a nearly rent-free home?

They did, however, agree on one thing they thought might make their life more secure—a guard dog. After visiting the dog pound several times, they selected a peppy mixed collie-shepherd puppy that was no more than two months old. Rudy was going to be the presence that, when mature, would eventually protect them and the house. He became the recipient of excessive affection, and when he grew up Darrel and Nancy were certain he would make the perfect watchdog. But Rudy would not be able to grow fast enough.

For Thanksgiving Nancy's parents came from Des Moines and Darrel's parents from the farm. Rudy was the hit of the party, and everyone delighted as he persistently dragged slippers and shoes around the house. Nancy and the two mothers prepared an enormous Thanksgiving dinner with both of the mothers defer-ring—perhaps at times reluctantly—to Nancy. In some ways it was a generational changing of the guard. When it was over Darrel thought it was the nicest Thanksgiving dinner he'd ever had. His mother always prepared a good enough dinner, but she never seemed to really enjoy it as Nancy did, always seemed to treat it like it was some sort of military drill, something to get done and out of the way. After dinner Darrel and his father engaged in a spirited game of pitch with the Morrisons. Mr. Parker seemed to genuinely enjoy the frivolity, which was a pleasant surprise to Darrel, for his father, like his mother, was never one to engage in something that could be too much fun.

In the wake of their parents' departure, Nancy talked with Darrel about how they should spend their Christmas—go to her family's house, travel to his parents' farm, or remain in Lincoln and spend their first Christmas together in their own home? Darrel gave it serious thought and finally said that he would just as soon stay home for Christmas and visit their parents on New Year's Day. Nancy happily agreed. There was something exciting to both of them about the prospect of spending their first Christmas together away from their parents. Another belated affirmation of their adulthood. Yes, that's what they would do.

Over the next two weeks Nancy spent her spare time shopping for Christmas presents. Her job was flexible. The hours she put in at Gooch's were up to her and Opal Closner as long as she took care of the television show and their recipe creations. It gave her time to shop during the week so that she didn't have to try to jam all her Christmas shopping into Thursday night, the one night during the week when the stores stayed open late, or on Saturdays when everyone crazily crowded into the stores all at once. But then she was always good about being prepared for any event well ahead of time, always organized. It was like life was one big recipe for her. If you had good ingredients, if the parts were prepared properly, and you followed directions, then whatever the undertaking it would succeed.

By the second weekend of December they had gotten into the Christmas spirit full swing. They bought decorations, installed a huge wreath on the front door, and purchased a ceiling-high Christmas tree that Darrel deposited in the basement, hydrating in a bucket of water until they had time to decorate it. They were too busy to give any more thought to the break-in. The Christmas spirit had over-taken them, and their energy was now spent in anxious preparation for the holidays. The first big snows had hit just after Thanksgiving and hadn't melted. It would be a white Christmas, that much was certain.

Tuesday, December 13, was a month to the day since the break-in. It was a cold and blustery day with swirling snow and a temperature that never got out of the teens. When Darrel arrived home that evening, he turned his car around in the drifted snow at the bottom of the driveway and backed it up the long, sloping, rock-covered driveway to the house. He had to jump-start the car at work and knew he would have to do the same thing in the morning. His battery had unexpectedly died, and he planned to pick one up the next day when he had to go downtown to get the decorations that were to adorn the state Christmas tree at the capitol building.

Once inside the door, Darrel smelled Nancy's chicken-fried steak, mashed potatoes, cream-style corn, and apple pie—the smells coalesced in the air and immediately magnified his hunger. *Boy, could she cook,* he thought as he went into the bathroom to wash up. They rarely ate the same thing twice in one month, and when they did it was to clean up leftovers from the night before, which Darrel didn't mind because he thought her food often tasted better the second time around.

After supper they played with Rudy before settling into the evening's tasks. Nancy had a pile of Christmas cards to write and address, and she'd assigned Darrel the job of wrapping two large packages—plaid shirts for Nancy's father and a crocheted tablecloth for Darrel's parents. He got some wrapping twine and butcher paper from the kitchen pantry and set to work. At the outset he decided that a lengthwise cord crossed by two cords precisely at the third points would be more than adequate to secure the boxes. When he was done with his part of the bargain, he leaned the packages against the wall in the dining room for Nancy to address and went into the bathroom for a bath. Nancy stayed up another hour until she had completed the cards. When she finished she had a stack of seventeen cards that she would mail in the morning along with the packages. After piling the cards neatly in the center of the card table she went to bed. Rudy scampered after her and plopped on his blanket at the foot of the bed.

On the morning of Wednesday, December 14, the alarm went off at its usual time of 6:25. Darrel stirred but did not immediately get out of bed. He pulled the covers up and lay in bed half-asleep for several minutes, as was his normal routine. Nancy changed from her pajamas into her jeans and a sweatshirt, put her bobby socks and white Keds on, and went to the kitchen to prepare breakfast. It wasn't long before the smell of bacon and toast filled the air. When Darrel finally arose he took Rudy outside. He came back in at 6:50 and turned on the radio so they could listen to Don Rumbaugh's morning weather report that came on at 6:52 on KLMS. The report was the same as it had been the day before—three to four inches of new snow, a high in the teens, and more blustery overcast conditions that would make for additional drifting.

When the weather was over, they listened to the seven o'clock news as they finished their breakfast. Darrel mentioned that he was going to pick up the Christmas decorations and battery. Nancy said that she would mail the Christmas cards and packages and then do a little more Christmas shopping for her parents and her two aunts. She was an only child and had no nieces or nephews to buy presents for. When it was time to depart, Darrel kissed Nancy good-bye for what would be the last time and went to his car. He scraped the frost off the windshield, opened the door, and put the key in the ignition so that it would be ready to start once he was rolling down the drive. With a hurried wave to Nancy he slowly pushed the Chevy on its way. Halfway down the drive he jumped in, put the transmission in second gear, turned the key, and popped the clutch. The tires firmly grabbed the rock drive and the engine immediately turned over. He made a slow turn out of the pavilion parking lot, making fresh tracks in the blowing snow, and headed toward park headquarters. As he turned west onto Sumner Street he did not notice the black Ford that sat at the curve behind him where Sumner curved south into Thirty-third Street a half block east of his house. Or, if he did see it, there was nothing about it that would cause him to remember it later.

It was still dark as Darrel made his way deliberately along Memorial Drive, the snow swirling in undulating wisps in his wake. He smiled as he drove, considering what he should buy Nancy for

Christmas—a cashmere sweater, a new purse? He leaned toward the sweater.

The eastern horizon had slowly started to brighten but not enough to appreciably lighten the darkly overcast sky. Darrel liked to arrive at work early and was always ten to fifteen minutes ahead of the 7:30 starting time. When he arrived at the office it was 7:20. Warren Andrews was already at his desk and about to leave for the stockroom, where the tree crew met every morning before going out to their appointed jobs. Darrel routinely went over the day's schedule with the men and reviewed any new assignments. The pair went to the stockroom together, where they met with Glenn Francisco, the foreman, and Bob Mays, Leon Snyder, and Glenn Suiker. When the meeting was over Darrel returned to the office, where he went over the accumulated correspondence from the day before. His desk was organized fastidiously, and he made it part of his daily routine to always finish his paperwork by 9:00 each morning so that he could get into the field and supervise his men. Dorothy Miille, the office secretary, usually arrived a little before 8:00, as did James Ager.

"Dorothy," said Darrel upon her arrival, "I have to go downtown this morning to pick up the Christmas decorations at the chamber of commerce. We're going to put them up at the capitol after lunch, and I have a half dozen volunteers to organize, so I doubt if I'll be back after lunch . . . While I'm down there I've also got to pick up a battery at Sears. I had to jump-start my car this morning, and if I have to keep pushing that thing around I'll have a heart attack!"

"Why do those batteries always seem to go dead in the winter?" mused Dorothy.

Once his desk was clear, Darrel checked out one of the park's International pickup trucks and headed downtown. He arrived at the chamber of commerce at 10:30, where he met with Kenneth McCaw, the president of the chamber, and his secretary, Lois Bogenrief. McCaw had sponsored Darrel's membership with the Junior Jaycees and they had become fast friends while singing in the choir. They went into the basement to retrieve the Christmas decorations and loaded them into the back of Darrel's truck, filling the entire bed. From there he went directly to Sears and purchased the battery for his car. He drove back to the park garage through an intensifying ground blizzard and met with Earl Jennings, the curmudgeonly park mechanic, who was in the shop slowly leafing through the pages of a grease-splotched parts manual.

"They said this would fit, Earl," said Darrel as he carefully placed the battery on the counter.

"Looks OK. I'll stick it in after lunch," replied Earl, quickly returning his gaze to the parts manual.

Darrel went outside, where he encountered Warren Andrews struggling to remove a taillight lens on one of the other pickups. It was a little before noon, but Darrel, after checking his watch, decided he had time to help Warren before he went home for lunch. He returned to the shop and reappeared with a larger screwdriver for Warren, who quickly removed the taillight lens and the burned-out lightbulb. They had the new bulb in and working by 12:00.

"Is the meeting still on for tonight?" Warren asked as Darrel got in his truck.

"Yeah, 7:00. Don't forget your forestry pamphlet," replied Darrel, as he backed into the driveway. He turned on the radio and cautiously drove down A Street as the snow continued to blow in gusts across the icy pavement in his path.

"It was announced today that Safeway's butchers threatened a strike unless they receive a wage increase and shorter hours similar to Hinky Dinky's agreement with their butchers."

Darrel switched the radio off as he drove past the city light plant that stood at the corner of A Street and Memorial Drive. He honked twice at a man eating his lunch by the window. The man waved back, holding his sandwich high in the air. As he rounded the curve just past the railroad underpass, Darrel glanced at the war memorial, a tall monolithic sculpture by Ellis Burman. It was a four-sided obelisk that depicted the soldiers of the four major wars the country had been involved in up to the time it was erected in 1936—the Revolutionary War, the Civil War, the Spanish-American War, and World War I.

He turned north off of Sumner and into the pavilion parking lot, passing between the two huge concrete pylons and the adjoining low walls that bracketed the entrance. From the blown-in tracks and the size of the drifts, it looked as though no one had been in or out of the lot since he'd left that morning. As he drove up the driveway he happened to notice that one of the shades in their bedroom was up about six inches, just as it had been after the November break-in. Once he'd parked by the back door he looked at Nancy's station wagon—the front door proclaiming, GOOCH'S BEST, FLOUR AND FEEDS. He was surprised by the fact that the windows were still frosted over and it appeared not to have been moved. He turned off the ignition.

Darrel got out of the truck deliberately and curiously peered up into the trees that surrounded the backyard. A flock of blackbirds was sitting in a scattershot formation on the limbs, motionless and silent. Normally they would be noisily raiding the bird feeder that Nancy had hung outside the dining room window. He started his key in the side door. The door was not latched and swung open with a slow creak. Darrel, vaguely alarmed, climbed the two steps that led up into the kitchen.

"Nancy?" he called quietly. There was no reply.

In the way that you can sense when there is someone else in a house even when you can't see them or hear them, Darrel felt just the opposite. To Darrel it didn't seem as if anyone was home.

He smelled the air and glanced at the stove. There was nothing cooking. A dish towel covered the loaded dish rack. A faint whimper rose from behind him. Darrel turned and looked under the roaster stand at the south end of the kitchen. He found Rudy lying flat on his stomach beneath the bottom shelf whining quietly. He grabbed the puppy and dragged him out.

"It's OK, Rudy," said Darrel, patting him gingerly. "What's-a matter, huh?"

Darrel moved slowly through the kitchen, carrying Rudy in his arms as he continued petting him softly behind the ears. On the counter he noted Nancy's purse with her wallet, checkbook, and the latest shopping convenience, credit cards, lying out. It wasn't like Nancy to leave the contents of her purse scattered about. His feet moved haltingly. He walked past the packages that Nancy was going to mail. They were still leaning against the dining room wall, unaddressed, exactly where Darrel had put them the night before. He didn't look at them, didn't notice that the larger of the two packages now had only one piece of twine remaining, the one that wrapped it lengthwise. He looked to his left into the living room. Nancy's Christmas cards were still stacked in a neat pile on the card table. Darrel moved ever slower. In the doorway to their bedroom, he stopped short. Someone was lying on the bed beneath their quilt. A pillow concealed the head. As he stood motionless staring at the bed, a gust of wind suddenly blew from the north, pressing against the house and causing it to creak and groan. In the silence, grains of snow could be heard lightly ticking against the window glass. The sheer draperies moved ever so slightly in the draft.

Darrel looked into the other bedroom, the baby's bedroom. A clothes bag was lying in disarray next to a hanger in the middle of the floor. He turned back.

"Nancy? Are you all right?"

Taking a step into the bedroom he turned to the right. He saw Nancy's glasses lying on the vanity beneath her Smokey the Bear figurine. Her jeans, neatly folded, lay on the floor with her socks on top and her Keds beside them. He took another step into the room.

"Nancy?" he asked in a whisper.

Moving closer to the bed, his hand moved shakily toward the pillow. He suddenly jerked the pillow away and, as he did so, his arm froze and his fingers tightly clenched the pillow.

"Oh, no . . . Ohhh, no. Nancy . . . what happened?" he said quietly, barely able to speak.

Before him lay his wife, strangled with a length of clothesline rope and a length of twine. Her entire head was morbidly discolored and swollen. She was nude with a bruised lip and a badly blackened eye. Her mouth was stuffed with handkerchiefs, and her arms were tied behind her back. Darrel raised the back of his hand to her cheek. The touch told him what he knew in his gut, she was dead.

"What happened?" he whispered again, as though she could still hear. In shock, he absentmindedly smoothed the sheet back over her face. The breath went out of him as he awkwardly placed the pillow beside her. Then he ran.

At a desk in front of a dirty double-hung window that overlooked Tenth Street in downtown Lincoln, a gray and balding man raised a half-eaten bologna sandwich next to a full cup of steaming coffee. He stared distantly out the second-story window of the red brick police department and dreamed of retirement as he watched the traffic lazily drift by on the street below, all moving one-way to the north.

"This one-way traffic's something else, isn't it, Ed," he yelled at the police dispatcher in the next room. "Do you think it's gonna last? Are there going to be more accidents, or less? I don't—" The telephone rang at his elbow. He answered it and without moving sat in silence.

"I see . . . yes," was his only reply as he wrote furiously on a legal pad. "We'll be right there . . . as fast as we can. Yes, sir."

Swiveling in his seat, he shouted at the dispatcher, "Send a black and white to 3200 Sumner, Ed! It's in Antelope Park next to the dance pavilion. Possible murder." He grabbed his hat and coat. "I'm on my way."

James Ager was also eating lunch when he received his call.

"I beg your pardon . . . you'll have to speak up. Of course, Darrel. Something's wrong with Nancy? Yes, I'll be right there . . . only a couple of minutes. I will . . . I'll hurry."

When Ager pulled into Darrel's driveway, Darrel was waiting in a frozen pose at the front stoop with one hand holding the storm door open and the other on the railing. Distraught, he grabbed Ager's arm and dragged him into the house. He went directly to the bedroom and, in tears, pointed to the bed. Ager lifted the pillow. He grimaced, knowing as Darrel did that Nancy was dead.

"Did you call the police? . . . a doctor?" Darrel nodded. "Then . . . that's all we can do. That's all we can do . . . I'm sorry, Darrel."

Ager led Darrel back into the living room where they sat heavily on the couch. Darrel put his head in his hands and began to cry hysterically.

A fire truck, with lights flashing and siren blaring, arrived first. Two firemen rushed through the front door. Ager pointed them toward the bedroom. Seconds later one of them returned to the living room.

"Why'd you do that?" he yelled at Darrel. "Why did you tie her up like that?"

"Leave him alone you dumb shit," Ager yelled. "He didn't do anything. He found her just like that a few minutes ago. It's his wife."

The fireman was retreating toward the bedroom when the resuscitation squad arrived.

"I don't think there's anything can be done, Bill," said the first fireman to the leader of the squad. "The body's back here in the bedroom if you want to take a look." The men awkwardly hauled their cumbersome equipment into the bedroom. Darrel continued to sob openly. Nancy was now a "body."

Another siren wailed mournfully, signaling the arrival of Detective Wise, the officer Darrel had talked to on the phone. Wise entered the living room reluctantly, removing his hat as a sign of respect in anticipation of what he knew he'd find. Ager had an arm gingerly around Darrel, who was pleading, "Why did they do that to Nancy, Jim? Who could do such an evil thing?" Ager pointed Wise toward the bedroom.

More cars drove up. A man with a doctor's bag, Dr. Rose, got out of one. Emergency lights reflected off the tree limbs, and finally the blackbirds who had begun cackling at the unfolding commotion below them took flight. After looking at the body, the doctor gave Darrel a small pill and handed Ager a bottle containing more of the sedatives. There was nothing he could do for Nancy other than pronounce her dead. After several more minutes Ager suggested to Darrel that they go to his house.

"We can't do anymore here, Darrel."

Detective Wise put a hand on Darrel's shoulder. "That's right, Darrel. You go with Mr. Ager. I'll make sure everything is taken care of here."

The house teemed with people as Ager and Darrel left. There were nearly twenty—police, firemen, and ambulance attendants, while on the front lawn there were now assembled a half dozen reporters. As Darrel and Ager left, the reporters stood in silence, a mute testament to the fact that Darrel was carrying a heavy burden. Without anyone telling them, they knew.

Wise entered the bedroom and waited in a corner near the closet while the ambulance attendants prepared to place Nancy on a gurney. She was wrapped unceremoniously in her own white bed sheet. Wise quickly surveyed the room, his eyes stopping at the statue of Smokey the Bear. What it must have meant to Nancy, he could only guess.

His gaze landed next on the picture of Nancy that sat on the opposite side of the vanity. Her short black hair was parted in the middle with a little more hair falling on the left side than the right. She had thick full lips with a wide smile that revealed flawless white teeth. Upon her nose rested glasses that bore the popular style of the day—wing-like protuberances at the outside top of clear plastic and silvered frames.

After the attendants loaded the body gingerly onto the gurney they began pushing it out of the bedroom and into the living room. As they slowly entered the living room, Chief of Detectives Gene Masters and Chief of Police Joe Carroll came in the front door and calmly took in the scene of controlled mayhem within the house. The two men were a nearly inseparable pair and had been since their days as beat patrolmen. It was said that in their younger and wilder days, on a bet, they had raced their police motorcycles up and down the front steps of the capitol building. It wasn't long after Carroll became chief that he placed his old friend Masters in the position of deputy chief. Masters wore dark-framed glasses that hung wearily on his nose and accented the morose, beagle-like quality of his face. He was number two, and he knew it. Older than Carroll, his slow walk and slow speech were an indication that he accepted his place in the order of things and aspired to nothing more than maintaining the status quo.

Carroll, on the other hand, was a hail-fellow-well-met glad-hander who was known throughout the station house as the "happy gooser," his main form of entertainment being to sneak up on some hapless fellow at the drinking fountain or deep in a hallway conversation at the police department and goose him. There was little the recipient could do, and it was more than one patrolman who said he would like to use his baton to bring a halt to the incessantly aggravating behavior. Carroll's other trademark, his even-brimmed beige Stetson, was always worn at a jaunty angle, off the job as well as on.

On this day, however, it was Carroll who followed Masters. Carroll didn't want to be out in front on this one. He didn't like murders. He would leave it up to Masters to handle the gruesome details. The attendants stopped when Masters approached the body and casually lifted the sheet from Nancy's face. He paused for a moment, his face blank, and then spoke.

"Boy, somebody sure beat the hell out of her." Replacing the sheet, Masters looked at Wise. "Accompany the body to the hospital. Make sure you save any evidence."

"What do you want me to do with the ropes around her neck . . . the knots I mean?" asked Wise.

Masters was silent for a moment, staring at the battered corpse as though giving Wise's question deep thought.

"Have them untied and . . . put the cords with the other evidence."

Wise looked puzzled and then slowly turned, following the body out the front door past the Christmas wreath that no longer signified holiday joy. Outside, the reporters moved as one, closer to the front step. They all knew Wise and hoped that at last they had someone who would answer their questions. At the head of the throng stood Virgil Falloon and Roy Campbell, both reporters for the *Lincoln Star*. Falloon stood six feet two while Campbell was much shorter and broader. Visually they made a Mutt and Jeff pair who always seemed to be present when a major story broke in the city. Over the coming weeks and months Falloon would follow the story closer and report it more accurately than anyone else.

The reporters chimed in: "Wise! How was she killed?" "Any leads?" "Hey, would you guys stop so we can get some pictures?" "Was she assaulted?" "Did it happen this morning or last night?"

They did not stop, and Wise answered none of their questions. In all his years on the force this was only his third murder investigation. He wished it had been none. He was glad he would be retiring in another few months. Let someone else handle these cases.

Inside the house, Masters hurriedly inspected the bedroom while Carroll talked with two of his patrolmen and two of the firemen in the living room. Everett Rudisil, the police lab man, was photographing the bed, the vanity, and the dresser with the open drawer that held Darrel's handkerchiefs. Masters saw something on the floor and bent over to pick it up. It was a piece of white paper with something printed on it. On closer inspection it read MILLER BRAND CLOTHESLINE ROPE, 25 FEET. He casually put it in his coat pocket and left the room.

At the hospital, Nancy's body was placed respectfully onto the autopsy table. William Hoagland, the senior member of the ambulance team, had volunteered to untie the clothesline rope and wrapping twine that encircled Nancy Parker's neck and bound her hands behind her back. With reason, he seemed unaffected by dealing with the dead on such an intimate basis. When the sheets were undraped from her body, a pair of panties fell from a fold in the sheets onto the floor. Hoagland picked them up and handed them to Wise, who haphazardly dropped them into a brown paper bag. They both cringed when they looked at her face.

"Looks like her nose is broken," said Hoagland quietly. "Her left eye is black and blue and swollen shut, and her lip is swollen like an egg on the left side. I'd say she put up a good fight until her wrists were—what's Masters want these untied for? By the time I get done he won't have any evidence of the knots. There'll just be a piece of clothesline rope and a piece of twine!"

"'Tis not mine to reason why," replied Wise sourly. "I just do what I'm told."

Hoagland leaned over the body and lightly touched the knots that bound the cords tightly around her neck. He hesitated a long moment before speaking.

"Well, you can tell him they're just regular hard knots . . . granny knots. One in each cord around the neck, but there are eight of them in the ones around her wrists. Whoever did this must have been afraid she might get loose."

"Maybe she did get loose and that's why she looks the way she does," replied Wise.

After forty minutes the knots were painstakingly untied and Hoagland started to cover her up again. When he moved the sheet, half a brassiere and a cut-up sweatshirt fell to the floor. Hoagland handed them to Wise.

To remove the last of the four handkerchiefs that were lodged in her throat, Hoagland had to call in an intern. Using forceps, and with some difficulty, the crumpled handkerchief was removed.

Wise had seen enough. He was ready to leave and took a long last look at Nancy Parker. The only things left on the body were her wedding ring and her engagement ring. He decided he would leave those for the funeral director. Across the room, almost without a sound, the autopsy doctor had arrived with a stainless steel cart upon which were spread the tools of his trade—scalpels, saws, hammers, and forceps. He stood silently at attention next to his cart as Wise eyed him skeptically before he turned and left. As Hoagland left pushing his gurney, the autopsy doctor noisily wheeled his cart across the tile floor, the instruments clanking on the shelves, and parked it next to Nancy. He threw the sheet onto another table and began his work.

At James Ager's house in the darkness of early evening, Darrel was asleep in an upstairs bedroom. He had taken another of the sedatives that Dr. Rose gave him and finally dropped off into a deep, yet troubled, sleep. His parents had arrived less than two hours before from Iowa. When it neared six o'clock his mother came up the stairs to wake him for supper. The oak floor in the room creaked loudly, signaling her presence.

"Darrel, are you up?" she asked quietly.

Darrel opened his eyes and groggily looked around the room. He didn't see his mother standing as stiff as a palace guard behind him in the doorway, her arms rigidly crossed over her waist.

"Where am I, Mother?" he asked quietly, almost to himself.

"You're at Mr. Ager's house, Darrel."

"Mother, what's happened? I feel like I'm in a dream. Like I am floating away."

Ignoring the question, Mrs. Parker moved closer to her son's side. "Let's go downstairs and eat some supper. Mrs. Ager and I have fixed a nice meal for you. It would be good to get something in your stomach."

As his memory of what happened achingly returned, Darrel sat up. His mother had come to his side, and he held her tight against him as he sobbed into her skirt. She stiffened and raised a hand to his shoulder.

"Come on, let's go downstairs. Father's waiting, too."

Darrel continued to cry. His mother looked blankly down the hallway.

"I'll wait until you're done."

That evening, at the same time the Agers and Parkers sat down to supper, County Attorney Elmer Scheele, Police Chief Carroll, Detective Masters, and Sheriff Merle Karnopp held a news conference at the police station. As he would continue to do in the coming days, Scheele led the gathering. From the outset Scheele said the main clue was a 1949 or 1950 black Ford two-door.

"We are pinning our hopes on finding the car that was reportedly seen parked near the Parker home early Wednesday morning." Police Chief Carroll added drily, "I think it is a good lead."

"Was there any evidence of a struggle?" asked Falloon.

"There was no evidence of a struggle," interjected Carroll fallaciously before anyone else could speak.

"Is there any connection to the break-in at the same house in November?" asked Roy Campbell. No one answered.

"How about robbery?" asked Falloon. "Was any money taken?"

"There was no evidence of robbery," said Masters.

"Was Mrs. Parker assaulted in any way? Was she raped?" asked another reporter.

"We're—" began Masters.

"We're unsure at this time," said Scheele, hurriedly interrupting. "We're currently waiting on the autopsy."

Despite the reticence of the authorities to reveal everything they knew about the crime, both newspapers would get nearly all the facts of the crime right in their first day's reports—what Nancy had been strangled with; the location of the body; the location of the panties and the rest of Nancy's clothes; the fact that she hadn't mailed her Christmas cards; that the dishes were washed; that she had been the recipient of a terrible beating; that the house had been broken into a month before.

Falloon and Campbell reported in the *Star* that "police were pinning their hopes on finding the car which was seen parked near the young woman's house." In the *Journal* two men who had been working in the Seacrest mansion the morning of the murder were quoted as saying that the car they saw "was dirty and did not have white sidewalls." They believed the car they had seen looked like a 1949 model Ford. A "dozen persons" were reported to have told police they had seen a car similar to the one seen by the workmen parked across from the Parker home on Sumner. The police had even made a cast of the track they believed was left in the snow by the rear tire of the car.

"The house was in a beautiful part of the park," said Mrs. Morrison, Nancy's mother. "There wasn't another house in sight and that always bothered us, especially after the break-in."

Although Chief Carroll had said on Wednesday, the day of the killing, that "there was no evidence of a struggle," by Thursday he had changed his statement. There was now the "possible theory that Mrs. Parker could have been knocked unconscious by powerful blows to the cheek."

Thursday morning Scheele, Carroll, and Masters picked Darrel up at Ager's house and drove to the other end of the park to his home. They wanted Darrel, although depressed and sedated, to walk through the house to see if anything was missing or out of place. When they entered the living room, Patrolman Gerald Tesch, who was guarding the house, sat on the couch reading a *Field and Stream*. He threw the magazine on the coffee table and jumped up when Chief Carroll entered. The house was still as it had been found the day before and was the way it would remain for the next several months. Shoes were scattered about, where they had been dragged from the bedroom by Rudy. The clothing bag was still on the floor in the baby's room, and some of the Christmas cards had been knocked off the card table onto the floor in the living room.

"Nancy wouldn't like this," said Darrel as he looked about the room. Under the influence of the sedatives, he was tired and appeared trancelike. Scheele told Darrel to "look for anything out of place or anything missing. Look around. Take your time."

They went to the bedroom, where Darrel looked through his dresser drawers. "Some handkerchiefs are missing," he observed, as he straightened the jostled contents. He checked every hanger in the closet.

"Nothing is missing here, but it looks like things have been moved around," he said after aligning the hangers in his usual precise manner. No one bothered to take notes as the group worked its way into the kitchen. Masters pointed to the counter where Nancy's purse stood open. The entire contents seemed to be lying out—her checkbook, two pens, a check made out by her father as a Christmas present, the two credit cards, a few green stamps, sunglasses, one lipstick, some Juicy Fruit gum, and an empty wallet.

"I think she had a ten dollar bill in her billfold. I know because she asked me for some ones and said all she had was a ten that she didn't want to break."

Going down the basement stairs, Scheele almost tripped on a roll of twine that was wrapped around a small stick and propped against the wall. In the basement, Masters was interrupted while cutting a length of rope from Darrel's clothesline.

"Why'd you do that?" Darrel asked, as Masters stuffed the rope in his pocket.

"It's OK, Darrel," said Carroll. "We just need a sample. We'll fix it later."

In the attic the group stood near two suitcases, a small one and a large one, as Darrel deliberately surveyed the room. He noticed nothing out of the ordinary, and they returned to the main floor. No one had noticed the dust-free rectangle on the floor between the two leather suitcases, a space that had been occupied by the medium-sized suitcase of a three-piece set. A suitcase that was now missing.

Thursday evening, one day after the murder, the Morrisons and the Parkers gathered at James Ager's house, each family preparing to start the long trip home to Iowa for the funeral. The Parkers would return to their Iowa farm by car. The Morrisons, accompanied by Darrel, were to be picked up by a limousine from the mortuary and, after visiting the chapel, would return to Iowa by train. The long black Cadillac moved slowly, yet steadily, down Normal Boulevard toward downtown Lincoln. A car sped past them. Darrel noticed that it was full of teenagers. They were laughing hilariously over something that Darrel could only guess at. It didn't seem possible to him that people could be merry after what had just happened.

Downtown, people were shopping late. The crowded sidewalks literally bustled; after all, it was Thursday night. Outside the big department stores, whose display windows were spectacularly decorated for Christmas, were the Salvation Army bell ringers. The Christmas season was reaching its frenzied apogee. Only eight more shopping days were left, and the holiday spirit was in the air.

When they pulled to the curb in front of the mortuary, a young man in a crisp black suit came out the front entrance and solemnly opened the door to the limousine. They were led inside to a small chapel where Nancy's casket stood. It was finished in a gleaming white lacquer and was left, mercifully, closed. They sat in silence, except for Darrel's and Mrs. Morrison's weeping. When the young man bade them to leave, for they had the train to catch, they all rose as one and wearily returned to the waiting limousine. As the big black car slowly lumbered toward the train station at the end of P Street, a block away to the north a black and white patrol car was pulling into the police department. A man was being delivered to the shadowy brick station for questioning and a lie detector test. He rode in the patrol car while his car, a black 1949 Ford, was driven in later by a patrolman. When the black Ford finally arrived and was parked outside the station, the patrolman driving it noticed that a brilliant white light shone on the brick wall in front of the right fender. When he got out and looked, he noticed that the right front parking light lens was broken. He shrugged his shoulders and went inside.

The grieving family was ceremoniously unloaded at the front entrance to the bustling train station. Their luggage was carried in by the young man from Roper's and handed off to a porter. Among the baggage were Darrel's suitcases, the two leather bags from the attic with Nancy's maiden initials on them—NEM. As they walked through the station, Nancy's coffin was being laboriously loaded onto the baggage car. When the grieving party went through the underground walkway that passed below the tracks, the dead fall leaves that had been held captive in the dark tunnel were blown into the air by a sudden breeze and just as quickly spiraled back down upon the concrete.

At the top of the stairs in the middle of the concrete platform, Darrel noticed a great white two-wheeled ice cart that stood next to a thick steel column beneath the glow of a dim hanging light. Water slowly dripped from it into a broad shallow pool. As he walked toward the train Darrel peered over his shoulder once more at the strange wooden vehicle. It looked almost like a caisson carrying a white coffin. The only thing missing was a team of horses.

On the train a porter announced, "Next stop, Omaha." Darrel was led to his own berth, where he unsteadily sat on the edge of a crisply prepared bed.

"Have you had your bedtime sedative, son?" asked a weary Mr. Morrison. Darrel shook his head. The train started to move just as Darrel tried to stand. He fell awkwardly back onto the bed.

"You wait here, I'll get some water," said Mr. Morrison as he trundled down the length of the car.

The train picked up speed, the wheels clicking ever faster on the joints in the track. The white "caisson" slowly receded beneath the faint shaded light that hung from the platform roof. Long after the train had pulled out of the station, a man emerged from the police station and got into the 1949 Ford. He pulled quickly out of the parking lot onto Tenth Street and headed north on the one-way. He was soon lost amid the late-evening traffic.

In a two-column lead story in Friday's *Star,* Falloon wrote that "late Thursday evening an ex-convict was released by the Lincoln Police. He owned a 1949 Ford—the type of car that has figured as a prominent lead to police—after he took and passed two lie detector tests. Earlier in the evening, he had been called by Chief Carroll 'our hottest suspect.'" He told police he had been sleeping at home on Wednesday morning when the murder was committed and then had gone to a locksmith to get a key made for the trunk of his car. The man questioned "had worked for a brief time for the Park Department following his release from the State Penitentiary last October."

In fact, this man was given two lie detector tests, one by Lieutenant Bob Henninger and the other by Sergeant Robert Nichols, a former state patrolman. Neither of the two men was an expert on the polygraph machine, and their tests were short and superficial at best. They both said that the suspect had passed, but they didn't say that together the tests were done in less than an hour. They said he passed, but he didn't tell them that he took a tranquilizer before the tests. They said he passed, but at least one of them, Lieutenant Henninger, said he just questioned him about generalities, didn't know he was a suspect in the Parker murder. They said he passed, but they didn't release his name. The man they released was Wesley Peery, the man who broke into the Parker home on November 13 and the man who killed Nancy Parker.

CHAPTER THREE

If, in the minds of the police, Wesley Peery had not killed Nancy Parker, then who did? From this point on Elmer Scheele would control the direction of the case, not the police. Scheele had once been in the FBI, something he did not let be forgotten, and the police would passively defer to his "experience" in the investigation from this point forward. Rather than follow the specific and factual information that had led them to Peery, Scheele and the police would now say they were "pursuing every lead," when in fact they weren't. Scheele had made up his mind as to who the killer was, and he would concoct an elaborate scheme to bring his quarry to ground.

At a Friday morning press conference, Carroll declared, "We're not back where we started! Definitely not. We're putting a picture of the crime together. We're working in a more concise manner." Scheele stated, "Robbery may very well have been a motive but we're also checking every known sex offender in the county."

Virgil Falloon assumed that comment meant the police had finally conceded that Nancy Parker had been raped, even though they had not heretofore directly admitted it. Chief of Detectives Masters said that "Mrs. Parker had died three to five hours before the autopsy." Falloon therefore concluded that since the autopsy was performed at Bryan Memorial Hospital at 3:00 P.M., the time of death according to Masters had to be between 10:00 A.M. and noon. To that Masters tersely replied, "I would place the time of death at 10:00 A.M. or before." Falloon looked incredulously at Roy Campbell.

Scheele then informed the press that all relevant evidence was being sent for analysis to the FBI laboratory in Washington, D.C. When Falloon asked Scheele where the investigation was headed, Scheele hastily replied, "After this amount of work it's getting to the point where it's beginning to narrow down. The investigation is now just one of plugging away."

The only bit of new information consisted of a report by Opal Closner, Nancy's coworker at Gooch's Mills, that she'd tried to call Nancy the morning of the murder at 7:50 A.M., 8:00 A.M., 8:10 A.M., and 11:00 A.M., before the police finally answered the phone at 12:30.

In the Friday *Evening Journal* it was reported that after having

> released the ex-convict who owned a '49 Ford and who had worked at the Park, Scheele said, "The car is still one of our most important leads. It is significant that no one has come forward to identify it and explain its presence.
>
> "The checking of fingerprints," Scheele continued, "has not gone far enough for us to know whether anything significant has been uncovered there. Investigation at the home has been completed and we have obtained all the evidence that could be found there.
>
> "All leads are being investigated and no particular phase of the investigation is receiving special attention."

The only hint that something might have been afoot, contrary to the news reports, was a single sentence buried in the middle of the *Journal's* lead story on Friday—just above a brief story whose headline read, KENTUCKY ENDS PARK SEGREGATION. "And throughout Friday morning Carroll and Asst. Chief Gene Masters conferred with Lancaster County Attorney Elmer Scheele on 'procedure' for continuing the investigation."

What the reporters didn't know was that the "procedure" involved the authorities following a completely new tack in their pursuit of the killer. At Scheele's behest, and unknown to the press, the authorities were considering an entirely new suspect. They had established their target and would plot their strategy in the pursuit of Darrel Parker. They had no evidence to support such a charge. They had no witnesses who could implicate him. Scheele just had the "feeling" that it must be Parker.

The meeting to plot this new strategy consisted of two parts. First was a decision that Scheele's deputy, Dale Fahrnbruch, in the company of Detective Clarence Schwartz, would follow Darrel Parker to Nancy's funeral in Des Moines. They would keep their new suspect "under tight surveillance." The second part of their plan was more involved and would require outside help. After the press conference, Masters entered Scheele's office. Scheele was on the phone and talking quite loudly, so Masters assumed, correctly, that it must be a long-distance call. "Yes . . . yes. Well, it's only the second murder we've had this year so we are quite concerned about getting it cleared up. If you could get here early next week that would work out fine. Just let us know a day ahead and we'll take care of the rest. Yes, yes . . . Thank you."

And the die was cast.

The papers continued to report what Scheele and Carroll told them: "The car is still one of our most important leads." "Checking of fingerprints has not gone far enough for us to know whether anything significant has been uncovered." "All leads are being investigated." "The doctors won't say if Mrs. Parker was sexually assaulted or fix the exact time of death." "Carroll said it was learned after a trip to the house that some items were missing."

Friday evening an agitated man was picked up by the police at Saint Elizabeth Hospital after he told a nurse that he was the one that "used a rope on Mrs. Parker." It was soon learned that he had been in the hospital since the day before the murder. Chief Carroll said that the man, like other suspects, was given a lie detector examination by Lieutenant Henninger and then released. Another man was arrested at the Lincoln Hotel after he told the elevator operator that he was the man who strangled Nancy Parker. A partially filled pint of vodka was removed from the man's pocket, and "he admitted having said the same thing earlier in a Ninth Street bar."

A reward of more than one thousand dollars was offered for more information leading to the arrest of the killer. However, when the papers printed the detailed reward offer in the Friday editions it sounded more like the qualifications for a lottery payoff: "Law enforcement officers and employees of the *Lincoln Journal* and the

Lincoln Star are not eligible to receive any portion of these rewards. The City, County, and the Lincoln papers are each offering $350, or a total of $1050." The qualifications continued: "To avoid any dispute between various informants the parties posting the rewards reserve the right and absolute discretion to determine which person or persons among several claimants shall be entitled to the rewards, and in what proportions. Judgment of the representatives of the parties offering the rewards shall be final and incontestable."

By Saturday morning, news of the murder was waning. The *Star* reported that the "County Attorney has tightened up on the release of news details and Chief Carroll stated that in the following week further information would be released only in daily news conferences at 10:30 A.M. and 4:30 P.M." Those times happened to coincide with the news deadlines of the two daily newspapers. Scheele concluded the Saturday morning news conference by stating that "a definite plan and specific assignments have been worked out so that the investigation of the case can go quietly ahead."

At 1:00 Saturday afternoon, December 17, in Des Moines, burial services were held for Nancy Parker. The snow fell in heavy wet flakes outside Dunne's Funeral Home as relatives and friends of Darrel and Nancy Parker filed solemnly into the chapel to hear Reverend Duane Ferris, the same man who had married the couple, speak the final words at Nancy's funeral.

"Death has overtaken one we knew and loved," he began quietly. "And how we accept death is often determined by the way death occurs. Occasionally I must counsel the elderly when they come to me in great pain or illness, with diminished abilities. They often tell me with great circumlocution that they want to leave this earth, that life has become too painful."

Two men entered at the back of the chapel and took their place uneasily among the standing mourners and the many flower arrangements that lined the walls. Dale Fahrnbruch and Detective Schwartz self-consciously removed their fedoras and attempted to fit in.

Reverend Ferris continued:

In my position, I must counsel them to accept life even in its most difficult and darkest moments . . . in the same way that they have embraced life's brightest moments. As a minister and as a human being who has compassion and love for my fellow man, I must say that at times death can be a merciful release. But what is not merciful is when death is not welcome, when it comes with startling alarm. Here was a life that was sadly unfulfilled, just ready to blossom . . . like the lovely flowers we see all around us here today. I must also say that although for most of us death comes peacefully after a long life, the sudden and violent loss of youth in its prime is always the most tragic of deaths.

I married this young couple little more than a year ago, and their love for each other was there for all to see and admire . . . I'm sure, Darrel, that your love for Nancy will not die and will continue for the rest of your days.

Darrel, sitting directly in front of Reverend Ferris, hung his head and sobbed openly. His father laid his worn and calloused hand upon Darrel's back.

"If there was some purpose in God's will for this tragedy, then I ask for His guidance, for none of us can see it. But there must be a reason."

Yet there was no divine reason. There was only the brutal theft, not of the few material things that were taken, but of life itself.

The organist began playing "Rock of Ages," and the silent throng mournfully filed out. Fahrnbruch and Schwartz remained at the back of the chapel until everyone had left. Then they slowly followed the others on the short drive to Resthaven Cemetery for the interment. Gathered inside a dark-gray burial tent, Darrel, the Morrisons, and the Parkers stood tearfully side by side as Reverend Ferris led them in the Lord's Prayer. When he finished, they each threw a small handful of deep-black Iowa soil on the white coffin that was slowly lowered into the grave. The contrast was like coal upon snow.

When Darrel unsteadily stepped out of the tent, he was sobbing uncontrollably. His mother supported one arm and Reverend Ferris the other. Darrel faltered for a moment and looked up into the falling snow. As they strode on, his mother quietly spoke to him: "Put your hat on, Darrel."

Fahrnbruch and Schwartz walked to their car, where they stood in the falling snow and had a brief conversation. When they were finished they got into the car, took down whatever information they thought they had gleaned from the funeral, and began the long return trip to Lincoln.

As the last person moved out the front of the tent, workmen quickly lifted a flap at the rear and entered the grave site. They each had a shovel, and in the frigid air they began to hurriedly complete the burial.

By Sunday the story was no longer the lead headline in the papers. The *Journal* had an encyclopedic piece on the murder that included a daily recounting of all that had transpired since the day of the crime. Mayor Clark Jeary was quoted as saying that rewards needn't be increased "because they're not needed." Chief Carroll repeated that the '49 or '50 Ford "is still a very important lead." In the "Public Mind" section of the *Star,* a Mr. Harold Warren wrote in to say, "There are two contemptible things about the recent murder—the bestial cruelty involved and the multitude of crackpots who confess to something they did not do. Another thing which may help someone in a grave emergency is this: Learn how to use the telephone in the dark."

Another reader wrote under the title BEHIND LOCKED DOORS: "Our town, like others, has always had its petty crimes and misdemeanors but we have never had to stay behind locked doors, afraid of the terror that might pass through them and having to look around every corner and down every alley, leery of every stranger and maybe even doubt friends."

The Morrisons, feeling it might help them to assuage their collective grief, asked Darrel to stay with them the following week. Mrs. Morrison confided in Darrel that, other than her husband, Robert, he was the only one who could comfort her and help her heal.

All references to the murder dropped off the front pages by Monday, except one. The *Journal* had a one-line lead on the front page: POLICE CHECK TRAFFIC AT MURDER SITE—PAGE 2. The story was sandwiched between an article about a woman's Chihuahua that had been nursed back to health by a veterinarian—the misspelled headline read BETERINARIAN'S GIFT IS BEST—and an article that described an elevator fire at the capitol building: CAGE SHOOTS UP TO 14TH FLOOR RIGHT AFTER 3 SCRAMBLE OUT.

On page 2, Scheele "revealed a 'device' that would be used by the investigators to obtain new leads—police would stop every car that passed through the intersection of Memorial Drive and Sumner during the day to see if anyone may have passed the Parker house the day of the murder."

Virgil Falloon, sitting in the front row at the daily press conference, raised his hand. Scheele gave him the nod. "Are the investigators operating on the assumption that the killer is still in Lincoln?" Scheele hesitated a moment, and that delay gave Falloon an inkling that there was something more to the two-word response—"No comment." The fact that Darrel was in Iowa was now only a temporary technicality as far as Scheele was concerned.

"Scheele renewed his plea to the public," reported the *Journal*, "to report anything they might know about the case, whether the information is considered major or trivial. The county attorney said the hunt is being continued for the two-door black Ford." When Scheele returned to his office after the conference, his secretary told him that "a Mr. Reid called from Chicago." Scheele went into his office and closed the door.

In Des Moines, Darrel took one of Dr. Rose's sedatives and went to bed. Before supper he had sat for a long time in a rocking chair by the picture window, rocking slowly and looking blankly onto the street as large flakes of snow cartwheeled lazily down. Darrel had tried powerfully hard to keep his grief in check. He wasn't in control of it, after all, and each night he dreaded going to bed because the only things awaiting him there were empty solitude and his memories of Nancy. The endless remorse, even being around the Morrisons, was beginning to take its toll. In a perpetual state of despondency, eating little, eyes darkened with sadness, he could see no way out of his current state. Deeply depressed, he felt his life was over, that without Nancy life was not worth living.

By Tuesday, the twentieth, the *Star* ran a small front-page article beneath the headline NOTHING NEW FROM AUTOPSY, NO CLUE GIVEN ON SEX ANGLE. As before, the reporters didn't know what was being suppressed. Everything in the report was a rehash of past news except the following: "County Attorney Elmer Scheele said the report by Dr. Frank Tanner, who performed the autopsy, added no additional information on whether or not the murdered woman had been raped." Dr. Tanner did know whether Nancy Parker had been raped. And so did Elmer Scheele.

The citizens of Lincoln were affected in a variety of ways by the crime. Foremost was the newfound practice of personal security. Few ever locked the doors to their houses prior to the murder. Now everyone did. Few people had ever bothered to lock their car doors at home or when downtown; some even left their keys in the ignition while they shopped. Residents were suddenly "lock conscious," according to the local merchants. Several hardware stores sold out of their door locks, hasps, and padlocks. "Several male customers commented that they found their homes locked when they returned home from work because their wives had changed or added locks." One of the store owners said, "I'm locking my own doors for the first time in years." Yet no one knew that Nancy Parker had locked her door the day of the murder, something she'd been particularly careful about since the break-in.

In Des Moines on Tuesday morning Darrel dropped off Mr. Morrison at his school for the first time since the murder. Mr. Morrison had taken off work on Monday—he'd been given the whole week if he wanted it, but he'd said no. He thought it would be better if he got back into his normal routine as soon as possible. The relatives had been there Sunday, that had helped, and Monday he'd spent the day slowly "pulling himself together." By evening he had decided that Tuesday he would go back to work.

When Darrel returned to the Morrison residence, Mrs. Morrison asked him to help her write thank-you notes to everyone who had sent flowers for the funeral. In the middle of the morning Mrs. Morrison, always called Mother Morrison by Darrel, made two cups of green tea, which they sipped slowly as they reminisced about Nancy. A few minutes before noon the phone rang. Mrs. Morrison answered it, saying nothing more than, "Just a minute, please," and handed the phone to Darrel.

"Mr. Scheele . . . Yes . . . Thank you, that's very kind of you. We're all doing better. It hasn't been easy . . . No, no it hasn't. I see, yes, certainly. You want me to come over tomorrow? . . . I'll do anything I can to help . . . If you don't want me to, I won't . . . All right, then. Tomorrow at highway patrol headquarters. Yes. I know where it is. Good-bye."

"Mr. Scheele has some new information that he'd like me to help him with," Darrel said offhandedly as he reached for another card.

"Did he say what it was about?" asked Mrs. Morrison.

"No, he just said to come alone and that I was to go to highway patrol headquarters so that we could avoid the press."

That evening, Darrel again rocked slowly by the front window. The movement seemed to calm him. He watched languidly as the shadows grew longer and the sky grew darker. What was he going to do, he wondered, when he had to go back to work, had to go back to the house. That would take an effort, a will, that he didn't know he could muster. No, he decided, he would never go back to 3200 Sumner to live. And he was right. He would go back only once more, but he would never live there again.

By the end of the day he was spent. It seemed for the last two days that by evening he was as tired as if he'd worked hard all day long. Yet when he went to bed, even though he'd taken sedatives, he had difficulty getting to sleep.

After supper, Darrel and Mother Morrison finished the last of the acknowledgments and placed them in a pile on the kitchen counter. Darrel looked at the pile and thought of the Christmas cards that Nancy had left on the card table the night before her death. He was tired, and he was profoundly depressed, an intensely disturbing feeling he'd never experienced before and something he knew nothing about. He felt like an automaton, going through the motions of life yet strangely detached from it. In the bathroom before bedtime, he grabbed the bottle of sedatives. He shook the bottle. The pills were gone and he'd forgotten to refill the prescription. Surely he could get to sleep one night without them. He would refill the prescription tomorrow, maybe in Lincoln.

It took more than two hours for Darrel to get to sleep. In the middle of the night he awoke in a cold sweat. He looked at the clock. It was 2:30. He lay on his back and thought of their honeymoon, the trip to the Black Hills. He rolled over, drifting wildly in and out of sleep. It didn't seem as though he'd ever fully gone back to sleep when the alarm went off at 6:00. He groggily rose and slowly pulled his pants on. At the breakfast table Mr. Morrison asked Darrel what information Mr. Scheele had.

"I don't know. That was all he told me, that they had some new information that he thought I could help with."

After breakfast, a little after 6:30 A.M. on December 21, Darrel was ready to leave. He put on a light tan zip-up jacket, too light for the freezing weather, and a brown fedora that made him look old beyond his years.

"Don't you want something heavier, dear?" asked Mrs. Morrison.

"I'll be all right. I'm going to stop and see the folks on the way, if it's too cold I'll get something heavier there."

He hugged them both and started for the door.

"Remember, we want to see you right back here tomorrow. We want you to spend the rest of the week with us."

"I will. I'll be back tomorrow."

But he wouldn't be back. He would never visit their home again.

That day in the *Star* a small article appeared on the front page—an article that at first glance had nothing to do with the Parker case. Its relevance would not be apparent for months.

Virgil Falloon, a Korean War veteran, was reading the article with special interest at his desk in the city room.

COL. LILES GUILTY OF AIDING FOE

Lt. Col. Paul V. Liles was convicted Wednesday of aiding the enemy by making propaganda recordings while he was a prisoner of war in North Korea, but he won leniency from the military court.

Liles won acquittal on the other charges against him. He was the 12th soldier to be tried on collaboration charges since the end of the Korean conflict. Two other officers and six enlisted men were convicted; two officers and one enlisted man were acquitted. Liles was the first West Point graduate to be tried on collaboration charges.

Falloon read nothing else on the page. He folded the paper, calmly laid it on his desk, and took a long drag on his cigarette.

"Brainwashing," he said and casually laid his cigarette, still burning, at the edge of the desk. He put a piece of paper in his typewriter and began typing. He quickly forgot the cigarette. Within minutes a coal dropped into the wastebasket below, setting it on fire.

Darrel stopped his car outside the front gate of Resthaven Cemetery. The gates were padlocked, so he walked along the black wrought iron fence that surrounded the cemetery until he could see Nancy's burial mound. The soil of the fresh grave, not yet covered by snow, stood out in the long line of grave sites and weathered tombstones. A rusted coffee can used to hold flowers clanked across the gravel road ahead of a gust of wind. The flowers that had been placed on Nancy's grave drooped, frozen and without scent, in their vases. The wind rattled overhanging branches against the fence. Darrel zipped his jacket up tight before he grasped the cold iron bars with his bare hands and said good-bye. He quickly returned to his car, turned up the heater, and headed west on Highway 6 until he reached Highway 59, where he turned due south toward Henderson.

By the time Darrel arrived home, the slowly scudding dark-bottomed clouds that pressed down on the landscape seemed low enough to touch. A light sleet-like snow fell softly. The chickens in the drive scattered in all directions as Darrel pulled up to the rear of the house. Another car was parked there, which he recognized as belonging to the Robbins family, their closest neighbors to the south.

As Darrel entered the kitchen all faces turned toward his.

"Hello, Mrs. Robbins . . . Mr. Robbins."

"Hello, Darrel," Mrs. Robbins replied, looking closely at Darrel's face. "We want you to know how sad we are at your loss."

"Thank you . . . very much. I just stopped by, Mother, to say that I'm on my way to Lincoln to help with the investigation. I got a call yesterday from Mr. Scheele, and he said they have some kind of new information. Robert thought it might have something to do with the car. So, I'm going over. I should be back home tonight, but in the morning I have to go back to the Morrisons'—they want me to spend the rest of the week with them. I told them I would. It seems to help them when I'm around . . . Well, I'd better be going. I told Mr. Scheele I'd be in Lincoln around 1:00."

Outside, Darrel's father spoke to him as they walked to the car.

"Do you want me to go with you, son? Keep you company?"

"I'll be fine, Father. Anyway, Mr. Scheele said I was to come alone."

A pickup truck drove by. The driver honked and waved. Darrel's father waved back and raised his head.

"Well, I've got chores to do anyway. They never seem to end and there's no one else to do 'em, you know that . . . You drive careful, now, there could be ice on the roads."

Darrel drove slowly out of the drive and looked back as his father began feeding the chickens out of a tin pail. Something about the scene made him start to cry, so he turned away. Inside the house Mrs. Robbins, who had been a nurse at Jenny Edmondson Hospital in Council Bluffs, looked at Mrs. Parker.

"If I ever had somebody that looked like that in the hospital, I'd have put them to bed on the spot . . . That boy is hurting."

Darrel drove straight south from Henderson until he hit Highway 34, which would take him all the way to Lincoln. Thirty miles down the road he passed Glenwood, its name written in huge black letters on the town's iconic white grain elevator. The Parker family attorneys, Kenneth and Edgar Cook, lived there and had just finished doing some legal work for Mr. Parker. Ken, the father, had started the law office not long after graduating from the law college in Lincoln. Their clientele consisted of store owners and residents in Glenwood and surrounding towns, but the bulk of their work was rural. There were many more prosperous farmers out there than most city folks realized, and they gave the Cooks a nice steady income—something you couldn't always say about a law practice in a big city.

From Glenwood the road dropped steadily down into the Missouri River valley. At the river's edge a bridge lay out before Darrel that carried him across the Missouri to Plattsmouth, Nebraska. At the same moment, unknown to Darrel, the California Zephyr out of Chicago was crossing the river in Omaha twenty miles to the north. It was running more than two hours behind schedule, and the engineer was running fast, trying to make up lost time between stops.

As the Zephyr screamed through one rural crossing after another, approaching Lincoln at breakneck speed, a heavy flaccid-faced man with long, wavy, brilliantined hair sat nervously in the dining car. After eating a sizable breakfast he hurriedly read the *Chicago Tribune*, jumping erratically from article to article. He continually checked his watch. As the train came within ten miles of Lincoln, he looked out the south window that was at his elbow. In the distance he could see the state capitol building looming high above the horizon, its gold-plated dome brilliantly reflecting the patchy morning sunlight. As if on cue, he got up slowly from his table, folded the paper, put it beneath his arm, and walked unsteadily up the undulating aisle.

At the train station in Lincoln, three men waited uneasily on platform number 1. Elmer Scheele and Gene Masters stood in heavy winter overcoats while a patrolman serving as driver waited in uniform behind them. Scheele paced nervously, the ever present cigarette in hand. Masters and the patrolman drifted together.

"Do you really think we need this guy, Gene?" the patrolman asked quietly.

"Hell no," answered Masters.

Scheele paced the platform, inhaled deeply on his cigarette, and nervously looked at his watch.

"Jesus Christ! Two hours late!" he cried.

The Zephyr's F Series locomotive suddenly screamed its arrival, entering the station like a juggernaut amid billowing clouds of steam and screeching brakes. Scheele immediately threw down the cigarette he'd just lit and stomped it out. Moments later the heavy man from Chicago stepped from the train with two bags in hand, one a suitcase and the other a glossy, heavy black case that was similar to a large salesman's valise.

"Mr. Reid?" asked Scheele.

"Yes," answered Reid.

"Elmer Scheele, county attorney."

Scheele extended his hand. Reid looked at his cases in response. Scheele signaled the patrolman. The patrolman took the bags, but as he did so he looked at Masters as if to say, "You're right, we don't need this guy."

"Put the black bag on the seat, not in the trunk," said Reid sharply. Reid brusquely straightened his coat, then pulled it down tight against his neck. The image he strove to maintain at all times was that of a man confidently in control. He managed himself and he managed events so that they always came out in his favor.

"Nice to meet face to face, Mr. Scheele, instead of over the phone," Reid said, as he finally offered his hand.

"This is Detective Masters," said Scheele anxiously. "We're running late. We should hurry."

They loaded into the police cruiser that had been idling in the no parking zone by the front door of the station. Reid rode in the backseat with Scheele, the black case between them. Once they were moving, Masters turned and passed a folder over the seat to Reid.

"You may want to look at this now," said Masters curtly.

Reid opened the folder slowly and looked grimly at the contents. There were photographs of the Parker house, inside and out, that Reid said, "tell me nothing." As they passed within a block of the capitol, Reid looked up the forty-story tower to the Sower—the twenty-foot-tall Lee Lawrie sculpture sitting majestically atop the dome. The driver noticed.

"The prick of the prairie!" said the driver in jest. Reid ignored him.

"Quite a building . . . for here," said Reid as he turned his attention back to the folder. The driver smirked.

"So, the twine around her neck came from this roll on the steps?"

"That's right," said Scheele and Masters at the same time.

The car pulled up to the stoplight at the intersection of Highways 2 and 77. At the southwest corner stood the state penitentiary and on the northeast corner highway patrol headquarters. Reid eyed the penitentiary, a dismal gray, weathered limestone complex with a faux Gothic design and castle-like guard parapets that sat atop the wall. It had stood nearly unaltered since its construction in 1876. Men who served in the Civil War had been incarcerated there.

"The state pen, eh?" he said sarcastically. "That's handy, isn't it?"

As the cruiser moved toward the entrance to the patrol building, they all laughed. The car pulled into the parking lot at the rear of the building. They hurriedly went inside as the patrol car's hood steamed in the cold late-morning air.

Deputy County Attorney Fahrnbruch, one of the two surveillants at the funeral, answered reporters' questions at the daily 10:30 press conference. The first question came from Virgil Falloon.

"Where is Mr. Scheele this morning, Dale?" asked Falloon.

"He's working on the case . . . Now, to get started, a young man was picked up yesterday downtown but we got nothing significant from the lie detector test that was given to him."

"You know, Dale," said Falloon, "if I was a criminal that had been picked up, I think that's the first thing I'd ask for, a lie detector test, because it seems like that's the one sure way to get released!"

Everyone in the room laughed, except Fahrnbruch.

"The man was picked up," continued Fahrnbruch, "after we got reports of certain activities."

"Can you tell us what those activities were?" asked Roy Campbell.

"I cannot spell them out at this time . . . all I can say is that the leads are being checked. The 1949 Ford is still considered to be the major clue."

Falloon shook his head in disgust.

"Hasn't the investigation run out of steam?" asked another reporter. "You haven't found the car. You haven't found—"

"We're working on new angles all the time."

"Where is Mr. Parker?" asked Falloon. "What's his reaction to the progress of the investigation?"

"Mr. Parker is with his parents in Iowa."

Darrel Parker pulled into highway patrol headquarters at 11:30. He parked his car next to the cruiser Scheele, Masters, and Reid had ridden in. The hood of the patrol car was still giving off faint clouds of steam. Darrel paused to steel himself before going in. He didn't want to break down in front of Mr. Scheele or anyone else. He sat motionless for a moment in his car with both hands on the wheel and his head bowed.

Inside the imposing red-brick structure he found a glass-covered building directory on the wall. Scheele had told him to go to Captain Smith's office on the second floor. When he arrived at Smith's office, the secretary seemed somewhat surprised.

"Yes, could you repeat your name, please? You have such a soft voice," she replied. "Oh, yes, Mr. Parker, they're— Mr. Scheele is expecting you. He'll be with you in just a few minutes. I'll tell him you're here."

She led the way into Smith's outer office. It looked downhill across the intersection and, since the building sat on an angle, directly at the penitentiary. Darrel sat on the couch and twirled his hat nervously in his hands as he waited. He looked at the prison and thought that it would certainly improve the looks of the drab place if they planted some trees around the front entrance. When he heard footsteps approaching, he stood up.

"Darrel, Darrel," said Scheele as he entered the office at a brisk walk. "You're here early! I thought you said you'd be here around 1:00? . . . Well, never mind. Come with me. I have someone I want you to meet. He's here to help us with the investigation."

Scheele led Darrel out of the office and downstairs. He said nothing to Darrel until they got to a door marked PHOTOGRAPHY LABORATORY. The door was partly open. Inside, Darrel was faced with the heavyset Reid, who stood beside a small table that held some sort of black machine with wires and tubes coming out of it.

"Darrel, this is Mr. Reid. He has some questions he'd like to go over with you."

With that, Scheele turned and went out the door, closing it quickly behind him. Darrel looked after Scheele with a lonely and puzzled gaze just as the door closed on his life.

CHAPTER FOUR

At 2:00 A.M. Thursday morning, December 22, Elmer Scheele called an impromptu news conference at the Lincoln police station and read a hastily prepared statement to a handful of gathered reporters who were seated in the pew-like benches of the municipal courtroom. With Scheele standing at a lectern at the front, backed up by Chief Carroll, Detective Masters, and others, the scene was reminiscent of a priestly sermon replete with acolytes.

"Gentlemen," he began in a self-consciously sonorous tone,

the Parker murder case is solved. Darrel Parker has signed a confession that after breakfast his wife refused his advances. He struck her a blow, knocking her unconscious and then strangled her. He tried to set the scene to make it appear that she had been raped—he removed her pants and underwear and bound her hands behind her back. Then he covered her and put a pillow over her head before leaving for work . . . Our plan worked, gentlemen. We let him attend the funeral in Iowa but we kept a check on him.

Deputy Attorney Fahrnbruch and Detective Schwartz went to Des Moines to conduct that surveillance. They then contacted R. W. Nebergall, Chief of the Iowa Bureau of Criminal Investigation, and asked him to check on specific leads in Iowa.

Virgil Falloon, sitting in the front row, deliberately wrote down the name R. W. Nebergall.

"Tuesday we got to the point where we were ready," continued Scheele, "and that was the time I put in the call to Mr. John E. Reid."

"But what about the movements of Darrel Parker the morning of the murder?" asked a reporter.

"He went about his normal activities all morning," answered Scheele tersely as he impatiently held up his hand. "I won't take any more questions now, gentlemen. I'll be happy to do that tomorrow. Right now, I'd like to introduce you to the man who got that confession, Mr. John Reid of Chicago. Mr. Reid is an expert with the lie detector and has run over 25,000 persons on the polygraph."

Falloon, incredulous at the number and without looking up, wrote furiously.

"He invented the Reid Polygraph," Scheele continued, "and is an attorney in Chicago with over fifteen years' experience as a criminologist. He is also coauthor of the book *Lie Detection and Criminal Interrogation.*"

Reid stood behind Scheele, smoothing his suit and tie as he waited. His jaw arched upward in a fashion that Mussolini would have approved. When Scheele finished he held out his hand to Reid, and the two shook hands as though they were old friends. Reid moved to the lectern, paused momentarily as he surveyed the room, and began to speak in a loud, self-assured voice.

"Parker cried the first time I saw him," began Reid, "when we discussed his wife's death. Then he never cried another tear all day. We—"

"Had you any prior knowledge of the case?" interrupted Falloon. "Did you know what to expect from Mr. Parker?"

"No, I had no knowledge of what Parker would say when I interrogated him. My only requirement or prerequisite was that I be able to conduct two interrogations."

Falloon leaned toward Roy Campbell. "So, they brought this guy all the way from Chicago and told him nothing about the crime, huh?"

"Parker had a definite reaction in the first test, but it was between sobs and crying when he talked about his wife's demise. I got the reaction, but I wasn't sure if it was a confession or because of his emotional upset.

"At 6:30, after we had something to eat, there were no more tears, and Parker was emotionally composed. All of the officials there were particularly interested in him."

Reid, reported Falloon, said he had "obtained confessions in a hundred murder cases in Chicago and never once visited the scene of the crime." The *Journal* reported that Reid said, "Parker broke down and confessed after being confronted with the test results."

At the end of the brief early morning press conference, Reid looked at his watch then suddenly whispered something to Scheele. Scheele moved to the fore.

"Mr. Reid has to catch his train back to Chicago, gentlemen. But I'd like to close by saying that the solving of this crime is the best example of cooperation between law enforcement officers I've ever seen. The investigators just wouldn't quit. They did what we asked and then went beyond that."

Scheele and Reid hurriedly exited through a side door. Falloon and Campbell looked at each other in mutual disbelief at the brief, one-sided nature of the press conference that was now abruptly over. They were flabbergasted at the manner in which John Reid had come to Lincoln, gotten his confession, and left, all in less than twenty-four hours, without ever having to account for anything. Reid would not return to Lincoln until the trial four months later.

Inside a dirty cracked window with rusting wire mesh that had been molded into the glass, a cobweb danced lightly on the breeze that filtered through. Corroding iron bars covered the window on the inside. Outside, on the snow-covered ledge, two pigeons cooed in unison. The birds were absorbing the first rays of the morning sun as it cleared the shadow of the capitol building four blocks to the east. A car honked on the street, then another, and another. It was morning rush hour. Inside the cell in the county courthouse, two feet moved beneath a worn, brown, government-issue blanket. The honking horns multiplied, echoing wildly in the air off of Tenth Street. A body stirred beneath the blanket. Darrel Parker was awakening from his first night in jail. He had no idea where he was. Slowly his eyes focused on the wall beside him. Breathing deeply, his face reflected his reaction to the cell's odor. A cockroach suddenly flitted across the sheets and disappeared beneath his pillow. He jerked up, pushed away from the wall, and fell awkwardly to the floor. With eyes now wide open he sat up, his back against the bunk. He looked up at the ceiling, then down the chipped, gouged, and graffiti-covered stone wall in front of him. He lifted his hands shakily, then rested his head on his knees. Now he remembered what happened. At least part of it.

Thomas McManus, a thirty-seven-year-old Lincoln attorney, was eating breakfast as he read the Thursday morning *Star*. McManus, intense, musically gifted, and wiry with a full head of wavy hair, was the son of an often despairing Irish father and an exuberant and caring French mother who started their married life in America in New York City's Hell's Kitchen. His father was a chauffeur for a limousine service and had often driven for Nathan Gold, owner of Gold's Department Store in Lincoln, when Gold was in New York City on buying trips. Gold eventually hired McManus as his full-time driver, and the entire family moved to Lincoln in 1927. Tom was a child prodigy on the violin and sat third chair in the Lincoln Symphony by the time he was eleven years old. Fearful that he'd never have a decent income if he stuck with the violin, after serving in World War II he went to law school on the G.I. Bill. After graduation he began his legal career with the law firm of Towle & Young in Lincoln.

Tom's wife, Lu, was cleaning the breakfast dishes when their two daughters ran upstairs to brush their teeth for school. In their absence, McManus felt free to read aloud from the front-page article by Virgil Falloon on the Parker murder.

"DARREL PARKER CONFESSES STRANGLE-SLAYING OF WIFE, HUSBAND SAYS MATE WAS COLD," read McManus. " 'Nothing that has happened before would make me believe this is true. Nothing,' said Mrs. Morrison, mother of Nancy Parker. 'I'm going to wait for some type of confirmation before I believe this.'

"Lynn Parker, father of Darrel Parker, said, 'I don't believe it. My son would never do such a thing. Never.' He said he 'had heard nothing from the Lincoln authorities involved in the case and finally became so unnerved by the news that he could not comment further.'

"Mayor Jeary said he was fully informed of Scheele's plan. 'I know the technique and its timing was masterful.' "

The telephone rang. Lu answered it.

"Hello . . . Sure, Max."

McManus laid the paper down and took the call. "Yes, I was just reading about it . . . I'll be damned. Sure . . . I'll see you there in thirty minutes."

"Guess what?" McManus asked Lu. "Max said to meet him at the county courthouse. We're going to represent Mr. Parker."

That morning at 8:30 A.M. Darrel Parker was led into Elmer Scheele's office, where he was told that he had given a full confession to the murder of his wife to John Reid. Scheele asked Darrel if he remembered signing it. Darrel said he "remembered signing something." After telling Darrel what would happen in the next several days, he let him make a telephone call. Darrel immediately called his parents and, after breaking down, told them what had happened and asked them to call Mr. Cook in Glenwood. Not long after lunch Darrel's parents arrived in Lincoln, where they went straight to the county courthouse to see their son.

"They say I confessed, Dad," began Darrel haltingly. "I don't know what happened. I remember leaving the farm. I remember seeing you and Mother. When I got here they put me in a little room with this Mr. Reid—I'd never seen him before. Mr. Scheele told me to come to Lincoln to help. This Mr. Reid wouldn't even shake my hand. He told me I looked guilty the minute I got in the room and then told me to sit down. He hooked up this machine of his, and then he put his face in mine and started to scream and yell."

Darrel began to cry.

"It was like a dream when I woke up in that cell this morning. I didn't know where I was. I didn't know up from down. But I knew that something bad had happened. I could remember enough to know that."

Tom McManus entered the room where Darrel was talking with his parents. Darrel glanced at McManus. A sheriff's deputy stood watch at the door. When McManus saw Scheele talking to his boss, Max Towle, in the opposite corner of the room, he waved. Towle saw McManus and signaled him to come over. Scheele went across the room to the Parkers.

"Tom," began Towle, "the paper made it look pretty bad for this fellow . . . the confession and all . . . You remember me telling you about the big bank robbery here in 1930, don't you?" Tom nodded. "Well, when we finally caught one of those guys, he was threatened with a lie detector, the first one in the state, and he confessed—before they even used the thing on him! Now, this Parker confessed. They used a lie detector on him, and this Reid fellow said he flunked it. So, I think he's probably guilty . . . but that doesn't mean we won't do our best for him. When Ken Cook called me this morning from Iowa, I said we would work with him on the case. He's an old friend of mine. In spite of the situation we'll still give Parker a good defense."

"Darrel," said Scheele, "your attorneys are here." Mrs. Parker glared with cold disdain at Scheele, who signaled Towle and left.

"Don't worry, Mother," said Darrel. "Mr. Cook and these Lincoln attorneys, they'll get this all straightened out. They have to. I'm innocent."

Max Towle, renowned head of the Towle & Young legal firm, had grown up in Lincoln. In his youth he was a star football player at both Lincoln High and the university. In 1912, as quarterback of the university team, the squat but powerful Towle—known as Bulldog by his teammates—threw the winning touchdown in the waning moments of the Nebraska-Minnesota game, a great rivalry at the time. After law school he served a stint in the Navy during World War I, and following his discharge he joined the Lancaster County Attorney's Office. After learning the ins and outs of the office and establishing an excellent record of prosecutions, Towle ran for the office of county attorney in 1926 and was elected in a landslide.

His most famous case was, without a doubt, the $2.5 million robbery of the Lincoln National Bank in 1930—the largest in the nation's history to that time. In the middle of the morning, five men rolled up to the bank at Tenth and O Streets in a big black Buick limousine. Four went inside while a fifth—later determined to be Big George Wilson—stood in the center of the intersection brandishing a Thompson submachine gun. Policemen called to the scene were immediately sent scurrying by the machine gun–wielding robber. The group loaded their take into the limousine and made a clean getaway. Over the next year Max was responsible for the recovery in Chicago of more than $500,000 in bonds—enough to have kept five smaller rural banks afloat. The negotiations for the return of the bonds were conducted with attorneys that had mob connections. The cash was never recovered, but it was established that the Al Capone gang had been behind the crime and had farmed out the actual robbery to Wilson and his associates.

In 1946 Towle was defeated in his race for reelection as county attorney after twenty years in office. He went into private practice and, in addition to his legal career, pursued several private interests, among which were the raising and running of race horses and avid participation in illicit cockfights.

A story that Max had never been able to live down concerned a sporting venture he had made to old Mexico. While there he bought two fighting cocks who were said to exhibit unparalleled prowess in the ring. Paying a premium price for them that was commensurate with their highly touted abilities, Max shipped the birds back to his law partner in Lincoln, evidently without including detailed instructions as to their proper care and use. Upon being informed by the freight office that some chickens had arrived, his partner gave instructions to send the birds to the food locker and have them cleaned and frozen until Max returned.

Max's favorite pastime, however, was horse racing. In his farmhouse hideaway on the outskirts of Lincoln, famous for all-night poker games, Towle had a twenty-five-foot-long wall that was covered with the pictures of his winning, and losing, Thoroughbreds—at least twenty of which he kept stabled at his farm.

Only a close circle of friends and coworkers knew of the other side of Max Towle, his compassion and the considerable philanthropy that went along with it. He often helped people in need by giving funds to them directly. One family had been supported by Towle for more than ten years after the father abandoned them. His secretary of fourteen years, May Robinson, respectfully observed, "Max gave a lot of money to a lot of people, yet never asked for anything in return. He had a real soft spot for people in need."

That evening the *Journal* printed brief snippets of man-on-the-street interviews. Richard Beers: "I was dumbfounded. I didn't believe it could turn out this way, but it sure is good to know that it's over."

Don Vavra, farmer: "I think everyone is relieved, especially the ladies." Jane Burgin, office worker: "I'm so relieved. I had every confidence in the people that were investigating it."

James Ager, park superintendent, was quoted as saying, "It seems impossible that Darrel could have done it. I've never received a greater shock in my life. His conduct was impeccable, he was popular with everybody at work, and he had no bad habits. He did excellent work and really took a load off my shoulders."

Ken Witt, president of the junior chamber of commerce, said, "I was completely shocked and taken aback by the whole thing. Darrel was meticulous and resolute in his work. We had the utmost confidence in him." Bernice Mallat, who worked with Darrel on the capitol Christmas tree committee said, "Darrel was the best one that ever headed the Christmas program."

Adjoining the Parker articles was one concerning an unsolved murder in Omaha. It seemed the Omaha police had been stymied by their case in the same way the Lincoln police had been by the Parker murder. They felt the need to seek outside help as well: "CRIME EXPERT ENTERS OMAHA MURDER CASE. A noted criminologist, Dr. LeMoyne Snyder, who had worked on the Sam Sheppard case in Cleveland, arrived in town to add his weight to the investigation of the December 10 murder of coed Carolyn Nevins." It was a virtual replay of the Lincoln investigation: "Police here are still running down leads in the slaying, many supplied by citizens at the urging of the police department." The two murders would find a brief convergence in the weeks to come.

At the bottom of the front page of the Thursday *Journal* was a one-line article—nearly lost beneath a Meadow Gold milk advertisement—entitled IOWANS DID NOT TRAIL HIM. It had a Des Moines dateline and said cryptically, "Dr. R. W. Nebergall, chief of the Iowa Bureau of Criminal Investigation said in Des Moines Thursday, 'We were not watching the movements of anyone.'"

Darrel pled not guilty at his arraignment. Elmer Scheele read the complaint against Parker charging that he "did feloniously, purposefully, and of his own deliberate and premeditated malice kill Nancy Parker."

County Judge Herbert Ronin set a preliminary hearing date for January 21. Conviction of first-degree murder in Nebraska was punishable by death in the electric chair or life imprisonment. When asked by Virgil Falloon at what point he felt Parker was the man they were after, Scheele replied, "Not until he signed the confession. An investigator has to fight against a single theory and look in all directions."

Darrel's father said, "If I'd thought Darrel was guilty in any way I would have had a lawyer on the job a long time ago."

After the hearing Darrel was taken to the penitentiary by Sheriff Karnopp. He was to be kept in a room in the prison hospital and would be out of the general population. "His only request was for something to read," said Deputy Warden John Greenholtz. "He can listen to the prison radio monitor with ear phones, or we'll let him listen to his own radio." His spartan room in the prison hospital contained two beds, a bedside table, and two chairs. The door to the room had a glass panel in it so that occupants could be kept under twenty-four-hour surveillance. Next door to Darrel's was the room of Loyd Grandsinger, a young California man who had shot and killed a Nebraska highway patrolman at a stolen car roadblock and was due to be executed in three months.

Marjorie Marlette, a *Journal* staff writer, wrote Friday of the travails that the city's lawmen had to endure during the investigator's "grueling week":

> In an unprecedented round-the-clock tracking of evidence, officers spent a sleepless week laying the groundwork for breaking the case. The time spent by the authorities was quantified—"Total police overtime reached 640 hours, or an extra 80 days of manpower."
>
> County Attorney Elmer Scheele was the man who coordinated the investigation, the central figure (a former FBI man). As for sleep, said Scheele, "when you have to you can get along without it."

After eating supper Friday evening, Darrel was visited by Salvation Army captain Walter Kennedy. "He already had a Bible," said Kennedy, "and he told me that he'd once been a Sunday school teacher." When asked by Kennedy what he would do for Christmas, Darrel began to weep. He had no idea.

"On Christmas Eve, Parker will be visited by prison officials," said Warden Joseph Bovey, "and will be given a Christmas package. On Sunday we're having a turkey dinner."

By New Year's, Parker had been absolved of any complicity in the Nevins murder in Omaha. "The whereabouts in Lincoln of Darrel Parker on the night Carolyn Nevins was slain have been satisfactorily established," said Chief Carroll. The same day it was announced by Max Towle that Darrel had told his attorneys he "had nothing to do with the death of his wife."

Virgil Falloon reported that Parker told his attorneys he had been "hounded by Reid into signing a false confession." County Attorney Scheele countered that "Parker was not abused in any way and was given every opportunity to rest. He made the confession entirely of his own free will and accord."

John Reid, during one of only two telephone interviews that he'd make before the trial, said, "Parker's statement was typical and par for the course in cases like these. I believe that at the proper time, testimony will reveal that there were a sufficient number of witnesses to the confession to disprove any claim by Parker of coercion."

Kenneth Cook, his son Edgar, Tom McManus, and Max Towle, the four attorneys who would make up the Parker defense team, met for the first time in Towle's office in the Terminal Building at the southwest corner of Tenth and O Streets, directly across the street from the old Lincoln National Bank building. After everyone was introduced they sat in heavy leather chairs at Max's massive antique oak conference table. The air was thick and blue with the smoke of Max's cigar and the combined cigarette smoke from the other three. Kenneth Cook began.

"Max and I went to law school together, Tom, but I haven't seen him since he was the county attorney here for . . . what was it, Max, fifteen or twenty years before Elmer Scheele?"

"True, but I'm a lot happier since I left that job, Ken. It's a little more interesting on this side of the aisle . . . Ken, you've known the Parkers a long time, you know Darrel better than any of us, why don't you get us started here."

"That's right, Max," said Cook, as he adjusted his hearing aid, "I have known the Parkers a long time—since Darrel was a child. I'm sure you've heard that he taught Sunday school, but he was also a choir boy, played on the high school basketball team, and was valedictorian of his high school class. He was quite a boy . . . he still is. And, outside of my own son of course, he's one of the most honest and forthright young men I've ever known. I have to say this right at the start, Max. You have to accept and believe with me that this boy is innocent. We're not putting up a last gasp defense for a guilty man here! He couldn't do anything like that—what he's accused of. He just couldn't. I know him too well."

Tom looked uneasily out of the corner of his eye at Max. Max stared straight ahead, betraying no emotion yet barely concealing his skepticism as he drew slowly on his cigar.

"We can believe that, Ken," Max said as he removed the ash from his cigar by slowly turning the end in the big square crystal ashtray that sat before him, "but we're going to have our hands full trying to show why on earth a man would confess to something he didn't do . . . Why did he sign the confession for crying out loud, if he was innocent? I just don't understand that. I've never heard of such a thing in all my years."

"A so-called confession, Max . . . Now, I don't know how this Reid got the damned thing, if he bullied Darrel or wore him down, or what he did, but goddamnit we're gonna find out. We're gonna get to the bottom of it. Darrel didn't confess to something he didn't do without being put upon or coerced or badgered in one form or another."

"But the paper said Reid got a reaction on his machine," interjected Tom.

"Reid didn't say *what* reaction he got. He never said, 'He's guilty, the machine said so.' Since that first news conference Reid hasn't said one word about that goofy machine of his. What we're going to have to deal with is the fact that they've got a goddamned written confession. And you know as well as I do, Max, that's all they're going to trot out come trial time. They won't need anything else."

"I don't think it's going to help for us to argue about that confession right now, Ken," said Max. "We've got to begin by going back and starting from square one. If he's innocent as you say, Ken, then we need to get our own lie detector man . . . a good one. He can settle this for sure if he's guilty or not, and it'll be an independent unbiased source that tells us. None of us knows beans about these crazy machines, and if we can't dispute how Reid got the confession, then we're going to be dead in the water. I've had Tom do some research on this, and tomorrow he can contact some of these people. We'll get the best man possible."

Within two days McManus had located the most renowned lie detector operator within a five-hundred-mile radius. George W. Robinson was a Keeler polygraph expert from Kansas City who had learned his expertise from the late Leonard Keeler himself, inventor of the modern-day polygraph.

After an examination had been scheduled, Max Towle told Virgil Falloon, "No results of these tests will be disclosed. They will be treated as confidential material because any premature release before trial might be prejudicial to Darrel's case." Max didn't tell his reasoning to anyone other than McManus, but he also wanted to keep a lid on the results in case they showed, as he expected, that Darrel was guilty.

The tests were administered by Robinson at the gloomily imposing Bailey's Sanitarium in southeast Lincoln. Converted into a sanitarium by Dr. Benjamin F. Bailey, the building had originally been a girls' dormitory on the campus of the defunct Normal School. The dark and aging building served as Lincoln's only private psychiatric hospital and was administered by Dr. Paul Royal.

On the day of the test, Towle stood with the press on the front steps of the hospital. With the foreboding hospital facade behind him, Max addressed a handful of reporters.

"Mr. Robinson did not want to examine Darrel at the state penitentiary," said Towle, "and Mr. Scheele's only alternative proposal was the Nebraska Safety Patrol building—the site of the original interrogation. Since that was obviously unacceptable to us, Dr. Royal kindly agreed to let us use his facility here."

Once he'd received the results of Robinson's examination, Max reconsidered his own statements from the week before and chose to release the results. He announced that the tests had shown

Darrel "definitely had no connection with the death of his wife! Mr. Robinson found absolutely no reaction of guilt to any of the questions asked." Since he had honestly believed Parker would have a guilty reaction to Robinson's test, Max was now a changed man. From this point forward, his approach to the case and his feelings toward Darrel Parker would be totally different. He could devote himself fully and without reservation to Darrel's defense.

"Furthermore," continued Towle, "Darrel steadfastly maintains his innocence and states that the confession he signed was obtained under conditions that were totally improper, while he was in a grief-stricken exhausted state, and after losing the will to live because of the loss of his wife. I should also add that this examination was conducted under normal circumstances and proper conditions—as they should be by any professionally skilled examiner."

When Towle asked Robinson if he would work for them on the case, Robinson declined. "For trial I know a much better man than me, Mr. Towle. In fact, for what you're after, he's probably the best there is. He has impeccable credentials and more trial experience than anyone I know of in the country. I'll give him a call when I get back to Kansas City. He's a California man, and his name is Dr. Douglas Kelley."

Scheele immediately reacted to the test results and Max's statement: "It came somewhat as a surprise since one of the defense attorneys was quoted as saying the results were not to be made public. I will only say that I am satisfied with our investigation and I'm completely ready to present the state's evidence in court under the prescribed rules of evidence at the properly ascribed time. This will insure the defendant of an orderly trial by an impartial jury."

When asked whether the results of the state's polygraph tests would be revealed, Scheele replied, "Any attempt to release or make public results of our own lie detector tests will occur, if at all, at the trial under proper rules of evidence and under the guidance of the court. We called in one of the best criminologists in the entire United States. His experience and reputation for integrity speak for themselves."

Reid commented for the last time before the trial by saying in a telephone interview that a repudiation of the confession by Parker was "typical of such cases. The attorneys are running true to form. We can only wait and let the trial speak for itself."

In the *Lincoln Star* on Thursday, January 12, a headline proclaimed, SHEPPARD HOPES SOMEONE WILL CONFESS. The Ohio Supreme Court was reviewing Dr. Sam Sheppard's case on constitutional grounds. Sheppard was represented by F. Lee Bailey in the case that would launch Bailey's famed career. Sheppard said outside the courtroom that he hoped whoever killed his wife would someday confess. "I feel very hopeful that the courts will decide in favor of my case." He maintained his innocence, as he always had, and admitted that if he was ever released he felt he "could never resume a normal life." He was released after the appeal, and he was right: he never resumed a normal life.

CHAPTER FIVE

Masked bandit robs lincoln couple in their home read the glaring headline in the *Star* on Monday, January 16. An article by Allen Edee described the serious, yet at the same time humorous, events:

A cool, soft-spoken masked bandit brandishing a gun calmly walked into the home of Mr. and Mrs. Charles W. Winkler shortly before 8 P.M. Sunday and robbed them of between $70 and $80.

The intruder, his face concealed by a white veil mask, slipped into the home at 3811 J through the back door while the occupants were watching television.

Calmly he robbed the Winkler couple, then disappeared a few minutes later out the same back door. He issued sharp orders in a soft-spoken voice, barely audible above the playing television set.

The couple told the *Star* this story:

The intruder ordered Winkler into the dining room and told him to throw his billfold on the floor, not knowing that two revolvers were lying on a dining room buffet. The cold glint of the bandit's gun, however, kept Winkler from pouncing on one of his own guns.

Escapes in Auto

The holdup man apparently escaped in an auto that was parked across the street from the Winkler home.

Mrs. Winkler said, "The man was as cool as a cucumber."

The bandit slipped in the back door of the home unnoticed. He went through the kitchen and was about three steps into the dining room before Winkler said he glanced up from the television set and saw him.

"We thought it was one of my son's friends playing a prank because of his peculiar dress," Mrs. Winkler said.

Cold Terror

The couple felt cold terror when the "darned fool in the masquerade outfit" pointed a blue steel revolver at them.

Winkler said he had barely spoken the words "Come on in" when he noticed the weapon.

"I want your billfold," the armed intruder said in a soft voice, hardly audible above the sound of the television.

Winkler replied, "Help yourself. It's on the book case."

Then the intruder ordered Winkler to "go get it."

Gets Billfold

Winkler then arose from the living room couch where he had been sitting with his wife and picked up his billfold from a dining room stand.

Winkler said he started toward the bandit, but the intruder, brandishing the gun, said, "Throw it on the floor."

Mrs. Winkler said the man squatted down and fumbled around on the floor for the billfold.

"He looked like he couldn't see through the veil," she said, laughing.

"I was so scared. I wanted him out of the house so I said, 'It's to the right of you.'"

Slips Out Back

The man scooped up the billfold without a word and slipped out the back door.

The Winklers quickly ran to the front door where they saw a car parked across the street. They called police and when they looked back out of the window again the car had disappeared.

The victims described the armed bandit as wearing a white shirt tucked in underneath blue bib overalls. The veil hid his face, they said.

Mrs. Winkler said the veil "looked like a white formal shawl or a lace curtain. It came to just below his neck," she said.

"Although the person had a soft high-pitched voice I think he was a man," Winkler said.

"He was medium build and about five feet eleven inches."

Lincoln police immediately sent out a broadcast on the robbery and sent a team of detectives to the home.

Winkler said the robbery occurred just before 8 P.M.

"The man wasn't here over two minutes."

Winkler operates a television shop and is consultant engineer for KLMS radio.

The *Evening Journal* added more fodder to the masked-bandit saga. Their headline read, ROBBERY GUN STOLEN FROM POLICE OFFICIAL.

Police came up with this new twist in Sunday night's robbery at the Charles W. Winkler home.

The gun used by the masked man was taken earlier in the evening during a burglary at a house a block away.

And who lives in the house down the street? Why, Gene Masters, Lincoln's assistant chief of police.

To top it off, the .38 caliber detective special revolver was clearly stamped: "Police Dept., Lincoln, Nebr."

Masters said the gun was taken from his house at 3743 J sometime between 5 and 6:50 P.M.

The assistant chief and his wife returned home to find the night lock on the rear door broken and the short-barreled snub revolver missing from a bedroom dresser.

"From the Winklers' description of the gun, there's no doubt in my mind it was mine," Masters declared.

But there's another element in the case.

Muslin Cover Taken

Mrs. Winkler told detectives the intruder seemed to have difficulty seeing through the white veil he wore over his face.

Masters reported a white muslin doily used to cover their washing machine was taken in the break-in at his home.

"But my wife doesn't think the guy could have seen through that," Masters said.

On January 19, in the *Journal*'s "Public Mind," a reader wrote under the banner MODERN IMMORALITY:

> We can't pick up a newspaper nowadays without reading about sex crimes, murders and robberies. Sex crimes particularly seem to be on the increase. They fill our days and nights with terror. It is little wonder that the women of Lincoln and Omaha are rising in indignant protest against the light penalties dealt out to offenders.
>
> Is there a reason for this state of affairs? There is, most emphatically. Several reasons, if one cares to delve into it. First of all we have become a nation in which beer taverns outnumber the churches. Wherever such a condition exists morality is on the down grade.
>
> It isn't juvenile delinquency that is the national problem half as much as it is adult delinquency. And we call ourselves a Christian nation!
>
> "FRANKLY SKEPTICAL"

The following Saturday, January 21, was the date of Darrel's preliminary hearing. At the end there would be a ruling on whether there was probable cause to hold a trial in district court. Max Towle was quoted as saying the hearing "would be a long one."

On the day of the proceedings a heavy, wet snow fell. A lone janitor shoveled the courthouse sidewalks at a little after seven in the morning as people were already beginning to gather at the entrance, even though the courtroom would not open for another two hours. The temperature was in the teens, and the breath of those waiting in line filled the air as they exchanged opinions about the murder and sipped cups of steaming coffee that they had brought in silver Thermos bottles. At 8:30 a deputy sheriff held up his hands to the court-goers and made a brief declaration: "When the doors to the courtroom open, you will enter in an orderly fashion. When the seats are full we'll allow thirty people to stand at the rear and the rest will have to come back out into the hall. If anyone leaves the courtroom for any reason, another person may then take their place." The deputies opened the doors, and the throng surged forward.

After the crowd had been seated and called to order by the bailiff, Darrel Parker hesitantly entered the room. Tom McManus gave him a legal pad and pen so that he could take notes. Darrel brought with him a tiny booklet of scriptures, only an inch and a half square, which he nervously placed at his elbow. The gray-haired and bespectacled Judge Herbert Ronin was next to enter the chambers, at precisely nine o'clock. Before the proceedings began, Towle leaned over to Kenneth Cook. "Remember when I said we'd be lucky if Elmer got us a copy of the confession by the preliminary hearing? He didn't, did he? The son of a bitch."

Detective Masters was the first person to take the stand, and he did so eagerly.

"Mr. Reid questioned Parker from 11:45 until after 3:00. He came out for a glass of water and then questioned him again from 6:45 until 8:00. When he came out the second time he said, 'I have your man.' Parker said she had refused relations with him the night before. When he asked her again after breakfast, at approximately 7:05 that morning, and she refused, he took her by the arm to the bedroom, removed her glasses, and hit her."

The gallery hummed. To the chagrin of those in the hall, no one got up to leave.

"He went into the kitchen and got two lengths of clothesline rope and tied a six-foot piece around her neck. He then took a piece of twine off a shoe bag and wrapped it tightly around her neck using what he said was a double bowline knot with a half hitch—which he demonstrated to me. Then he wrapped the clothesline around her hands and cut her sweatshirt down the front with a paring knife from the kitchen. Last, he washed the dishes to make it look like she'd done them, and then he took the money from her purse. He said he did all those things to make it look like rape and robbery."

Dr. Tanner, the doctor who performed the autopsy, was next on the stand for the State. Towle asked him about the results of the autopsy: "Dr. Tanner, when you completed the autopsy had you found any evidence, anything at all, that indicated there had been a rape?"

Tanner answered simply, "No."

"Your Honor," said Towle, "I'd like to ask now, since this case will rest on the so-called confession of Mr. Parker, that the defense be given a copy of that document. I don't know why we haven't been given a copy. We can't properly prepare—"

"We object," said Deputy Attorney Fahrnbruch. "The request is irrelevant. It's a fishing expedition."

"How can it be irrelevant, your—"

"The confession is not germane," answered Judge Ronin forcefully. "Denied."

"Can we have the autopsy report?"

"Objection."

"Sustained," said Ronin.

"Can we have the photographs of Mrs. Parker before she was removed from the house?"

"Objection," repeated Fahrnbruch.

"Sustained."

Towle had only one question for Chief Carroll. "Chief Carroll, did you ever locate the black '49 Ford that was seen by several witnesses outside the Parker house on the morning of the murder? The one you said was the best clue."

"No, it was never located."

Towle questioned twenty more witnesses, most of them character witnesses. Dorothy Miille, secretary at the park office, was typical in her praise of Darrel: "He was perfectly normal at work that morning. I was told he arrived about 7:20. After I got there he just went about his duties as he did every other day. He did complain to me about his car battery being dead and said that he was going to pick one up at Sears when he went downtown."

When Max asked her about the relationship between the Parkers, she said, "I'd never seen any signs of jealousy, they never argued, there was never any animosity between them at all that I witnessed."

When the last witness had been dismissed, Judge Ronin made his ruling, the conclusion of which there was never any doubt. "There's probable cause to believe the defendant committed the crime. The trial date will be 9:00 A.M., April 9."

The next day the *Journal* ran a recap of the preliminary hearing on the front page. There was a picture that took up a quarter of the page showing Darrel flanked by the Cooks, Tom McManus, and Max Towle. There were no new revelations, but, separate from the hearing report, in the lower right-hand part of the page was a small article beneath the headline WOMAN CLAIMS WAS ASSAULTED: "A 27-year-old woman told police Saturday that she was forced from her car by a man with a snub-nosed gun west of Omaha. The man took her into his car, a 1946 or '47 Chrysler, and drove onto a side road where she was raped. The man returned her to her car, after taking one dollar from her purse, and threatened her if she reported the incident."

On Sunday, January 29, a small man wearing wire-rimmed glasses, a topcoat, and hat and carrying a worn but fully loaded briefcase entered the cracked and fading front doors of the penitentiary. A minister, Bible in hand, hurriedly followed the man in. A short while later, Darrel, lying on his bed awaiting church services and a visit from his parents, was aroused by a guard opening the door to his room.

"Someone to see you, Parker."

Darrel assumed his parents had arrived. He was taken to a conference room on the main floor, where he was confronted by the little man in the wire-rimmed glasses.

"Hello, Mr. Parker," the man said as he nonchalantly shuffled papers on the table. "I'm Dr. Stein. I'm a psychiatrist representing the State."

"My attorneys have told me not to meet with anyone from the State, Dr. Stein. They don't think I've been treated quite—"

"Oh, I understand. You don't have to answer any questions if you don't want to. I just wanted to ask you about your personal history. That was the agreement, you know, between Mr. Towle and Mr. Scheele . . . and myself."

Darrel looked around the room with weary, depressed, and darkened eyes. He looked toward the front entrance, wondering if his parents had come yet. He knew he shouldn't agree, yet he seemed unable to tell the man no.

"What do you say?" goaded Stein. "You don't have to answer anything you don't want to."

"Well . . . just the history then."

Violin music. Holst. *The Planets.* A bow inlaid with ivory was drawn across the strings of a violin handmade by Tom McManus's musical mentor, Carl Steckelberg, who had once been head of the university's music department. The play was flawless. McManus was in his basement playing next to a running, open-topped washing machine. Bubbles rose lazily from the washer, some going clear to the floor joists above before bursting. Clothes were drying on a line, and dirty ones lay in sorted piles on the floor. Although he'd gone into law, he never gave up his music. Years before he felt he had been snubbed for the position but had recently become the concertmaster with the Lincoln Symphony. Dressed for church, eyes closed, he was lost in the music. The telephone rang in the kitchen above him.

"Tom, telephone," announced Lu at the top of the stairs.

"Tell them I'll call back, Lu. I'm playing! . . . Are the girls ready for church?"

Lu stepped down the stairs and shut the door.

"It's Max, Tom. It sounds important."

Tom hurriedly put the violin in its case and rushed up the stairs two at a time. On the phone, he just listened. Max had been tipped off by one of his contacts at the prison that Stein had cornered Darrel.

"I'll be right there, Max . . . I have to go, Lu, it's an emergency."

At the prison, Darrel and Dr. Stein were still talking.

"The most fun we had then was furnishing the house," said Darrel. "We did it on a budget of just eighty-five dollars. We'd go to sales and we'd—"

McManus, winded from running, rushed headlong into the room. Stein, in an immediate guilt reaction, quickly began replacing his papers in the briefcase.

"What's going on here?" shouted McManus. "Darrel, we told you not to talk to any of these State doctors, didn't we?"

Darrel looked at Stein, who looked at no one. Calmly, Stein replaced his papers, closed his briefcase, and headed for the door. McManus shouted after him.

"Dr. Stein, Mr. Scheele didn't check with us on this. You know that!"

Stein didn't answer. He casually put on his hat and walked out the door. McManus slumped into a chair opposite Parker.

"What did he ask you, Darrel?"

Beneath a leaden sky on a frozen dirt-covered street in north Lincoln, a police cruiser slowly followed a 1946 Chrysler four-door. Another cruiser blocked the intersection ahead of it. The Chrysler driver pulled to the curb and stopped. Policemen got out of both cars with guns drawn.

"Put your hands on the wheel," said the first policeman to arrive at the car. He looked inside then slowly smiled. "Well, who do we have here? None other than Wes Peery, Lincoln's one-man crime wave. Get the hell out, Wes!" The other policeman approached.

"Cuff him up while I look in his car," said the first policeman. He inspected the car and immediately found a snub-nosed revolver under the front seat. After scrutinizing the barrel on both sides he yelled at his partner.

"Well, looky here, Frank. Would you like to give Masters his gun back, or should I?"

The next day Masters sheepishly reclaimed his gun. He said he had questioned Peery, whose name was not immediately released. However, when the story made the papers it was reported that "the man arrested would also be questioned in connection with the January 22 rape of a Council Bluffs woman."

By the next day Wesley Peery was revealed as the thief who had taken Masters' gun. He was also charged with the Winkler robbery and the rape in Sarpy County near Omaha. His identification by the rape victim was "definite." Detectives, as they had done with so many other suspects, questioned Peery about the still unsolved Carolyn Nevins murder in Omaha. However, they didn't question him again about the Parker murder. Masters said, "A lie detector test cleared the Lincolnite of any connection with the Nevins case."

Detective Beave of the Lincoln Police Department said of Peery, "The suspect was released last fall from the state penitentiary, where he served a 10-year sentence. The man has a juvenile record going back to 1935, when he was only ten years old. In 1943 he was given a 15-year term for grand larceny and burglary at the Washington

State Reformatory, but was paroled in 1946. In 1946 he was picked up for auto theft again here in Lancaster County."

Two weeks later in Lancaster District Court, Wesley Peery appeared for his preliminary hearing. Masters identified the handgun taken from Peery's car as being his service revolver, and Winkler identified it as being similar to the gun used in the holdup. Virgil Falloon and Roy Campbell were both seated in the courtroom when Peery stood, smiled, and waved at a middle-aged woman seated directly behind him who was wearing silver glasses and had short black hair.

"Who's that Peery just waved to?" said Falloon.

"That's his mother . . . Does she remind you of anyone?" Campbell replied. Falloon looked more closely at the woman, then at Campbell. He shook his head in disbelief.

"He told me," said the victim on the stand, "if you scratch me, I'll kill you."

"Pretty slick," said Campbell. "Peery gets arrested, charged, and arraigned all in one week. The law can sure move quick when it wants to, can't it?"

"And how much of this do you think was intentional on Wes's part?—take himself out of the limelight. With his record, the car, the rape in Omaha . . . Max has a pretty good idea he's the one that killed Nancy Parker," said Falloon. "He probably wanted to get caught for something else—trade a few more quick years in the pen, which for him is like going back to his apartment, instead of getting the electric chair."

Poverty. Deprivation. Abuse. Neglect. A person like Wesley Peery could be understood only by looking at his entire life, not just his criminal record. Such a look back would tell anyone why he had become the type of person he was in 1956. You didn't have to be a psychiatrist to know the signs. As with so many violent criminals there is a commonality to their past, their early years. There was a dire beginning that foretold an even darker ending.

As a boy he was thin and undernourished—understandable since his father had been on welfare since Peery was three years old. He said his father—before he left the family high and dry—"beat me every day from the time I was five." His mother had drily observed, "Wesley was slow to learn to walk and talk, was always quiet, and seldom cried when hurt." He developed an obsession for stealing and hoarding small articles of worth, such as coins, watches, rings, and jewelry. This eventually led him, at least in his eyes, to what was a seminal event in his life.

His father had accused him of stealing money, small change and a handful of foreign coins, off his dresser. Peery vehemently denied the accusation and swore that it was his older brother, Floyd, who had taken the money. Regardless of who had actually taken the coins, Wesley took the punishment for it. And what ultimately stuck in his mind was not the accusation of theft, and not the beating, so much as his feeling that his mother had known it was Floyd and had not intervened, had not stood up for him. He never forgot what he saw as an unforgivable betrayal by his mother. When his mother was notified of his incessant thievery at school, he candidly told her, "I don't know what it is, but when I leave home something makes me take things."

As his behavior continued to worsen, according to his mother, "punishment had no effect." One evening after a particularly heavy beating by his father, Wesley waited for his parents to leave and then set the house on fire.

A year later, his father's cousin moved in with them. The man was an established burglar and often carried a concealed gun. Enamored of the man, Wesley followed him one evening when he broke into another house in the neighborhood—"From that time on, I wanted my own gun." He was eight and a half years old.

When he was ten years old, he was caught taking money out of the open till of the cash register at the neighborhood gas station. For that, he was at last sent to a home for delinquent children.

In his early teens he continued his acts of petty crime. He stole bicycles, hubcaps, and any items left in unlocked cars that he could lay his hands on. He kept his cache of stolen goods in a friend's storage shed. When he was fifteen he was finally arrested for his accumulated petty thefts and sent to the State Industrial School in Kearney, Nebraska, a home for wayward boys. When he was seventeen he was picked up for burglary and a parole violation and returned to Kearney. At eighteen he was taken in as a foster child by a charitable farmer who lived on the outskirts of Lincoln. As part of a scheme to steal what he thought were hidden assets, Peery shot the farmer from ambush with a shotgun but was later charged only with assault, not attempted murder.

In 1943, at the age of nineteen, he stole a car in Seattle, where he'd been staying with his older brother. He was later apprehended in Roseburg, Oregon, still driving the stolen car. Under the seat was a pistol. Years later he would falsely claim that he had committed several murders on this supposed crime spree from Washington to Oregon. Yet what was established by newspaper accounts was that within a two-day period he drove south from Seattle. First, there was a bowling alley break-in where fifteen dollars worth of coins were taken from a pop machine. The police said that whoever broke into the bowling alley "had to be a small, slender person to fit through the broken window." At that time Wesley was lean and lithe. In the same town on the same evening there was a pistol taken from a car in the parking lot outside a large restaurant—the same pistol that he was caught with the next day and one that he saw fit not to pull on the armed highway patrolman who stopped him for running a stop sign. He was sent back to Washington to serve out a sentence for grand larceny at the Washington State Reformatory.

The success, the outward happiness of others, seemed to arouse nothing but anger within him. What he couldn't have, what others had, he would steal. When he was older he began to take what he wanted when he wanted, regardless of the penalty. Consequences meant nothing to him. He would get out of prison, commit more crimes, and in short order return to prison again, his only home. Once there, he would revert to a model life, always getting out early for good behavior.

After his incarceration in Washington he was released on parole in October of 1946. He returned to Lincoln, where he promptly stole another car and committed two holdups. He was sent back to prison for ten years in the Nebraska State Penitentiary. While there, he was given the Minnesota Multiphasic Personality Inventory. He "had a high score in the paranoid area." It was noted that "the subject feels he is constantly being unjustly treated by others and tends to be a person who consistently overstresses his potentiality."

In fifteen years, from March of 1941 until he was released on October 12, 1955, Peery had been out of jail a total of less than ten months. When he was released in October of 1955 he immediately fell back in with an old group of Lincoln friends—Richard Brockman, Ira Brockman, and Edwin Lundy, all of whom had prison records and who at the time were involved as a group in a rash of burglaries that targeted small businesses. Lundy had a job working on the garbage truck detail for the city's park department and, based on his recommendation, had gotten Peery a short-term job at the park. Lundy told James Ager that his friend needed money so that he could visit his brother in Washington. He didn't say that Peery had been in prison or that Peery's brother was in the state prison in Washington.

James Ager had no knowledge of Peery's background, but when the work ran out, he let Peery go during the first week of December.

Peery's presentation of himself to the public was quixotic. He had a blank expressionless face that betrayed no emotion, but his eyes gave a dark reflection of what went on behind them. Lazy, sleepy eyes with an opaque serpentine quality always seeming to be focused beyond what he was looking at. The white that ran between his lower eyelids and the bottom of his iris was a condition that some native tribes say reveals a man's spirit of evil.

One thing was certain. However underprivileged he was as a child, however much he'd been abused, however much he'd been incarcerated, he had never been rehabilitated. He was beyond rehabilitation. One could no longer feel sorry for Wesley Harms Peery by the time he'd become an adult. He had moved beyond sympathy, was irreparably and deeply damaged, and had become an unrelenting criminal who reverted to increasingly sadistic acts of lawlessness each and every time he was released from prison back into society. He had grown beyond redemption, and for the acts he committed he was forever beyond remorse.

CHAPTER SIX

A frigid and windy day in February. The drone of a propeller-driven aircraft hummed in the distance. Tom McManus waited inside the tiny Lincoln airport as a twin-engined Convair arrived. A light snow swirled in the propellers' wake as the plane approached the terminal. At the airport entrance McManus watched as the passengers hurriedly disembarked in the cold late-afternoon air. A tall man with intense eyes and a confident gait deplaned carrying a small suitcase and a shiny black case that looked very similar to the one that Reid had carried. When he came through the doors McManus approached him.

"Dr. Kelley?" asked Tom.

"Yes. And you are?"

"I'm Tom McManus, Max Towle's partner."

Dr. Kelley was the man recommended by George Robinson. He was a professor at the University of California at Berkeley and a man with a colorful past. McManus had heard of him when he was in the service in Europe at the end of World War II. Kelley headed up the thousand-bed psychiatric hospital in Belgium that dealt primarily with victims of shell shock—a phenomenon that McManus had experienced firsthand when his unit was mistakenly bombed near Saint-Lô by Allied planes in the infamous Operation Cobra. Kelley also served as the chief psychiatrist at the Nuremberg Trials when the war was over. In the previous weeks Kelley had talked with Max Towle extensively by phone, and they had arranged for an entire day of testing on Darrel on February 24. He informed Max that before he would agree to take the case he wanted to meet with Parker and give him his own polygraph test. Based on the results of that test, he would decide whether or not he would work on Parker's defense.

The next morning Towle, McManus, and Dr. Kelley were waiting for the arrival of Darrel at Bailey's Sanitarium. They talked in a small glass-enclosed office that overlooked a large assembly room where Kelley would examine Darrel. Kelley was given the evidence and briefed by Max as to what Darrel had said about Reid's interrogation. As they talked, Kelley slowly compiled a list of the questions he would ask Darrel during the lie detector examination. When they were finished, Kelley answered Max's question about who might have committed such a crime.

"The person who committed this crime doesn't have to be crazy, no, Max . . . The motivation behind such acts is to have someone at their mercy, under their control, perhaps just as they were once a victim while at someone else's mercy."

An orderly entered the office.

"Dr. Kelley, Mr. Parker has arrived."

Kelley followed the orderly into the observation room, where his lie detector had been set up on a table, alongside a stethoscope, a blood pressure cuff, and a legal pad. Muffled laughter and screams erupted from various parts of the building.

"Can some doors be shut?" Dr. Kelley asked the orderly. Darrel calmly entered the room and sat where Dr. Kelley directed him. He looked apprehensively at the lie detector.

"I can understand your hesitation about taking another examination with a lie detector. Let me assure you that we're going to proceed slowly and deliberately and there will be no yelling or screaming on my part, that's not how a proper examination is conducted. Is that understood?"

Darrel nodded without looking at Kelley.

"Now first, Mr. Parker," began Kelley, "we're going to perform a medical exam to make sure there's nothing wrong with you physiologically that would affect your answers to questions on the polygraph . . . I understand you have asthma?"

From the office Max and Tom watched Dr. Kelley meticulously conduct his medical and lie detector examinations. It was the first time either of them had seen a lie detector in operation.

"It doesn't seem like that big of a deal," said Tom as he watched Kelley casually begin to ask questions of Darrel.

"I don't suppose it is," replied Max, "if you know what you're doing."

When Kelley was finished, he turned the machine off and unhooked the apparatus. As he did so, he talked with Darrel. "Now that she's gone, Darrel, how do you think of your wife?"

Darrel, still in a state of depression, answered slowly. "I have my memories. They are always with me. They can never be taken away . . . I still love her."

A patient's faint scream was heard from the floor above. Darrel looked up. "To some people, I'm sure just being here—at a mental institution, being tested—means I'm crazy . . . means I did it."

"Sometimes we have to ignore what other people think."

"That's hard," said Darrel. "At least it is for me."

The orderly notified Dr. Kelley that lunch was ready in the cafeteria. Darrel, accompanied by a sheriff's deputy, followed the orderly into the hall. Kelley entered the office where Towle was looking out the window at a towering oak whose limbs were being wildly navigated by a pair of courting squirrels. Max removed a chewed-up, half-smoked cigar from his mouth and turned to hear what Dr. Kelley had to say. He wanted to be proven wrong a second time.

"My polygraph test showed Mr. Parker innocent, Max, just like Robinson's did. He couldn't have done it even if he wanted to. He's just not that kind of person. Based on my interview his reaction to any serious problem would be to internalize it, not act on it. It just would not be in his nature to commit some form of externalized aggression."

"There's no doubt about your findings?" asked Max. "No chance that—"

"No doubt in my mind whatsoever. I'm as sure as I can be about such things. I asked him every question I could think of based on the information you gave me. Every response was negative—meaning he had no knowledge of the crime, nor any culpability. His answers were totally consistent."

"Robinson said you've worked a lot of trials," said Towle. "You've had experience with this kind of thing."

"I've had a lot of trial experience, Max. But I've never experienced a situation like this, where someone as innocent as Darrel has signed a confession. If you're going to ask will I work on this case with you, the answer is yes. You're going to need all the help you can get."

"There's one other thing I'd like to ask, Doctor. You know your machine, and I guess Reid knows his if he's done twenty-five thousand exams like they say—I still don't believe that—but I have a question for you. Darrel has told us that he held up during Reid's first interrogation, the one that lasted three hours or more. Even though he broke down and cried several times, he said he didn't crack, never admitted anything. But he said that at the start of the second interrogation, after he and Reid ate their sandwiches and had the milk in the photography lab, that he felt strange—became extremely tired and woozy. He said his head was spinning, he even tried to lie on the floor and Reid wouldn't let him. And after that he says he remembers very little, just bits and pieces, and went into a kind of fog. The confession became just a blur that he remembers very little of. Do you have an explanation for that?"

"Something like that, a reaction like that, could be caused by being in a tranquilized state—brought about by the ingestion of tranquilizers or some other drug, if that's what you're suggesting. If so, that would obviously negate any test on a lie detector, but then, as we've said, the prosecution won't have to rely on a lie detector exam anyway. They've got the typed confession, and that's all they're going to go by at trial. My guess is you'll never hear about Reid's polygraph test again, even if the judge were to allow it. With the tactics he used, Reid couldn't have gotten a reliable polygraph test anyway. If it was some kind of tranquilizer he was given, its effect, especially on someone like Darrel who's probably never been on medication other than for his asthma, would have been significant. He would have felt disoriented, tired, woozy, and detached; he would have been easy to manipulate. You told me that witnesses who saw him after the interrogation said he seemed subdued, in a trance. Pills would have just made Darrel that much more vulnerable to the same tactics Reid had employed in the afternoon interrogation that he'd then been able to withstand. That could very well have been the cause of his manipulation by Reid, but proving it is another question altogether. And we have to know that Darrel's breakdown might have eventually happened regardless of whether he'd been drugged or not, just due to his mental state. I'm sure you know that medical proof of any kind of drugging will at this point be impossible, as will any other definitive proof of what Reid did, since there were no witnesses. Whatever went on in that little room will just be Darrel's word versus Reid's. And that's obviously why Reid wanted no witnesses. My opinion is that the entire defense process should revolve around revealing the tactics Reid employed to get the false confession, aside from any drugging that may have occurred."

Before McManus drove Dr. Kelley back to the airport, Virgil Falloon, McManus's neighbor and longtime friend, talked with Dr. Kelley in his hotel room. Falloon interviewed Kelley while he packed his bags. As Falloon would write in the next morning's paper, Kelley told him that

> Darrel Parker made a false confession and has no guilty knowledge of his wife's slaying. He has a passive personality that is putty-like to suggestions when he is emotionally upset.
>
> My lie detector test not only showed his innocence but more important to me was the psychiatric side of the examination which gave me an understanding of his personality makeup. Mr. Parker's emotional and psychological makeup clearly explains why he could have burst forth with a false confession.
>
> Furthermore, Mr. Parker is the type of person who could be easily induced to give just such a confession. From my psychiatric evaluation and findings on the lie detector, it is my opinion that is what happened. If he had killed his wife there is no way he could have gone to work, as he did, and shown no signs of being emotionally disturbed the rest of the morning.

Dr. Kelley's final statement to Falloon was that the "investigation of this case should be reopened and all available information and clues should be rechecked."

At the airport Tom escorted Kelley to the plane. On the tarmac just before boarding, Kelley said, "I've got an extra copy of Reid's book back at my office, Tom. I'll mail it to you. Before trial you and Max should go over it with a fine-tooth comb. It'll tell you a lot about what Reid does, how he does it, and why he does it."

During the month of March both sides prepared for the trial. Scheele found two more doctors to analyze Darrel's mental state in order to counter Dr. Kelley's considerable expertise and that of the other two defense psychiatrists. One was Dr. Don C. Fitzgerald, the chief of psychological services at the state hospital. He had received his undergraduate degree at Brigham Young University and his doctorate at the University of Iowa. When he examined Darrel he gave him the Minnesota Multiphasic Personality Inventory, the Wechsler Adult Intelligence Scale, a Rorschach test, and the Word Usage Test. The other man, Dr. C. H. Farrell, was an Omaha psychiatrist who was in private practice after working several years at the state hospital in Hastings, Nebraska. He had received his medical degree at Creighton University in Omaha and began his practice in 1946. When their meetings with Darrel were complete, Scheele said he would make their findings public only during the trial.

Darrel continued to spend his days in the prison hospital, continued to complain to his parents that "for a man used to being busy on a daily basis, there is nothing to do." Along with his radio, his parents brought him a bevy of reading materials—books, magazines, comic books, crossword puzzles, and newspapers. He covered the other bed in the room with them, dividing them according to category, in effect creating his own library. His only physical activity was a daily half-hour walk around the hallways of the hospital. He wasn't to mingle with the general population of the prison. Other than his sporadic visitations it was solitary confinement; his only interaction was with the guards who served his meals.

Max sat in a booth in his favorite bar on Ninth Street, waiting. He nursed a martini, chased the olive around the bottom of the glass with his finger, and occasionally checked the door. Carl Wise entered the bar and took the seat opposite Max. They had known each other for more than thirty years. "Hi, Carl. Thanks for coming." Max signaled the waitress. "Two martinis, Lois."

The papers were preparing the citizens of Lincoln for the upcoming trial. Judge John Polk had been selected as the presiding judge. One of the older county judges, the white-haired Polk had been known to nod off during trials, a habit that was most disturbing to the attorneys arguing in front of him, defense attorneys particularly. The trial was to be a long one, "at least two weeks or more," according to the *Journal*. As many as one hundred witnesses were expected to be called, and a similar number might be called before a jury would be selected. Of considerable interest was whether the lie detector tests, which had been so much in the public eye for months, would be admitted into the record. "To date, such tests have generally not been ruled admissible as evidence," reported the *Journal*.

In Towle's office, three days before the trial started, Tom McManus gave Max a running summary of what he'd been able to find out about Peery. He read from a yellow legal pad: "When Peery came out of the pen in October he got hired on at the park department after a friend told Ager that Peery needed a few bucks to get to Washington State to see his brother—just happening to omit the fact that Peery's brother was in the pen there."

"What about the break-in at the Parker house?" asked Max.

"Probably Peery. He knew the house from working with the park department. Had probably seen Nancy when she stopped by the office to pick Darrel up. The Tuesday after the break-in, when Ager had a crew start work on a security fence around the house, guess who was on the crew?"

"Peery."

"That's right. That gave him a chance to check Parker's schedule and routine. Nancy fed the crew cookies, so Peery would have had a chance to check her out, too . . . Our snitch said Peery's girlfriend saw her husband at the pen toward the end of December. She was wearing a different watch, and when the husband asked where she got it, she came up with some cock-and-bull story that he didn't buy."

"What about the car? The Ford."

"He sold it to a farmer from Milford after the Winkler robbery. He may have already bought the Chrysler by then since the Ford was so hot."

"Call the farmer. Set up a meeting for next weekend, and tell him we'll bring a photographer."

After church on Easter Sunday, McManus sat on his back porch with Virgil Falloon, his neighbor. They had hidden Easter eggs and chocolate bunnies for their children. Lined up at the bottom of the steps the kids anxiously awaited the signal to look.

"One, two, three, go," yelled Tom to the excited throng. The kids took off screaming in all directions. Around the corner of the house stepped Max Towle, with an Easter basket in each hand. "Max is such a soft touch. He's always bringing the kids stuff on the holidays," Tom whispered to Falloon.

"Hello, boys. Looks like I got here just in time. Here, Virg, you take one of these for your kids. Who's got the most eggs? My money's on Kitty. She runs faster than the boys."

Max plopped on the porch and painstakingly opened a chocolate Easter bunny.

"How do you feel about tomorrow, Max?" asked Virg. "Are you ready?"

"You're never totally ready, Virg. There's always something you want more time on. Always. You just have to do the best you can with what you've got. Things constantly change, like the car. We only found out where the Ford is two days ago."

Tom's youngest daughter approached, crying false tears.

"Daaad. Kitty won't let me find any eggs. She's got 'em all."

"Kitty, let your sister get some eggs, too . . . OK?"

"Aaaall right."

"Don't you just love kids," exclaimed Max.

CHAPTER SEVEN

On Monday morning, April 9, Darrel sat dressed in his suit, bolt upright on a gray-enameled government-issue chair in the corner of his antiseptic room. It was 6:00 A.M. A guard entered the room with a worn metal tray upon which were scrambled eggs, two pieces of undercooked bacon, a piece of burned toast, a cup of pitch-black coffee, and a glass of watered-down orange juice. A special breakfast for a special day.

"Today's the big day, eh, Parker?" asked the guard casually.

Darrel nodded and quickly turned to the tray. He ate it all. He'd gained nearly twenty pounds since December from eating the bland and starchy prison food. Eating had been the only thing to look forward to, even if it was often indigestible. The daily walk he was allowed was not nearly enough exercise to burn off the number of fat-inducing calories he took in each day.

His day in court. This is what he'd been waiting for.

It had finally come. He was certain that once the facts were out, once a jury understood what had happened to him with Reid in that interrogation room, that he would be acquitted. He had told as much to Kenneth Cook, who could do nothing but say, yes, if they could lay the facts before the jury and they understood what had actually transpired, he was sure that Darrel would be acquitted. But inside, Cook wasn't so confident.

In its unfolding, in the laying out of all the minutiae, Darrel knew the truth of the murder of Nancy, his interrogation, and the confession would come out. The truth would be there for all to see and hear, he was sure of it. It would be there, but it would be apparent only to those who were truly open to it. It would be there, but it would have to be discerned through the boring, repetitive questioning by Elmer Scheele that would intentionally and relentlessly come in the wake of each witness's testimony. In spite of everything it would be there in the end. The evidence would be there.

After months of press coverage, however, there wouldn't be many in the city who would be open to new interpretations of a truth that was already "known." The trial would involve weeks of testimony—the State would call a witness, the defense would call a witness, there would be rebuttal witnesses, there would be cross-examinations and recross-examinations, there would be special proceedings. By the time it was over the trial transcript would reach 1,752 pages. For many, especially the jury, the trial would become a mind-bending, tedious, and procedurally baffling exercise. Max Towle knew that if the defense could just get the jurors to listen they would have a chance. All they had to do, after all, was to get just one juror to accept the truth. The truth as Max now knew it to be.

On his way to the trial, Max had his briefcase in hand and was about to leave his office with Tom McManus. He paused at his secretary's desk. He could always count on her for an honest opinion.

"May, I would like to ask you a question—as a woman . . . If you were on this jury, how would you feel about Darrel? Right now, before you've heard any of the evidence? What would you say if I had you in *voir dire*?"

"If you're asking me, Max, I would have to say that I would have an open mind. I would listen to all of the evidence before making any conclusions. But if you're asking me what I think most women in town would think, then I'd say most women in town have probably bought the confession. And they might even be more strident in their judgment of him than men would because of the nature of the crime."

"Thanks, May . . . I think."

It was a cool spring morning, forty-one degrees, as Darrel and Sheriff Karnopp loaded into the backseat of Karnopp's unadorned patrol car. On the way to the courthouse they each looked out their separate windows. Karnopp had come to like Darrel. He had his misgivings, had a hard time believing that someone as different as Darrel was from his normal clientele could be guilty of the crime he was accused of. He was thus not entirely sure of Darrel's guilt, but he soldiered on and did his job as he knew he had to.

"I tell you what, Darrel," Karnopp began slowly, still looking out the window. "If you promise me you won't try anything, I won't put the handcuffs on you at the courthouse. OK?"

"I promise."

The car pulled up at the back entrance, the west side, of the Lancaster County Courthouse. The old building had seen better days. More than fifty years earlier they had to remove the "copper" statue of Abraham Lincoln that had adorned the dome, because it was prematurely deteriorating—the figure turned out to have been made of something other than copper, was severely corroded, and ready to topple. Now all of the building was deteriorated. The marble steps inside were worn concave from the thousands of footsteps of people who had trod up and down them for more than seventy years. The fading and cracked paint on the walls and wood floors had been covered with a fresh coat for the trial, but that did little to hide the fact that the building was worn out. The courtroom, likewise, had a fresh coat of paint on the walls and a fresh coat of varnish on the faded and worn woodwork. All of this was done because it was known that this was going to be "something more than just another trial." It had attracted the attention of the entire city and far beyond.

Darrel got out of the car looking haggard and puffy with dark circles under his tired eyes and wearing a dark-gray suit that had grown tight on his body. He was faced with a group of photographers who shouted at him beneath bursting flashbulbs. Spectators lined the sidewalk as Darrel looked up into the budding trees in an attempt to avert their gaze. The sun shone brightly through scudding spring clouds that moved to the east ahead of a cool and steady breeze. As he walked with Karnopp to the rear entrance of the courthouse, members of the crowd whispered behind gloved hands, one or two shouted obscenities, and the rest watched in quiet sympathy. Once Darrel was inside, the crowd hurriedly rushed to the main entrance and joined the line waiting for the courtroom to open, where the same attendance rules that were applied at the preliminary hearing would be in force.

Further evidence of the unique status given the trial was noted inside the courtroom, where the press were given unusual and preferential treatment. Chairs marked REPORTERS were located immediately inside the rail, an area normally reserved for only the defense and prosecution tables. Virgil Falloon was the sole representative of the *Star.* Other seats were taken by the *Journal,* the *Omaha World-Herald,* the midstate papers—from Kearney, Hastings, and Grand Island—the *Des Moines Register,* and two television stations, KOLN from Lincoln and WOW from Omaha.

Darrel sat uncomfortably at the defense table between Tom McManus and Kenneth Cook. He smiled meekly and said a quiet hello to his mother, who sat directly behind him. She was immaculately dressed in a long purple print dress with a wide black patent belt, black purse, and a tight black hat with a fine lace veil wrapped in on itself atop her forehead. Spotless white gloves covered her hands, which she folded calmly on her lap. She was stoic in a resolute yet serene way. She was an unemotional, unflappable rock. Mr. Parker, on the other hand, appeared to be nothing more than what he was—a lifelong and weather-worn tiller of the soil. Without his hat on, the white skin above his tan line was starkly visible. In the big city he was truly out of his element. He had done all he could. His faith was now firmly placed in the four men who sat in front of him, flanking his son. He knew the Cooks; he knew the Cooks trusted Towle and McManus, and that was good enough for him. He was content in the notion that he had the best people he could get for the job, and he, as well as anyone, knew that the job was going to be a big one.

At the prosecution table Scheele stood shuffling papers in a deliberately authoritative manner. He was resplendent in new Florsheim wingtip shoes, a crisp black pin-striped suit, and a colorful, wildly patterned tie. The overhead lights reflected in the glistening pomade sheen in his hair, which was combed straight back without a part. At his right hand was Deputy Attorney Dale Fahrnbruch, the surveillant of Des Moines, the funeral follower.

Towle, in contrast to Scheele, looked like a short but stout and aging truck driver with his meaty neck, paunch, and huge workman-like hands. Edgar Cook sat deferentially to his father's left and Towle to McManus's right. They would hold these positions throughout the trial, except for those occasions when Max and Ken sat together so that they could compare observations during testimony.

Judge Polk entered the courtroom at exactly nine o'clock. After brief opening statements, the jury selection was under way within minutes. Five of the first eight potential jurors were rejected—four by the State and one by the defense. One man said he had formed an opinion that couldn't be changed. Two women were dismissed because they said they were opposed to the death penalty. The guidelines Scheele followed were: "Are any of the people involved in the case known to you? Has publicity caused you to form an opinion that can't be changed? Are you opposed to capital punishment?"

Max Towle took a different tack: "Do you know you can't always believe what you read in the newspapers? Do you realize that sometimes people make false confessions, as some of our GIs did in Korea? Have you heard of false confessions being obtained by force, coercion, or intimidation?"

Towle's question about not always believing what you read in the newspapers was probably the most important one of *voir dire*, for nearly everyone had read the accounts of the murder and Darrel's subsequent confession and arrest. Of those jurors who were rejected, most said, "I've already formed an opinion." Those opinions were formed almost exclusively by what had been read in the newspapers. No one was asked if they had not read of the case.

The prospects were equally varied in their responses: "I don't know if I believe that people can make false confessions." "Either you did something or you didn't." "I don't see how a confession can be false if someone confesses." "If they do that, make a confession, then it has to be true." "A confession is a confession." "Because of all the publicity these past months, especially about the confession, I'm afraid I've developed an opinion that I can't lay aside." "I have an opinion, but in spite of that I'd certainly follow the instructions and try to reach an impartial verdict."

Towle's last question of each potential juror was all-encompassing, meant to cover any possible subjects that he might have overlooked.

"Do you know of any reason, any reason at all, why you can't be a fair juror?"

At least one prospect would not answer that question truthfully, and once seated on the jury his role in reaching the final verdict would be decisive.

After the first day of jury selection Towle met with the press and told them that "brainwashing tactics were used to obtain the so-called confession and that some people are more submissive than others and will admit to something under duress even if they aren't guilty." Elmer Scheele declared in an immediate rejoinder to reporters, "We are not trying a lawsuit here in the examination of jurors."

On Tuesday Emma Groth, a Lincoln housewife, was the first juror selected. Henry Wieskamp, a farmer from the small town of Hickman just outside of Lincoln, was second. Then Dorothy Karlmagen. Peremptory challenges by the State eliminated two jurors before Clyde Blackledge, a semiretired, white-haired contractor, and Emil Joe Hynek, an auto mechanic, were chosen. The defense eliminated three jurors and the State one before John D. Cejka was seated. Evelyn Watson, who worked at the state's motor vehicle department, was chosen seventh. The number would not be a lucky one for her. She would not soon, nor ever, forget her experience as a juror in the murder trial of Darrel Parker. George Walters, who worked at the veteran's hospital on the east side of Lincoln, was chosen next. He would be elected jury foreman. Dale van Landingham, another farmer; Conrad Kammercell, a janitor; Mary Carlson, a nurse; and Lillian Murphy, another housewife; plus two alternates completed the jury selection from the thirty-four-member jury pool. The jury had been selected much sooner than was expected.

The trial would now begin. Witnesses would be called who would reveal what had happened, or at least what they thought had happened, while others would give their expert opinion as it applied to the "reality" as defined by either the defense or the prosecution. That reality would in turn be seen and heard by twelve different jurors—twelve who would see and hear different things from the same witness. One thing was certain: not all would enter the jury box, as they had said during voir dire, with an open mind.

After the jury was seated Elmer Scheele rose stiffly, strode confidently to the jury box, and began the trial in a voice that could be heard clearly throughout the courtroom.

After all this questioning and talking the lawyers have selected you twelve ladies and gentlemen—and the two alternate jurors—to consider the evidence in the case of the State of Nebraska versus Darrel F. Parker.

These opening statements are not supposed to be, under the rules of the court, in the form of an argument, but simply an outline of the evidence that each side expects to present during the course of the trial.

It is true, and Judge Polk will tell you, that the burden of proof is on the State to show Mr. Parker's guilt beyond a reasonable doubt. And the State will present the evidence to meet that burden of proof. As has been told to you over and over again, the defendant is given the presumption of innocence until the State has proven its case. And that is the way it should be.

Now, to begin. After arriving in Lincoln, Mr. Parker and his wife became quite active socially. The couple became well acquainted with the people he worked with and others and enjoyed the company of their newfound friends.

But their house, recently refurbished by the park department, had been moved to an area of Antelope Park that is quite isolated. After the incident on November 13, the break-in at their home, Mrs. Parker became very apprehensive about staying in the house alone.

At a little after 12:00 on Wednesday, December 14, of last year, Mr. Parker called Detective Wise at the police station and said his wife had been strangled. The investigation was undertaken right away . . . When they arrived at the house the investigating officers found that there was a very peculiar and unusual method used in tying the cords around Nancy Parker's neck and wrists. Around her throat was a piece of brown twine, sort of like wrapping twine, and on the basement step was a stick with that very color of twine.

Tom McManus printed *color* in large block letters on his legal pad. After it he made a question mark and wrote, "What the hell does that have to do with anything?"

As the investigation progressed and Mr. Parker went to the funeral of his wife, he was told by me that he might be asked to return to Lincoln and help with the investigation. When I did call him I suggested that he meet me at highway patrol headquarters, in order to avoid any undue publicity. He agreed to come.

When he arrived I asked him to accompany me, and I then introduced him to Mr. John Reid. By eight o'clock that evening Mr. Reid came out and told me he had Mr. Parker's confession and that I should get someone to take it down. I made arrangements to have Miss Audrey Wheeler, Judge Polk's official court reporter [Scheele moved toward Polk, smiled, and graciously held his arm out in the judge's direction], come out to highway patrol headquarters.

After that was done, Mr. Reid, Miss Wheeler, Assistant Chief Masters, Captain Beave, and Mr. Parker and I were all in Colonel Sand's office. Mr. Reid told Parker that, "As I read this statement, if there are any mistakes or errors, correct them as we go along." And that was done; he corrected all the errors as he found them. He then signed his name to the confession with no hesitancy, no reluctancy, freely and voluntarily. He then did the same thing to the other copies . . .

Now there is considerably more evidence to be heard, but it is impractical for me to try and go over every detail at this time. I would rather you hear it from the witnesses themselves.

Finally, I know that you folks, because of the importance of this matter, will be extremely conscientious, and I know you will be very attentive at all times to everything that is said during the course of the trial. That is very important.

We want you to give this case fair and very careful consideration, and I know you will.

Thank you.

Max Towle had listened intently as Scheele spoke. He took few notes and, when it was his turn to speak, did so extemporaneously. Ambling slowly to the jury box he paused to look at each of the jurors before he began.

My duty as defense attorney will be to tell you about all of those things that happened that Mr. Scheele conveniently omitted telling you about, things that haven't yet been reported about what occurred when this so-called confession was taken. We'll tell you what really happened to Darrel Parker in that little room without windows, without witnesses. I don't think any of us would want to be questioned in the manner that John Reid used when he interrogated Darrel Parker! There is a reason why Mr. Reid wanted to be alone with Darrel Parker, why he wanted no witnesses, and we will explain that in due time.

Now, Mr. Scheele said in his opening remarks that John Reid was a kind and considerate man. When Darrel arrived in Lincoln that morning he had been taking sleeping pills the whole week before. He was so depressed he said he felt as though he didn't want to live anymore. He had driven over two hundred miles that morning and was in a state of grief, depression, and severe shock. He was exhausted and fatigued.

After he arrived at highway patrol headquarters he was taken immediately to that little room and introduced to John Reid. He wasn't told who Reid was. He wasn't told what was about to happen to him. He wasn't told what the machine was that was on the table. Left alone there, he would eventually fall under the spell of Mr. Reid's interrogation techniques. Mr. Scheele doesn't want to talk about the methods that were used by Mr. Reid in getting that confession, but we will.

Right from the start Reid told Darrel he "looked like a criminal." He quickly took advantage of Darrel's mental state, abused him physically and verbally. Yet, despite his condition, despite the shock at the treatment he received, Darrel resisted Reid's barrage of accusations. When Reid came out of that room in the afternoon, he said, "I can't get anywhere with this fellow. He is upset, he is grief-stricken, and I can't tell anything from the lie detector." I know that is what he said because he said it to some of the police officers waiting outside the room, officers I know, and I have talked to them.

Mr. Reid told him, "I've had experience with crimes like this. The trouble in your home was sex. Your wife wouldn't submit or succumb to your desires for sexual intercourse, so you killed her." Darrel insisted over and over that he hadn't done anything wrong, that they were happy in their marriage, that there was nothing to confess to.

Before Reid questioned Darrel again, sometime between 6:00 and 7:00, he took him back to the little laboratory room and, with his back to Darrel, poured him a glass of milk. He then gave Darrel the milk and a sandwich and told him to finish them both. Reid waited then, watching Darrel and talking casually to him for twenty or thirty minutes before he began his questioning again.

Darrel says he seemed to lose his equilibrium, something seemed to come over him and he couldn't control himself. He just doesn't know what happened. He even wanted to lie on the floor he was so tired. But Reid wouldn't let him and kept on relentlessly. By 8:00 he had his "confession." Yet no one knows what went on in there. No one except John Reid and Darrel Parker.

If Darrel wasn't a submissive type, a milquetoast, why, he would have had the courage to get up and walk right out of there. You and I would.

Reid got Darrel to say that the night before Nancy would not have sex with him. In fact, the night before they wrapped Christmas presents and wrote Christmas cards. They'd just bought a Christmas tree and had put up a wreath on the front door. They were preparing for the holidays. When they went to bed that night there wasn't one word mentioned about sex.

And when Mr. Scheele says, "Miss Wheeler will tell you here on the witness stand that she never saw a kinder, more courteous man with so much patience as Mr. Reid." I will tell you that Miss Wheeler came into the picture long after Mr. Reid's browbeating was over, long after his work behind closed doors was over. Reid would be a terrible stupe if he continued his bullying tactics in front of anybody, now wouldn't he? If his tactics were so aboveboard, why didn't he allow someone to be present in that room to verify his version of events?

Mr. Reid grilled this boy for a period of nine hours, continuously saying to him, "You're going to fry if you don't confess. Tell me about it and I'll help you out. You don't want to be tried in the newspapers . . ."

When you hear the accusations Mr. Reid made to Darrel, I want you to decide whether or not you think those are the words of either of the Parkers. I don't think you will.

And the missing watch . . . no one seems to know what happened to it. Now, I say this, whoever killed Nancy Parker has that watch. And concerning the search for that watch, I have to say that I have done more investigating than the Lincoln Police Department in an attempt to locate it—and I'm still looking.

Finally, I would like to say that we are going to bring before you the findings of a celebrated international man who is an expert like no other and who operates the lie detector machine just as Mr. Reid does, some would say even better. He is the last word in psychiatry and criminology. When he was in Lincoln in February we went with him to Dr. Royal's hospital and gave a test to Darrel that—

Elmer Scheele jumped up and immediately objected.

"Comes now the State of Nebraska and objects to any reference to the results of any polygraph or lie detector test by defense counsel for the reason that the results of such a test are inadmissible as has been held by the Supreme Court of the State of Nebraska."

"Our lie detector tests showed the defendant was innocent!" Towle responded loudly. "Furthermore, in this case, lie detector tests were used over and over to show the supposed innocence of every single suspect that the authorities released!"

Polk ruled that the admissibility of a polygraph examination would be determined at the time it was submitted during the trial. Towle continued.

"I can only hope, Your Honor, that when the time comes the court allows Dr. Kelley to tell us how his lie detector machine showed that this boy is innocent . . ."

Virgil Falloon, in his summary of the first day of the trial, reported that Towle "predicted that the State will have to rely almost entirely on the alleged confession, about which there will be a serious dispute as to its being voluntary or not."

The only witnesses to testify on the first day were Glenn Hill, the first fireman on the scene, and Carl Wise. Wise, retired and the proud owner of Deluxe Billiards on O Street, testified that Mrs. Parker was bound with more than one cord and said simply that they were "tied with lots of knots."

"Do you know, Carl," asked Towle, "that in Darrel Parker's confession he told Mr. Reid that he tied a forester's knot around his wife's neck and that it was a double bowline?"

"I wouldn't know a double bowline if I saw one," replied Wise.

When Towle had Wise demonstrate the type of knots that were in the ropes, Towle said that they appeared to be "just common knots that people tie packages with, granny knots."

"Don't you think, Carl, that the police made a serious mistake by untying those knots at the hospital, instead of cutting them off and preserving the knots?"

"What difference would it make what I thought?" said Wise, glancing uneasily at the prosecutor's table. "It might have been better if they were cut, but my instructions were to see they were untied and that's what I did."

"When you left the house to go to the hospital, Carl, how many people would you say were left in the house?"

"There were probably twenty or more."

"Not the most conducive conditions to conduct a police investigation under," remarked Towle. "And during that investigation you checked on a young man who was released from the state penitentiary in October and who had worked for the park department within a week of this murder, didn't you? You know who I'm talking about, don't you?"

"I think I do."

"Sure you do, he is the one being charged with rape in Sarpy County as we speak? Isn't that right?"

"I haven't followed his activities for some time."

"But you followed them for fifteen or twenty years, didn't you?"

"Yes."

"What I'm getting at, Carl, is the fact that he owned a black Ford just like the one that had been seen near the Parker house the morning of the murder?"

"I think he did."

When Towle asked to see photographs of the knots tied around Nancy Parker's neck and wrists, he was told by Deputy Sheriff Zieman, "They didn't turn out."

The next morning, in the lower left-hand corner of the *Star's* front page, right next to Virgil Falloon's recap of the trial's first day, was a two-paragraph article entitled PEERY RAPE TRIAL OPENS. When Falloon saw the article, written by Campbell, he knew his prediction about Peery had been correct.

Thursday's testimony began on a distinctly somber note with Mrs. Morrison, Nancy's mother. She solemnly appeared in a dark-blue paisley dress with a small white hat laced with cloyingly sweet lilies of the valley. She sat erect in the witness chair and held her purse tightly in both hands, hard upon her lap. Although she would testify honestly and without apparent rancor, she had been gradually convinced by Scheele over the last few months that Darrel was guilty. As she spoke, Mrs. Morrison never turned her gaze in the direction of Darrel Parker.

She stoically told of Nancy's love of music—she played clarinet in the band, orchestra, and the marching band. It became a longing lament. She had, after all, lost her only daughter, her only child. At their church, Nancy belonged to the youth group. Active in Girl Scouts, "she had achieved their highest honor, the Curved Bar." Her grades came as "the result of disciplined hard work, and were always in the top twenty-five percent." During high school she worked at Iowa Methodist Hospital as a dietician's helper. Her first big trip away from home came during the summer after her high school graduation, when she attended a music camp in Gunnison, Colorado.

"She spoke of that often, and it gave her a love of the mountains which she never lost. It so impressed her that while she was going to Iowa State she spent a summer working in the Black Hills of South Dakota. That's where they went on their honeymoon."

When asked whether Nancy ever discussed any of her "close, private, personal problems," Mrs. Morrison said, "If you mean marriage problems, no, she never discussed anything like that."

"Concerning the loss of her watch, could you tell us what type of watch she had?" asked Scheele.

"She had a Hamilton watch that we gave her for a graduation gift from high school. I know nothing more than that except to say that she'd bought a new band for it because she said the snap wasn't holding."

"Mrs. Morrison, when I called Darrel at your home, did he seem normal to you, perfectly normal?"

"Yes. We had put in all of our spare time writing notes of appreciation. Our car wasn't working, and he took Mr. Morrison to school and back and just made himself generally useful about the place."

"As far as you could determine on your visit here," asked Scheele of Mrs. Morrison, "did everything seem to be happy in their home?"

"Yes, I noticed nothing to the contrary."

"Was Nancy your only child, Mrs. Morrison?"

"That's right."

Mr. Morrison told Scheele that he was a music teacher in the Des Moines public schools.

"And did Nancy play in the band and orchestra?"

"She played in junior high and high school."

"From the visits which you had with Darrel here in Lincoln, so far as you could tell everything seemed to be perfectly harmonious between them; is that correct?"

"That is true."

"In your contacts with Darrel, and conversations and observations, what type of a personality did you observe him to have?"

"That's a rather difficult question. I believe I was favorably impressed."

"Was he a submissive, milquetoast type of individual?"

"I would not say so."

Scheele ended his questioning. Towle declined to cross examine either of the Morrisons.

The ambulance attendant who untied the knots, William Hoagland, stated that it had taken him thirty to forty-five minutes to undo the knots that were tied in the twine around Nancy Parker's neck and wrists. A. L. Delaney, a Lincoln police detective, said that he walked around the entire perimeter of the Parker home the day of the murder and found no tracks in the snow.

Everett Rudisil, the police identification officer, testified as to the fingerprints he'd found.

"Did you, in your search for latent fingerprints," asked Scheele, "find any that could be identified?"

"Yes, sir, I found two."

The gallery suddenly buzzed with excitement, sure that they were about to hear the first revelation of the trial.

"And whose prints did you determine those to be?"

"They were Carl Wise's."

An outbreak of guffaws rose from the gallery. Polk let it run its course. Scheele asked a few more questions and sat down.

Towle asked Rudisil if he tested for prints on the washed dishes— two plates, two juice glasses, Darrel's cup, the pan Nancy had poached their eggs in, and a plastic Tupperware pitcher that she had made juice in—that were all in a drain bin by the sink.

"They are important, Everett, because Detective Masters said that Darrel told him that he had washed the dishes after strangling his wife 'to make it look like she washed them.'"

"No, I didn't test them . . . Maybe I slipped up there."

Frank Tanner, the autopsy physician, was not asked by Elmer Scheele if he had found any evidence of rape. He was not asked if there had been evidence of semen found on Nancy Parker's body. It would be up to Towle to broach the publicly sensitive subject.

"In your examination of the body, Dr. Tanner, you examined the vagina, I suppose, for the purpose of determining whether or not sperm fluid was there?"

"Yes, sir."

"Did you find any evidence?"

"No, sir."

"But you did find a light colored substance on the outside of her person, near the vagina, didn't you?"

"Yes, sir."

"It looked like dried semen?"

"Might have been."

"Isn't that what you thought at the time?"

"That is one of the possibilities, yes. I didn't make any further comment except to say that it could have been semen."

Vernon Byler, the police photographer, told of the photos he'd taken inside and outside the house—pictures that would for all time freeze the condition of things as they were on December 14, 1955. The pantry closet in the kitchen was as representative as any—there was a dog brush and a hammer and nails on the top shelf. Below that a jar of Mazola oil, Kellogg's Krunchies, two rolls of Reynolds Wrap, and a partially filled bottle of vinegar. The third shelf held a box of Malt-O-Meal, a box of Quaker Oats, a box of Gooch's Best buttermilk pancake mix, a jar of Skippy peanut butter, and a small can of Folgers coffee—Darrel didn't drink much coffee. On the last shelf was a box of Nutrena dog food meal for Rudy, a box of Niagara instant laundry starch, and a tin of Johnson's floor wax. Resting on the floor at the bottom were five empty six-packs of 7UP along with a broom and dustpan, a dust mop, and a sponge mop. Common things that had meant something to Darrel and Nancy, if only in a utilitarian sense. What was perhaps most important about the pantry was what was not there. That had been where the clothes-line rope that was left over from the basement had been stored.

When the photos of the strangled Nancy Parker were passed to the jury, it was readily apparent by their individual reactions who had been less than truthful during voir dire. Towle watched each juror closely, disturbed but not surprised by what he saw. One by one, as the pictures traveled through the jury, the angry stares several of the men directed toward Darrel revealed that some had already formed an opinion. The women had little stomach for the photos, staring into the open courtroom in an effort to maintain their composure, or quickly handing them off. When they were passed to the defense table, Darrel wept openly and hurriedly passed the photos to Tom McManus. The photos forced them all to view the heinous deed that had been committed and, coming near the start of the trial, would be the single piece of evidence that would cause most of the jurors to form an opinion, even though they had vowed to reserve judgment until the end of the trial.

Gerald Tesch, the tall heavyset patrolman who had gotten Darrel a sandwich and milk the day of Reid's interrogation and the same officer who had watched the house in the days after the murder, told Scheele that he had found two ropes in the attic at 3200

Sumner—ropes that had several knots tied in them. Scheele had seized upon them and suggested that they were "practice knots" tied by Darrel in preparation for the murder. Yet when asked what kind of knots they were, Tesch replied, "I studied knots when I was in the Navy, but, no, I can't identify any of those knots."

"These so-called practice knots, then, don't resemble the knots described by Detective Wise or Mr. Hoagland," observed Towle. "You know . . . tying practice knots in preparation for a murder, Gerald—like Mr. Scheele suggests—seems a little like playing baseball before you go bang somebody over the head with a baseball bat. Somehow, practice just doesn't seem necessary."

The gallery erupted in laughter. This time Polk's lips tightened and he banged his gavel several times for order.

"Do any of the exhibits Mr. Scheele showed you look like the forester's knots that Mr. Parker 'confessed' to—the bowline knots or forester's knots?"

"No, sir."

Towle, holding up a small looped string, asked, "That's also true of the knot in this string, the alleged 'murder knot,' that Detective Masters had Darrel Parker tie after his interrogation with Mr. Reid?"

"That's true. None of them are forester's knots."

Towle returned to the defense table, where he sat heavily next to Tom McManus. As Tesch left the stand, Towle turned to McManus.

"So much for the 'peculiar, unusual, and complicated knots!'"

On Friday the thirteenth—a date that seemed to appear ominously and often in the Parker case—Virgil Falloon authored a three-paragraph article that was tucked away on page 2: PEERY DECLARED GUILTY ON RAPE CHARGE. As Falloon said at Peery's preliminary hearing, Peery would now be "out of the limelight." He would be back in the state penitentiary before the second week of the Parker trial had begun. Out of sight, out of mind.

Bennet Hites, a diminutive bookish man and chief chemist for the Nebraska Agricultural Inspection Board, testified for the State. At the preliminary hearing he had said that Nancy Parker had eaten forty-five minutes to an hour before her death. That did not now fit the prosecution's time line of events that led up to the murder—it meant that Darrel would have had to kill Nancy between 7:45 and 8:00, times when he was already proven to be at work. The prosecutors had obviously talked with Hites about revising his estimate, for he now said, "I would certainly change it downward if I had it to do again."

Dr. Victor Levine followed Hites with testimony that attempted to dovetail even more closely with the prosecution's scenario. A professor at Creighton University's School of Medicine in Omaha, Levine had been given a sample of Nancy Parker's stomach contents by Dale Fahrnbruch. His analysis, he said, led him to conclude that her death occurred fifteen to twenty-five minutes after she ate breakfast. Although the prosecutors had now reduced the time of death by fifteen to twenty minutes so that it more closely matched their theory of the murder, it still did not fit the time frame as dictated by Darrel's schedule on the morning of the murder. Levine's estimate would have put the time of death between 7:20 and 7:40.

Gene Masters was next on the stand. With his usual morose look, and wearing a drab, rumpled brown suit that matched his smoker's stained teeth, he ambled slowly to the witness chair, where he sat stiffly upright and affected an air of hearty self-confidence.

"Was any money or currency found in Nancy Parker's purse?" asked Scheele.

"There was two pennies."

"No currency?"

"No."

Masters went on to describe at length the details of the house and its contents—the furnishings in the bedroom, the northeast bedroom, the clothes in the closets, the Christmas tree and clothesline in the basement, where the dog was, and the location of all the items in the kitchen and dining room. It was a tedious preamble that led up to the question by Scheele concerning the ropes around Nancy Parker's neck and what had been done with the knots at the hospital. The fact that they had been untied had turned into an embarrassing element of the investigation for the prosecution.

"Will you explain, Mr. Masters, why the decision was made to have the ropes untied at the hospital?"

"That was a question we wasn't sure on just what to do; and it was finally decided, after a conference, that it would probably be better to untie the ropes so that at a future date it might be possible to match them with some other rope—which can be done—and we thought it would be better, more possible, to trace the rope if it was all in one piece rather than cut up in numerous pieces, and would determine where the ends were."

Since the decision had been Masters' and the prosecution knew that untying the knots had since become an issue regarding the loss of evidence, Masters' response and the circumlocution it entailed made it obvious that this explanation had been prepared with Scheele specifically for the trial.

Roy Rasmussen and Charles Warren described the ins and outs of knot tying. Rasmussen was the longtime groundskeeper at Boys Town, and Warren was the city forester of Omaha. Parker had gone to Omaha earlier in the fall to meet with Warren to pick up pointers from his work as a forester. Warren took Parker to visit Rasmussen in order to get a demonstration in knot tying for use in tree-trimming work. When shown pictures of the knots used in Nancy Parker's murder, both men concluded they were completely unidentifiable and "definitely not forester's knots."

Court was recessed until Monday. The jurors were not sequestered but were told by Polk "not to converse with anybody about the case and not to form or express an opinion until the matter is finally submitted to you."

Tom McManus, Max Towle, and Folmer Rank, a photographer, drove west on O Street near the town of Emerald early on the sunny Saturday morning of April 14. The threesome was on its way to the farmstead of S. J. Miller near Milford, a small farm town twenty miles southwest of Lincoln.

McManus had discovered that Peery's car had been sold on January 19, four days after the Winkler break-in. The black Ford two-door had been registered to both Wesley Peery and Marzetta Carter, Peery's mother, whose last name had changed for at least the third time.

When they arrived at Miller's white frame house, neatly surrounded by a four-foot black wrought iron fence, they found the car sitting in the center of Miller's turnaround. While Max had a cup of coffee and questioned Miller, Rank immediately set up his camera and began photographing the car. When he completed taking a picture of one side of the car, McManus would get in and turn it around so that the next side to be photographed would face the sun.

On the front windshield was a Kappa Sigma decal. On the upper center was an octagonal university parking sticker. Affixed to the rear window was a university football sticker. The decals established, if nothing else, that a previous owner had gone to the university. But the main reason they had come was the tires. Even though it had yet to be given to the defense attorneys, Towle knew that the police had a tire cast taken in the snow on Sumner Street the night of the murder that showed distinctive tread markings.

The right front tire was a Lee, and the left front was a Hood Deluxe. But it was the rear tires they were after—two Goodyear six-sixteen, four-ply Deluxe All-Weather tread tires. The tire had been discontinued in 1950, so their existence on a car in 1956 was extremely rare. The tires had a unique design of diamonds, or X's, that crisscrossed the center surface. Rank lay on the ground in order to get a good picture of the tread on the black-walled Goodyear tires. Although the tires were worn, the diamond pattern was clearly visible.

On Monday, Robert Duckett, a tall, slender man with a short flattop and a receding hairline, took the stand as a witness for the prosecution. However, by the time he was done his testimony would be more beneficial to the defense than the prosecution.

"Assigned to the FBI," began Duckett, "in Washington, D.C., my duties are to examine hairs, fibers, body fluids, and related materials. I have been doing this work since 1944."

Scheele gave Duckett exhibit 3, which was noted as "Neck cord from body of Nancy Parker," and asked him to comment on it.

"This exhibit is a piece of jute twine," replied Duckett. "It is constructed of two plies twisted together."

"Mr. Duckett," continued Scheele, "I will now hand you what has been marked exhibit 61, an envelope containing twine and marked with the words, 'Picked up from the second step on basement stairs.' Will you tell us if you have ever seen that before?'"

"Yes, I have. It is jute twine that was wrapped around a stick. It is composed of three plies twisted together."

"Is the twine appearing on the stick that you have just described of the same type as the brown twine that was taken from the throat of Nancy Parker?"

"No, sir."

"Always ask the damaging question yourself, right, Tom?" Towle said disparagingly to McManus.

When Duckett was asked to analyze the clothesline rope that also bound Nancy Parker's neck, he said there were two ends that "were too frayed to determine whether they had once been of the same piece."

When handed the sweatshirt that Nancy Parker had been wearing, the one that had been severed down the front, Duckett said the "severed area of the sweatshirt, in my opinion, had been caused by cutting and tearing."

Scheele presented exhibit 56, the quilt taken from the double bed. "My examination showed that there were seminal stains on the quilt." Duckett made a similar conclusion when he examined the scraping of pubic hair and a dried secretion taken from Nancy Parker's left vulva and thigh: "I identified semen in the dried material."

"Mr. Duckett," asked Towle, "you just told Mr. Scheele that the brown twine found on the steps does not match the brown twine found around Mrs. Parker's neck. Isn't that right?"

"That's right."

"But in Mr. Parker's confession when he was asked where he got the twine, he said he got it off the roll of twine on the steps."

"I can't speak to the confession, Mr. Towle. All I can say is that the twine around her neck did not come from the roll on the stairs."

Dorothy Miille, the park secretary, repeated her description of the Parkers' relationship as being "harmonious"; "they got along well"; and they "were kind and considerate, with no discord."

James Ager defined Darrel's job as one of "taking care of the city's trees—those between the sidewalk and the curb and, also, the trees in the parks. He supervised five to six men, and he took extreme interest in his job. He was an excellent employee."

"Tell me, Mr. Ager," asked Towle, "you observed the mannerisms and speech of Mr. Parker the day of the murder. And you were the first person to arrive at the house after Darrel discovered his wife's body.

"When he was grief stricken, when he was crying and you sat with him there in his house, did you have any idea, any idea at all, that he was faking his grief?"

"I had no idea he was faking. His grief certainly seemed genuine to me."

"You believed then and you believe now that his grief was real?"

"Yes."

Opal Closner, Nancy's workmate at Gooch's, was a short stocky woman who appeared in court with a smug self-absorbed air about her. As others had done, she was wearing her best Sunday dress for her testimony and seemed to eagerly await her time in the witness chair. Scheele brought her to court as the only witness for the prosecution who would attempt to cast doubt on the loving relationship between the Parkers that had been described by all the other witnesses. When asked by Scheele to explain an argument that she had witnessed between Nancy and Darrel at her house, she said, "Well, it was over the covering of their table. He had made this table and he wanted to get something to cover it with, a linoleum, but Nancy didn't like the color he'd picked. He was rather disgusted about it."

"Did he display a temper on that occasion?" asked Scheele.

"Not exactly a temper. You could say he was just disgusted, wasn't happy about it."

"Did Nancy seem to be anxious to do what her husband wanted?"

"It always seemed to me that she was."

Max Towle began his cross-examination by asking, "Did you and Mr. Closner ever visit socially with the Parkers?"

"No."

"Your contacts then were purely related to your business affairs?"

"That's right."

"And they seemed to get along except once when Darrel showed Nancy some covering samples which she didn't like. He seemed a little put out and left and then she shopped around until she found what she wanted?"

"She said she got some that night; I suppose what she wanted."

"And that is the 'quarrel' they had, kind of a discussion?"

"Yes."

"Whether to use red or green or blue or yellow?"

"Yes."

When Closner's testimony was reported in the *Star*, it was stated that a CO-WORKER SAW CHANGE IN NANCY, with a subheading that read, UNUSUAL BEHAVIOR OF VICTIM TOLD TO PARKER MURDER JURY. Scheele's ploy had worked. Doubt had been cast and as such was duly reported.

At the start of the second week of the trial, in Monday's *Star*, Virgil Falloon wrote THE MOMENT HAS ARRIVED. On Tuesday there would be testimony by "two of the nation's top criminologists who are about to cross paths in the Parker murder trial. Spectators are expected to jam the courtroom to glimpse the action." The focal point of that confrontation would be the "confession" and how it was obtained— whether it had in fact been voluntary, whether it had been legally taken by Reid. When he wrote about the murder and trial, Falloon was the only reporter who had seen fit to continually put the word *confession* in quotes.

"The State contends the forester 'freely and voluntarily' gave the statement detailing the crime. But the defense contends it's a false confession obtained by a 'prepossessing bully' who browbeat a submissive Parker into saying what authorities wanted him to say."

Falloon described the two foes, Reid and Kelley, and announced that they had both arrived in town. He also mentioned that the missing watch had yet to be found. "Darrel didn't know where the watch was because he hadn't taken it off her arm," Falloon quoted Towle. "I'll say it again, the man who has that watch is the man who killed Nancy Parker."

CHAPTER EIGHT

Tuesday morning, April 17, had arrived. It was the first so-called confrontation between John Reid and Douglas Kelley, "head to head" as Falloon put it. At the close of Monday's testimony, Judge Polk had advised the jury that "we have a procedural matter in the morning that will require the presence of only the court and counsel."

The "matter at hand" was described by Falloon as a "trial within a trial" and would entail testimony from both sides as to whether the confession, exhibit 66, would be allowed as evidence. A ruling would then be made as to whether or not the confession had been voluntary. Dr. Kelley and John Reid would both testify, as would Darrel Parker. In Towle's words—spoken to Falloon off the record on Monday—"This isn't a 'trial within a trial,' it *is* the trial and it won't be decided by a jury, it will be in the hands of only one man, Judge Polk."

John Reid began his testimony at 10:15 A.M. In the dock, he sat upright, leaning slightly forward in the witness chair, chin up, with his hands awkwardly crossed in his lap.

"I am a graduate of DePaul Law School and was admitted to the bar in the state of Illinois. In addition to my business, I lecture at Northwestern University's Law School. I am coauthor, with professor Fred Inbau, also of Northwestern Law School, of the book *Lie Detection and Criminal Interrogation*."

When Scheele asked if he had any military experience Reid replied, "No, during the war I was given a deferment to lecture to the army and navy intelligence officers, and I also served as a policeman in the Chicago Police Department. I am presently a criminologist specializing in lie detection."

"When you first got to Lincoln," asked Scheele, "how did you become acquainted with Mr. Parker?"

"I met him about a quarter to twelve in the morning on December 21, 1955, at highway patrol headquarters. We were in a little laboratory when I told Mr. Parker why I was in Lincoln and asked if he would cooperate and submit to a lie detector test. To the best of my recollection that interview lasted until about 2:45. I talked to him again at approximately 6:30. We took two sandwiches and some milk back to the laboratory where we ate and I questioned him some more until about eight o'clock. At that point he told me that he had killed his wife, and I went out and reported that to you."

"What did you do between 8:00 and 10:00?"

"I talked to him some more until Audrey Wheeler arrived a little after 10:00, and she then transferred the oral confession into writing, which she then typed up. When that was done we met in Colonel Sand's office at about 12:30 A.M. I told him what this statement was and that I wanted him to verify it. I said I was going to read it to him and I wanted him to take the original copy and follow along. I said if there were any errors or anything wrong that he could correct it. And I gave him a pen and told him to write down the correction and mark 'OK' and put his initials beside it."

"And did he make those corrections himself with his own hand?"

"He did, yes. I then asked him to sign his name, and he did. And then—we, you and myself and I think Mr. Masters, went down to police headquarters in one car—"

"Could it be," interrupted Scheele, "to refresh your recollection, Mr. Reid, that Chief Carroll drove Mr. Parker, you, and me—"

"Yes, that's right. That's right."

"Now, during the entire time you questioned Mr. Parker, at any time, did you make any threats to him, any inducements or promises to him?"

"I did not."

"Did you strike Mr. Parker, pull his hair, or abuse him in any way?"

"No, sir."

"Finally, did Mr. Parker sign this statement freely and voluntarily?"

"He did."

Kenneth Cook slowly rose to question Reid for the defense. As Cook walked toward the witness chair, Reid looked around the packed courtroom and half smiled to himself at the spectacle of which he was the center. He was confident in the thought that any question he might be asked he would be able to answer to the satisfaction not only of himself but of the prosecution.

"When you arrived at highway patrol headquarters, did the authorities give you a briefing of any kind regarding the case?" began Cook.

"I suppose you could call it that. I saw some photographs and was briefed quite sketchily."

"After you got this confession from Mr. Parker at around eight o'clock, what did you do then?"

"I just walked around out at the police headquarters. I knew the statement was going to speak for itself after that."

"Some time after you were done taking this confession, at around eleven o'clock, Mr. Masters and then Chief Carroll went in with Mr. Parker?"

"That's right."

"But you don't know what happened while they were in there together, do you?"

"No, sir."

"And about 12:30, when Miss Wheeler reported that the transcription was complete, you all gathered around the desk in Sand's office and Darrel signed the copies. Were any suggestions made by anybody as this reading proceeded?"

"No, everybody kept quiet. Mr. Parker made the corrections— wait, now that you mention it, I do recall something. Mr. Masters said that Darrel told him it was a double bowline knot, so Darrel made the correction and put in 'double bowline' instead of 'slip knot.'"

"Mr. Reid, I notice in the confession that you asked Mr. Parker, 'And where did you get that brown twine?' The answer was, 'We had a ball there that was wrapped around a stick we used in our garden, and the puppy would drag it around. It was down in the basement. That is where I got it.' That wasn't true, was it?'"

"That was a voluntary statement on the part of Mr. Parker."

"That isn't what I asked you, Mr. Reid—you are enough of a lawyer to know you shouldn't respond, aren't you?"

". . . I am."

"What I particularly want to know is, was that statement accepted by Mr. Masters in its final form without objection?"

"That's right," replied Reid.

"That's all," said Cook.

Reid testified for what amounted to thirty-four pages of the trial transcript. The *Lincoln Journal* reported that evening that "Reid, under questioning by Scheele, said he never struck Parker, pulled his hair, made threats or promises to induce him to sign the confession, and he was not abused in any way."

One sentence. That is all the *Journal* had to say concerning Reid's testimony. And that is how the public, at least those who didn't attend court on a daily basis, would get their information on the trial. They would take such reporting as gospel.

Miss Audrey Wheeler, one of only five women who would testify in the trial, was fully prepared for her day in court. A prim and plain-faced woman, she was Judge Polk's regular court reporter and the stenographer who took down in shorthand, and then typed, Darrel Parker's confession after Reid's interrogation. She told Elmer Scheele that the confession was given "without any hesitancy or reluctance." John Reid, she said, "did not raise his voice to Mr. Parker," "did not make any promises to Mr. Parker," and "did not touch Mr. Parker."

"Of course, you hadn't been present," asked Ken Cook, "and you didn't know what had transpired there prior to the time you arrived?"

"That is correct."

A hesitant, anxious, and still depressed Darrel Parker walked deliberately to the witness stand, as though his feet were cast in concrete. His eyes were downcast, dark, and hollow. No matter what Kenneth Cook asked him, no matter what he answered, he knew he would still have to eventually face Elmer Scheele, the man he had once trusted and who, he now knew, had masterminded Reid's surprise interrogation of him.

"When you found your wife's body on December 14, what effect did that have on you?" asked Cook.

"The world ceased to have meaning. As far as I was concerned there was nothing for me to live for any longer."

"And after the funeral, did you feel the same?"

"Yes. I was dazed, like I was in a trance. I didn't care what happened to me. As far as I was concerned, they could take everything I had. With Nancy gone there was no reason in living . . . That's how I felt."

"Before you left for Des Moines for the funeral, had any of the authorities said anything to you that caused you to think you were in any way required to return to Lincoln?"

"No."

"When Mr. Scheele called you at the Morrisons', what did he say?"

"He said new information had come up and that they had to have me come to Lincoln to help out with the investigation. He said I shouldn't stop at Mr. Ager's or anywhere else because he did not want the newspapers to know that I was in town."

"Did you have any idea at that time that you were the subject of their investigation?"

"No, sir."

"Now, on your way to Lincoln you drove right past Glenwood, Iowa . . . my town. As you did that did you have any thoughts that you should stop and see me about this trip you were taking? Did you have any idea at all that you might need an attorney?"

"No, sir."

"Once you got to Lincoln and Mr. Scheele introduced you to John Reid, did he tell you who Reid was, or where he was from, or what his business was?"

"I was told nothing."

"He didn't tell you that Reid came from Chicago for the sole purpose of questioning you?"

"No."

Cook then asked Darrel what the first words were that Reid spoke to him after Scheele had left the room.

"He told me to sit down in the chair that was next to the table with the machine on it. Then, the first words he said to me were that I 'looked like a criminal the minute I came in the room.'"

In the gallery Reid listened to the testimony as he sat next to his partner, Fred Inbau. They had been whispering back and forth as Darrel spoke to Cook. Reid had been smiling after his comments to Inbau, and finally, after Darrel had glanced their way, Reid's reaction had been one of outright, though subdued, laughter. Cook had noticed Reid's behavior and approached him immediately, erupting without bothering to make an objection to Judge Polk.

"Is there something funny about this, Mr. Reid, that you have to smirk and laugh!"

Judge Polk suddenly jerked up and immediately came to life, not bothering to scold Reid but instead castigating Cook.

"Mr. Cook, if you have any remarks to make, I want you to address them to the court."

"I would like the people who are prosecuting this young man to maintain a sense of dignity and refrain from making snide comments and asides!"

"All right, Mr. Cook. You've made your point, now go ahead," said Polk, leaning back in his chair once again.

Returning to his questioning Cook asked Darrel if he had any idea that he was about to be subjected to a lie detector test.

"No. I had no idea what was about to happen. I'd never seen one of those machines before."

"Did Mr. Reid or Mr. Scheele ask your permission to give you a lie detector examination?"

"No, they didn't."

Asked how long Reid waited before hooking up the machine, Darrel said, "Right away. He pulled his chair up to mine, faced me with his knees bumping into mine, and with his face about a foot from mine. Then he began constantly making derogatory remarks about Nancy and about our marriage.

"He accused Nancy of refusing me sexual relations and of being the type of girl that ran around with low-cut dresses. He said the officers showed him pictures of Nancy and her breasts, and he said 'the boys would play with them but she wouldn't let me touch them.' I told him that was a lie, that my wife and I were very happy together."

"What did he do to you physically as this was going on?"

"If I dropped my head he took his hand and put it under my chin and pulled my head back up. Then he began stroking my head as if I were some kind of animal saying, 'Look at me, look at me, look at me!' I'll never forget those eyes. Every time I looked away he pulled my head back around."

Asked if he had any idea that he was suspected of killing Nancy, Darrel said no. When asked how long this type of questioning lasted, he said, "I would say twenty or thirty minutes of continuous and steady accusations. Then I became emotional and I began crying because of all the things he said about Nancy that weren't true. She was not that kind of girl. I laid my head on the table and cried. It befuddled me and confused me . . . I didn't know what to think. I couldn't figure out why he was accusing me!"

"Did you realize that this treatment was made to obtain an admission from you that you killed your wife?"

"After a while I began to figure that out, but I was so far out of it by then that I didn't know what to do. He asked if I strangled my wife, if I was running around with other women, if I had killed Carolyn Nevins in Omaha, and he asked me one thing over and over—was I trying to fool his machine? Then he turned the machine off, pulled his chair closer, took hold of my chin and pulled it up, and told me that I was lying."

"In other words when he said, 'Are you trying to fool the machine?' the machine hadn't showed what he wanted it to show, that you were guilty. Is that it?"

"I don't know what the machine showed. He just told me I was lying and couldn't beat his machine. I became emotional and started crying. I laid my head on the table. Then he took hold of my hair and pulled me back up and told me to look at him.

"He kept repeating that I had hit my wife. When I told him I did not kill her, he said, 'You're trying to convince yourself of that.' He said he had seen the likes of me before and that I wasn't being satisfied. He said the Catholics called it a sin when their wives refused their husband intercourse. I asked him where he was getting all of this information, that it was not true. And he said there ought to be a law against women who refused their husband relations."

"Did he say anything about your religion?"

"Yes, he accused me of belonging to a radical religious order. When I told him that my wife was a Presbyterian and that I was a Methodist, he told me again that I couldn't beat his machine. He told me they didn't find any semen on Nancy—'Who else could it be, Darrel, but you?' He insisted that I blame my wife—'Put the blame on her! You've got to build a defense. You don't want a trial by newspaper.' I couldn't figure out why I needed a defense when I hadn't done anything. Then he began drilling me about the missing watch. He insisted that I knew where the watch was and that if I didn't produce it, I was going to fry. I told him I didn't take it and had no idea where it was. It seemed he asked about the watch hundreds of times."

When asked if he had become afraid of Reid, Darrel said, "Yes, sir. He told me he would get a confession from me if it took three days or a week. I'd had no lunch. I was getting hungry, and I asked if I could have something to eat. He said that he was hired to obtain a confession not to feed me."

"Had you anything to eat from six thirty in the morning until six thirty that evening?"

"No, sir."

Darrel stated that after the first session had ended Reid took him into another room, another office, where Reid talked to Scheele.

"Mr. Reid told Mr. Scheele that I had told him several facts about the crime and he thought I knew how it happened. He said I got mad at Nancy and hit her and then got scared."

"Had you told him anything like that?"

"No. I told him I did not kill my wife."

Darrel told Cook that by this time he had become quite afraid of Reid and had come to believe he was being held against his will.

"When I was sitting in that other room I got up to go to the restroom and Captain Smith came running in and said, 'Oh . . . I thought you were going to . . . oh, OK, that's all right.' I think he thought I was going to leave."

At 6:30 Officer Tesch brought Darrel his sandwich and a quart of milk. When Darrel began to open the sandwich, he said Reid "came over and took the milk and the sandwich out of my hands, grabbed them, and said we were going back to the laboratory. He told me to follow him, and I did. When we got back to the little room he told me to sit in the chair again while he went to the counter and poured the milk."

"Could you see him pour the milk?"

"No, he had his back to me, so I couldn't see. When he was done he told me to drink the milk."

"And while you ate, what did he say?"

"He told me he had been working on the Nevins case in Omaha—which I found out later wasn't true. Then he said these Nebraska police—he called them 'corncob cops'—he said they weren't experts and that's why they had to call him in. By then I knew he was some kind of expert. When we were done eating, he seemed to wait a while before he did anything—just sat there making small talk. I began to feel tired, and then he hooked up the lie detector again. He pulled his chair up and took off, repeating the same accusations—that I was mad because Nancy was running around with another man, asking about the wrist-watch, and said if I would just confess he would help me get a good deal."

When Cook asked about his physical condition after the questioning resumed, Darrel said that he "began to feel so sleepy and tired and groggy that I just wanted to lay down on the floor, if he would let me."

"Did you try?"

"Yes, sir."

"Did you succeed?"

"No, sir."

"Do you have any recollection now of this second interrogation?"

"Time seemed to mean nothing to me."

"Do you remember how long this second phase lasted?"

"I couldn't tell you. I don't know."

"Do you remember Masters coming into the room?"

"No, sir.

"From then on it seemed like he was constantly talking about the wristwatch. He told me over and over that if I didn't produce it I was going to fry. Time . . . meant nothing.

"Everything just ran together. Then it seemed this lady was there and there were questions, and then I was talking to Mr. Masters and tying a knot. I was dozing or drowsy, and then I was in another room where people were constantly jumping up and down and saying, 'Change this, change that, add this, add that,' and I did. I was just doing what they said."

He remembered little if anything about signing the confession and remembered nothing about what was in it. The first time he read it was when Cook "brought it out to the penitentiary weeks later. When I read it I thought it was some kind of joke. I couldn't believe I'd said those things. I remembered signing something—but it seemed like only three or four times."

"You don't remember signing sixty or seventy times?"

"No."

"When these people were talking to you and you were answering their questions, did you realize the significance of what you were saying?"

"Not at that time, no, sir."

"Can you explain why you would say to Mr. Reid that you didn't know where your mother was born when you had known that fact all your life or that you were asked where your father was born and you said, 'I can't tell for sure'? Can you explain that answer when you've known all your life that your father was born in the very house you were raised in?"

"No, I can't. I didn't realize until the next morning what had happened, what I'd signed."

Elmer Scheele cross-examined Darrel in the slow, repetitive manner that had by now become his trademark, resulting in a virtual replay of all the same information, worded slightly differently, that Darrel had given Cook.

"Mr. Reid pounded you under the chin more or less continuously, is that correct?"

"It wasn't a pounding, it was more like a bumping and lifting."

"I just can't understand why you didn't complain about this treatment. I can't understand why you didn't tell me," said Scheele.

"I was too befuddled and confused to know what was going on. No one had taken the time to tell me what was coming off."

"Why didn't you ask someone?"

"I expected to be told . . . I expected someone to tell me."

"Darrel, what happened after Mr. Reid shut his machine off at the completion of the test?"

"As I've said, it seemed that from then on he was dwelling on the watch, what had happened to the watch, where had I put it."

"And you say he hit you under the chin repeatedly? Grabbed you by the hair, pulled your head up on numerous occasions?"

"Yes, when I became emotional at what he said to me and laid my head on the table."

"How many times would you say he jerked your head up by the hair like that?"

"Over and over."

"Yet you did sign and correct the confession. Those are your initials and your writing?"

"Yes, sir."

"No question about that?"

"No."

Tom McManus entered Max's office at the end of the long day to replace a file. He and Max had just finished their last meeting with Dr. Kelley. McManus found Max standing alone by the window, deep in thought, silently looking down on the slow-moving evening traffic. The multicolored neon lights below reflected on his face, giving it an eerie iridescent quality. Max held his old football squeezed loosely against his thigh and nervously fingered the seams.

"Worried?" asked McManus.

"Goddamned right I'm worried," Max said, his eyes still fixed on the street below. "We're about done with this question concerning the 'confession' . . . and we know what the old fart's going to do. He'll allow it and that'll be that. If he 'legalizes' an illegality that's the basis for this whole goddamned trial—the only reason why things have gotten this far—then what the hell have we got? We'll be swinging at shadows."

"Dr. Kelley testifies tomorrow. Maybe he'll—"

"I wish he could win it for us . . . single-handed, I really do. And maybe he will, but I don't have a good feeling about it . . .

"You know, Tom, when I played ball in the distant and foggy past I used to feel like I was a big deal, like my actions alone could make a real difference—like I was in control of the situation. And then I graduated. There was the war . . . coming back . . . starting all over. When I became county attorney it kinda felt like I was a big wheel again. Like I was back in charge of something. But by that time everything left a little different taste in my mouth. It wasn't all black and white anymore. There was a lot of gray . . . a lot of gray. And that's when I realized life isn't one big football game."

Max turned and deftly flipped the ball high atop a file cabinet, where it landed softly and didn't move. Next to the ball was a picture of Max standing at a football game in Memorial Stadium dressed in a beaver-skin coat and wearing a Stetson pulled down to his ears. He had a wide grin on his face and was holding a cowbell high in the air with one hand and a Nebraska pennant on a long bamboo cane in the other.

When they left the building by the O Street entrance, each went his separate way. As he neared the corner, Max approached a dwarf selling newspapers in the cool, crisp evening air. The man had a stack of papers beside him on the sidewalk, wore a worn white canvas money apron, and held aloft a paper folded in half. "Get your *Liiiincoln Eeeevening Jourrrrnal* paaaper*," shouted the man in a rhythmic cadence that could be heard far up and down the street.

"Hi, Max. How's the trial going?"

"You tell me, Billie. You probably know better than I do."

"You mean 'cause I know the herd mentality? . . . I'm afraid most of the people think he's guilty, Max. They believe what they read in here," said Billie, holding out the paper.

"Billie, he's innocent, you know."

"If you say so, Max, I believe it."

"I say so."

Max lit one of his cigars as a tall man carrying a briefcase, obviously in a hurry, bought a paper from Billie on the run. Max looked after the man as he walked away.

"He'll probably buy the line, too. Don't you think?"

"Yep."

"Good night, Billie," said Max, flipping him a fifty-cent piece. "Keep the paper. I'm not reading the *Journal* much these days."

"Thanks, Max. G'night."

Max went around the corner of the building with blue cigar smoke billowing upward in his wake.

"Get your *Eeeevening Jourrrnal* paaaper."

CHAPTER NINE

Tall and plain-faced, Dr. Kelley had the studious and serious manner of a college professor about him as he approached the witness chair. In a light brown three-piece herringbone suit, he was a man who exuded a reserved self-confidence, and when questioned, he delivered his testimony in such an assured and straightforward manner that to the listener there could be little doubt as to the validity of what he said. Totally at ease, he meant what he said to be taken as fact.

Dr. Kelley arrived in Lincoln on Sunday and sat through Reid's entire testimony on Monday. He took notes throughout Reid's time on the stand and reviewed those notes in detail with Max and Tom. After the "trial within a trial," Parker, Reid, and Kelley would then have to repeat their testimony before the full court, and Kelley wanted Max to be fully prepared for Reid's second appearance. It would be the defense's last chance at Reid if the confession was in fact ruled admissible, as Max expected it would be.

"A psychiatrist is a person who has taken the medical degree of doctor of medicine and then spends considerable time in postgraduate study in the specialty field of psychiatry," began Kelley. "As a professor at the University of California, I am head of the Law Enforcement Section, where I teach the psychiatric aspects of crime and also a course—that is the only one in the country—on interrogation and lie detection. In addition I also lecture in the Law School and the School of Medicine.

"When World War II began I went to England and was put in charge of the main psychiatric unit. I developed the psychiatric treatment pattern for the entire American army. When the war was over I was immediately sent to Nuremberg, where I served as chief psychiatrist to the Allied War Crimes Council. I was in charge of the twenty-two Nazis indicted plus all the others who were in jail there. I had complete responsibility for the psychiatric appraisal of Goering, Hess, von Ribbentrop, Streicher—everyone who was under charges.

"When I returned to California after the war, I became a consultant to the attorney general of California and the Berkeley Police Department—the best rated small-town department in the country. I also became consultant to the district attorneys of Alameda and Marin counties."

In reference to the tests he had administered to Darrel in February, Kelley said, "It is my first imperative to determine whether the subject has any physical problems that might interfere with the test. When I was told Mr. Parker was asthmatic I gave him a medical examination but found he had no active asthmatic symptoms at that time. In addition to the polygraph examination, I gave him a Rorschach test, a psychological blank test, the Minnesota Multiphasic test, the California Mental Health questionnaire, the Cornell Index, and the Johnson Temperament Analysis. I also had him write out a life history or autobiography, and when these were complete, I believed I had a good overview of his personality and state of mind.

"My conclusion was that Darrel is an intelligent and hardworking person who reacts to situations inwardly without exploding. He is what we call a tender-minded person—an individual who rarely loses his temper. He doesn't like to hurt animals, doesn't like to hunt, a person who has never inflicted any pain on animals or people. He is a sensitive type who has some feelings of insecurity, which he has adjusted well to. Well adapted socially, he is friendly and tries to join organizations and inside is trying to show himself he can do these things because he is a person who has never been around much. Finally, I found he is extraordinarily honest. He impressed me as one of the more honest persons I have ever run across."

"Doctor, assuming the facts as you know them," asked Cook, "and assuming the reaction of Darrel Parker to the crime as disclosed by his testimony, are you able to form an opinion as to his mental state at the time the confession was obtained?"

"Of course. It is my opinion that at the time he gave the confession he was suffering from what we would technically call a reactive depression of the psychotic type. When I examined him on February 24, I found he was still profoundly depressed, *two months after the fact.* He had reacted to the crime with sufficient severity so as to require medical attention and sedation, and after the funeral he was functioning at a very minimal level. I believe him when he says that he didn't want to live. A person who doesn't blow up at other people, who is tender-hearted and turns his hostility inward can become severely depressed and may even become suicidal.

"When he was interrogated, when accusations were hurled at him in such an unexpected manner, this triggered a complete depressive reaction characterized by confusion, automatic behavior, profound suggestibility, and a complete unawareness of the nature of his actions.

"There are statements in the confession which are not even important, that are wrong—like where his parents were born, where he was born. This suggests that he was in a confused state. The confession admits a basic fact, the murder, and then errs in many of the details, which suggests to me he was simply parroting in an automatic way material which he had no real knowledge of. When people make mistakes in a confession, they only make them in false confessions. We found that over and over during the war. A person who is smart enough to plan errors is smart enough not to make the confession in the first place. The kind of person who commits such a crime would have these details literally burned into his brain forever. They don't tell one person one thing and something else to another person thirty minutes later.

"Mr. Parker was profoundly depressed, and the sudden pressure of an interrogation drove him into an automatic state where he responded parrot-like to anything put to him. When questioned later, the information was given back as though it was his own."

"But if we substitute what Mr. Reid claims to have taken place, would that change your opinion?" asked Cook.

"Not at all. I heard Mr. Reid testify that he touched Mr. Parker's head and stroked it, pulled his chin up, and made Parker look him in the eye. That's a persuasive technique, a form of hypnosis that would have put Darrel, or anyone else, over the edge at some point."

"They say that Darrel made oral statements to Chief Carroll and Detective Masters that were different than the written confession. Would that make you alter your opinion?"

"Absolutely not. It only reinforces it. He was hopelessly confused."

Cook noted that on the night of the confession several people saw Darrel and noted that he "appeared to be without emotion."

"People in such conditions act like a robot, the living dead. They are almost frozen. It's a break with reality that has no outer manifestations. Everybody can be broken by such an interrogation, but each person has a different breaking point. Darrel is the type who would tend to break before most people."

Tom McManus sat passively beside Towle at the defense table. He looked first at Polk, then to Max.

"Why doesn't Polk wake up?" Tom whispered.

"Because he's a goddamned geezer and shouldn't even be on the bench!" Max replied tersely.

"If what you say is true, can you tell us, Dr. Kelley," continued Cook, "why an innocent man would confess?" In what would be one of the most important questions of the trial, Kelley paused before answering. Recognizing the significance of the question, Kelley turned and faced the judge.

"Some people try to save somebody they think might be guilty. Others are mentally ill and try to get their name in the papers. In the Black Dahlia case in California, we've had thirty-seven such false confessions. The final group are depressed persons who are innocent and go along with whatever's said to them in an interrogation. They don't know what they're doing. That's the group Mr. Parker is in."

Cook calmly leaned one hand on the defense table.

"What's your opinion then, Doctor, as to the personality of the person who did commit this crime?"

"This was a *sex crime* committed by a psychopathic deviate. There is no doubt that psychopaths commit such crimes in order to gain their sexual pleasure. Semen was found at the scene in two places, on her person and on the quilt. The position and condition of the body make it obvious to anyone that this was a sexual assault. A sadistic, hostile, antisocial person with deviant sexual patterns committed this crime. He wouldn't be a normal person. Normal people just don't do such things. But he would not be insane because insane persons never get so complicated in their assaults."

When asked if Parker's particular personality type could have led him to commit such a crime, Kelley said, "Darrel Parker is the exact opposite type of person who would commit this crime. He has no hostility, no aggressive or sadistic structure whatsoever."

Cook next asked if a person could exist who could kill his wife, act normal for five hours at work, and then break down in a genuine grief-stricken collapse when he discovered the body.

"Such a person cannot exist," replied Kelley.

Cook, leading up to Kelley's lie detector results, asked if Kelley could discuss his "other findings."

"I found that Darrel is almost pathologically honest. He goes out of his way to tell the truth . . . and I know that because I ran a lie detector test that showed—"

Scheele immediately jumped up and raised his arm in the air. Surprisingly, before he could speak, Polk spoke up.

"Are you trying to say what that is, Dr. Kelley?" asked Polk, leaning forward in his chair.

"Oh, no, sir," answered Kelley disingenuously, "just that it supported my impression of his truthfulness."

"I see," replied Polk thoughtfully, leaning slowly back as he tried to fully digest Kelley's response.

Max elbowed McManus. He had a smile on his face.

"Not bad. He just succeeded in entering the results of his lie detector examination. But I don't think anyone was sharp enough to pick it up. Polk sure as hell didn't!"

"Can you give us the results of that—" Cook began again before Scheele cut him off.

"Objection."

"Sustained."

"Your Honor," said Scheele, who remained standing. "I'd like to question the witness about this subject, if I may."

Polk nodded his assent.

"How many qualified lie detector operators would you say there are in the United States today, Dr. Kelley?" asked Scheele loudly as he strode quickly to the witness chair for emphasis.

"You must remember," Kelley began calmly, "my premise includes an operator who works with a psychiatrist, or who is a psychiatrist himself . . . Any good operator can do that."

"I understand," said Scheele, boldly crossing his arms over his chest. "But outside of that assumption, how many people are there in this country who possess the qualifications that you say a truly qualified polygraph operator should have?"

"Not more than five or six."

Taken aback, Scheele moved before the bench. "Including yourself, of course?" Scheele stated, chuckling to himself.

"That's right," answered Kelley soberly.

"Your Honor," said Scheele, turning toward the judge after a long pause, "I object again. There isn't sufficient evidence to show that the polygraph has received scientific recognition to the point where it possesses efficacy."

"Sustained."

Returning his focus to Kelley, Scheele continued.

"Doctor, isn't it true that a personality of the type you described Darrel Parker to be would tend all the more to explode?"

"He's never exploded in his life! There is no history of this at all in his background. The type of behavior you're talking about would've occurred over and over again before this incident and would have been obvious to anyone who knew the Parkers. These things don't just drop out of the blue!"

"But couldn't a resistance, a refusal," persisted Scheele, "heighten the desire and intensity to release the compulsion to get access to what he felt belonged to him?"

"He doesn't have a compulsive force to release," replied Kelley assuredly.

Scheele moved closer to Kelley. "Does it matter that Mr. Parker was trying to impress you with his honesty? Does that have any significance to you, Doctor?"

"He didn't *try* to impress me, Mr. Scheele, he couldn't help it. It's just naturally the way he is," said Kelley.

Scheele stopped. He had been caught off-guard by Kelley's series of rapid replies that seemed to turn each of his questions topsy-turvy. He looked down at his legal pad, passing his finger down the page as though closely studying his notes.

"Dr. Kelley . . . you know Mr. Reid personally, don't you?"

"I know Mr. Reid very well."

"And weren't the methods used by Mr. Reid similar to the standard methods used by criminologists and interrogators everywhere?"

"Not at all. As I've said, Mr. Reid testified that he touched Mr. Parker during the interrogation. At that point I repudiate his statement completely. Where I come from if a person is touched during questioning, we totally discount what's said. We simply don't do it that way on the West Coast."

"Do you mean you want us to believe that a mere pat involving slight physical contact is not a proper method of interrogation?"

"In approved police departments, no. But then I can only speak for California. I don't know what happens in Nebraska!"

"Why should Nebraska be any different than California?"

"It shouldn't, but I heard Mr. Reid testify as to what he did. It produces false confessions."

"And, again," said Scheele, smiling broadly, "you accepted Parker's—"

"No," interrupted Kelley tersely, "I'm accepting what Mr. Reid testified to! I wouldn't believe it if I hadn't heard him say it in this very court. I heard Mr. Reid say that he touched Mr. Parker's head and stroked it, put his arm on his shoulder, held his chin up, and made Parker look him in the eye. That is a persuasive technique that can cause an almost hypnotic trance pattern."

Scheele abruptly changed the subject. "What do you mean when you say someone is 'tender-hearted'?"

"A person who is tender-hearted is an individual who, for one reason or another, has directed his hostility inward."

"You said that this young man was dependent in his early life upon his parents?"

"Most of us are, yes."

A few chuckles were heard scattered about the courtroom.

"And you felt that after he married he transferred that dependency to his wife?"

"As an adult I would classify it more as support from his wife."

"Did he appear to you during the course of your examination," continued Scheele, "to be attempting to put himself in the most favorable light possible in your eyes?"

"No. Because a lot of things he went out of his way to tell me were unfavorable things."

Scheele, realizing he was consistently losing ground in his skirmish with Dr. Kelley, quickly ended his cross-examination.

Kenneth Cook returned to his examination with but one last question: "Why did you take this case, Dr. Kelley?"

"Because I like to believe in the cases I work on and I don't usually take one unless I'm convinced of the defendant's innocence."

Scheele recalled John Reid for direct rebuttal. Reid returned to the stand, still exuding his previous confidence and answering Scheele's questions in a calm, quiet voice.

"Did you say anything," began Scheele, "to Mr. Parker after you were introduced to him and I left the room?"

"Yes. I explained that I had a lie detector and would like very much to give him a test. I told him it was relating to the death of his wife."

"Did you first obtain his permission to proceed with the test?"

"Yes, I did."

"Did you say anything to him about looking like a criminal?"

"No, sir. I shook hands with him, and he sat down in the chair there."

"Now, you heard the testimony of Mr. Parker as to the eating of these sandwiches and drinking the milk. Did you pour the milk that the two of you drank?"

"Yes, I did. I poured it in the laboratory."

"Did you put anything in the milk?"

"No, sir, of course not."

Reid left the stand, and Scheele addressed the court.

"The State renews the offer of exhibit 66, Your Honor."

Cook stood and objected on the grounds that "it clearly appears the confession was the result of promises, threats, and coercion, and to have been given at a time when the defendant was not mentally responsible for his actions."

Judge Polk overruled. He paused, then said tersely, "The court holds that exhibit 66 is admissible and the objections thereto are overruled and the exhibit is received into evidence.

"We will recess for lunch and resume at 1:30."

Miss Audrey Wheeler, in a deliberate and decorous manner, sat stiffly upright in the witness chair when court resumed before the jury. It was obvious that, like others, she also reveled in the moment while she awaited questioning before the full court and press. She had on a new light green dress, a tightly curled and permed hairdo, and what appeared to be a new pair of black lace-up medium height heels. Having served as Polk's court reporter for twelve years, she was totally in her element. In any other environment she would undoubtedly have been shy and retiring, but in this setting, in this arena, she was at home perhaps as in no other part of her life. She was not an old maid here; she was Miss Wheeler, court reporter.

"What happened when you and Mr. Reid entered the laboratory room?" asked Scheele.

"Mr. Reid introduced me to Mr. Parker and explained to Mr. Parker that I was there to take his statement."

"Did Mr. Parker say anything?"

"I don't remember that he did. I don't think he did."

"Did Mr. Parker cry at any time during the taking of this statement?"

"No, he did not."

"Did he show any visible signs of emotion at any time during the time of the taking of the statement?"

"None at all."

"Tell the jury, just like you told me, what Mr. Reid's conduct and manner of asking questions was and what Mr. Parker's manner was in answering them."

"Mr. Reid was very kind, very gentle, in asking his questions. Mr. Parker at times hesitated about answering—seemed to be thinking over his response. But at no time was there any pushing or any hurry. It was all very smooth . . . very easily done."

Scheele asked Miss Wheeler if at any time Reid struck Parker with his hand or fist or pulled his chin up, if he pulled Parker's hair, or if he stroked Parker's hair. Wheeler answered no to all three questions.

When asked if she could describe Darrel's conduct and demeanor during the entire time the statement was taken, Wheeler said, "He appeared to me to be very unemotional. He was very calm. In fact, he showed no emotion whatever."

"Is it true Mr. Reid asked you to make some errors deliberately throughout the typing of the statement?"

"I don't remember if it was asked in exactly those words, Mr. Scheele. He told me not to correct any typing errors. And I think there may have been something said like, 'You have taken these before, you know there should be some errors'—something of that sort said."

"Did Mr. Parker then call attention to the misspelling of the errors?"

"Yes, he did."

"Was any other error called to his attention verbally by anyone in the room during the course of the reading of the statement?"

"The only one I remember, Mr. Scheele, was when you spoke up from the back of the room and said, 'How do you spell *jeans*?'"

"I wasn't sure, apparently," said Scheele, innocently referring to his notepad again. "And what occurred after he signed the statement, Miss Wheeler?"

"After he signed the statement, the next thing I remember was Mr. Reid saying to Mr. Parker, 'There is some discussion about the type of knot in the rope, and I don't know anything about knots. What kind of knot was it?' And I think Mr. Parker said it was a bowline knot, a *double* bowline knot. And Mr. Reid said, 'Would you mind changing it then?' And he changed it."

Again Scheele asked if Darrel showed any display of emotion "during the course of the reading of the confession and the correcting and signing of this confession."

"He did not."

"Did he cry at any time?"

"No, sir."

"Then he signed the statement freely and voluntarily, without any hesitancy or reluctance?"

"Yes, sir."

"Can you tell the jury generally what was said in my office the next morning to Mr. Parker?"

Miss Wheeler looked up as though carefully considering the question, measuring her response before she spoke.

"As I remember, you were the only one who spoke to him. You explained that you were intending to file a charge of first-degree murder, and you explained his rights and asked him if he wanted to contact anybody. Then he asked to call his folks, and you gave him that permission."

"When you saw him in my office that morning did he appear to be emotionally upset?"

"Yes, for the first time he showed emotion. After he talked to his mother on the phone, he had tears in his eyes."

Kenneth Cook cross-examined Miss Wheeler by stating that "any questions I might ask are not intended in any way to reflect upon your truthfulness or good character . . . but you did make some mistakes on purpose in that statement, didn't you?"

Miss Wheeler hesitated. "That's right."

"Mr. Reid has said that he requested that you make mistakes in your typing and he left the number of mistakes to your discretion. Is that what happened?"

"As I said before, Mr. Cook, I don't remember that that was actually told to me, to deliberately make errors. Mr. Reid did say something like 'you have taken these statements before, you know there should be an error here and there,' and not to correct any typing errors."

"Well, you are an expert typist, I'm sure, and yet some of these mistakes were made three times over. I don't think that was coincidence. Some of those mistakes were made on purpose, weren't they?"

"Yes. I am sure they were deliberate."

Two police officers who had been in the room the evening the confession was signed and "corrected" testified. Scheele asked Captain Smith of the highway patrol, "Did several of your men participate in the search of Mr. Parker's car that night at patrol headquarters?"

"Yes, sir. They did."

"You know, Captain Smith," Max Towle asked, "from your work on this case you knew that Joe Carroll called Robert Nichols in to perform a lie detector test on the man he thought committed this crime and the type of man who was most likely to commit it. You know that don't you, Captain?"

"I know that."

Chief Carroll testified that on the evening the confession had been taken that Darrel Parker "was very calm and collected, to my estimation. Very different, as a matter of fact, than he was the day of the murder when I seen him."

Under cross-examination by Max Towle, Carroll was asked if Darrel, on the fourteenth, was crying most of the time.

"Yes," replied Carroll.

"He was grief-stricken, and it all appeared to be genuine, didn't it?"

"Apparently so."

"In the middle of the night when he was questioned at highway patrol headquarters, you told us you and Masters and Mr. Parker just sat around having a nice little chat . . . a visit?"

"Yes, sir," said Carroll, smiling gently. "Everyone was calm and collected."

"And this was his story, as he told it to you then: First, he said he had breakfast. Did he tell you what time he finished breakfast?"

"He said around 7:00."

"Then they listened to the news at 7:00. Did he say that intercourse was mentioned?"

"He mentioned intercourse, yes, sir."

"Then you say he told you that he made an advance toward his wife and mentioned that he thought maybe she would be willing to have sexual relations with him, and she said no."

"I don't recall that."

"Did he tell you how long they discussed it, how long they argued, five minutes, ten minutes?"

"No, sir, except that she refused."

"Then he took her by the arm and led her into the bedroom—that's the story. And after leading her into the bedroom he reached up and took her glasses off. Did he tell you why he removed her glasses?"

"No, sir."

"Then he hit her in the left eye and knocked her on the bed, and after that he unzipped her jeans, pulled them off, but carefully folded them up and laid them on the floor beside the bed and then took her socks off and laid them on the jeans?"

"That's what he said, yes."

"Yes, and after being so careful about folding the jeans, he proceeded to tear the sweater and brassiere off, did he tell you that?"

"He didn't say anything about that to me."

"Well, my question is, did you ask him how long it took to do all of this?"

"No, sir."

"Didn't you think it was important?"

"I thought it was probably covered in the statement that was being transcribed in detail."

"He told you that he tied her hands behind her, went to the kitchen closet, got some rope and tied her up—tied her hands behind her—and tied two ropes around her neck?"

"Yes, sir."

"Then he told you he washed all of the breakfast dishes and pans and laid a tea towel over them?"

"Yes. He volunteered that information."

"And after arriving at work at 7:20, you want to tell this jury that all of these things we just talked about happened in a period of ten minutes or less?"

"Yes, sir."

Towle hesitated, fumbled with a legal file at the defense table, and then looked at Carroll.

"Chief Carroll, it didn't take you long to point the finger of suspicion at another party, did it?"

Scheele objected. Polk sustained him.

"Well, you arrested Wesley Peery, who is now in jail for rape, didn't you?"

Scheele objected. Polk sustained him again.

"In the newspapers you were quoted repeatedly, during the first three or four days of this investigation following this murder, as saying that a black Ford car parked right south of the Parker home was the most important lead you had, weren't you?"

"I object to that as improper cross-examination," said Scheele.

"Sustained," added Polk.

"I offer to show by this witness, Your Honor, that an ex-convict by the name of Wesley Peery was convicted of rape within the past ten days, that near the time of this murder he was an employee of the city park department, and at that time he owned a black Ford car."

Scheele objected. Polk sustained him again. Towle sat down.

"What was the purpose of Mr. Reid being in Lincoln?" Kenneth Cook asked Gene Masters.

"The purpose of Mr. Reid being here was to interrogate Mr. Parker."

"This change in the confession from 'slip knot' to 'double bowline,' when was that made?"

"After he signed the final page of the confession. I pointed out that he'd told me it was a double bowline."

"So, you want to sit here now and say that you permitted this statement to be read and signed by Mr. Parker, and then you objected to it?"

"That's right," replied Masters.

"What did he say during the questioning by you and Chief Carroll about the kind of knot he tied?"

"He said he would tie a double bowline if I got some cord. I found some string, and he tied a knot."

"That's the knot that Mr. Hoagland, Mr. Rasmussen, and Mr. Tesch all said was unidentifiable, wasn't a double bowline?"

"That's what they said."

"So Darrel, at the time the confession was signed, OK'd a kind of knot which, so far as the facts are concerned, didn't exist?"

"He OK'd the change to the double bowline knot. That is correct."

"And that wasn't the fact, was it?"

"No," replied Masters testily.

"Mr. Masters, you were the person actually in charge of this case and you mean to tell me that you don't know how many knots were in that brown cord?"

"Not in the brown cord, no. I don't know how many knots were in the brown cord."

"Let's move on to something else. How many stories did Mr. Parker tell you about where the watch was?"

"He told four."

"Yet, he finally ended up saying he didn't know where it was, didn't he?"

"He said he didn't remember."

"In your testimony at the preliminary hearing, you said he 'couldn't decide.' That's different than saying he didn't remember. When you looked where he told you, you didn't find the watch. You didn't find it in the toilet, or the pipes—you tore the pipes up in the basement of his house looking for it, didn't you?"

"No, we didn't find it there."

"And you didn't find it in the yard. And you didn't find it in the cedar box. And you didn't find it in the back of his car, did you?"

"No, we didn't find it."

Cook asked Masters if he had questioned Parker about the semen that was on his wife's body, a subject that the prosecution seemed to continually dance around without mentioning.

"No, I didn't ask him in regard to that."

"But you knew of a report by Dr. Tanner that mentioned semen or the possibility of semen on the body?"

"No. Dr. Tanner knew nothing of any semen on the body."

"Well, here is his report," said Cook, holding it up by the corner in front of Masters. "Where did he get the sample of semen?"

"That was taken that day at the hospital."

"Yes, but where did he get it?"

"From her body."

"That's right. And yet in all of your conversations with Mr. Parker you never inquired about the possibility of what that was or if he knew anything about it, did you?"

After Masters answered no, Cook asked again how Parker's demeanor had differed from the day of the murder to the evening of the confession.

"He appeared normal, more normal than I had seen him at any time that I had come in contact with him."

"Did he display any emotion during the reading of the confession?"

"He did not."

"That'll be all, Your Honor."

By the end of the day the State rested its case. The trial transcript would be at that point just over a thousand pages in length.

Tom McManus drove his 1953 Buick Special at exactly the speed limit—as fastidious in his driving as he was in his music. He flicked up a cigarette out of a pack of Camels and grasped it with his lips. He pushed in the lighter on the heavily chromed dashboard, lit his cigarette, and handed the lighter to Max so he could fire up a cigar. The headlights lit the asphalt in a lonely white beam. They had not passed another car in miles. Dim lights from far-away farmhouses twinkled like stars in the clear, cool night air.

"This Sidladjzek's a character, Tom," said Max, his eyes riveted on the road ahead. "Wait'll you see his place. On top of being a junk collector and a fence, he's a kleptomaniac, too. Wise told me they caught him once with stolen goods and threw him in the clink. He bailed out, then he broke back into the jail to steal the same stuff back and they caught him again."

A silo caught Max's eye. He leaned forward on the dash, looking for the place to turn.

"This is it, Tom . . . turn here."

Tom braked hard and made a sudden turn onto a worn gravel road. They drove a half mile before they came to a long hedge-lined driveway. A weather-beaten farmhouse was barely visible through a clutter of junk—scrap metal, rusting tractors, aban-doned trucks, wrecked cars, and assorted refrigerators and washers. Tom, awestruck, parked the car at the rear of the house. The scene was made even more eerie by the yard light that was attached to a defunct windmill in the center of the turnaround. A scraggly elm grew up, in, and around the windmill. Its branches, whipped by the cold spring breeze, flicked in and out of the light's path, throwing a ghostly moving glow of light and shadow upon the mounds of wildly scattered refuse.

"You're right, Max," said Tom. "You do have to see it."

An old man stepped onto the back porch of the house. He carried a shotgun. Tom hesitated, waiting for Max to lead the way. As Max approached the house, a dog roared out from beneath the porch, growling viciously. Before the dog reached Max, it was yanked to a halt by a long rope attached to a choke chain.

"Hi, Sid. How are you?" said Max, as he cautiously skirted the dog. "This is Tom McManus, I told you about him."

The two arrived at the porch and were met by a worn-out man in his late fifties who could have easily passed for seventy. He was stooped and walked with a hesitant shuffle. He led them inside to a scene just as jumbled as the one outside.

Despite having electricity, the interior was dimly lit by an old oil lamp that rested atop an aged rolltop desk stuffed with opened and unopened envelopes. A wood-cased radio was tuned to a scratchy religious broadcast. Sidladjzek sat carefully on a swiveling oak chair, its seat softened by a soiled pillow.

"Piles," said Sidladjzek, pointing to the pillow. He leaned back, gumming an unlit cigar.

"I din't like 'at sombitch the first time I seen 'im, Mr. Towle. Over the years he's brought in a ton a junk, a ton . . . but it was always penny ante stuff mostly. Watches, bikes, radios, old coins—dinky shit. But coins and watches are his favorites—always talking big and always dealing in pissant junk."

Tobacco juice drooled down the side of his mouth as he spit beside his chair. McManus craned his neck to see a coffee can near the chair. It looked as though he'd missed the can as often as he'd hit it. Spinning in his chair, Sid hit the light switch on the wall beside his desk. Suddenly illuminated were piles of tires, batteries, clocks, radios, and dressers with drawers full of watches, tools, silverware, and knives.

"I don't 'member if he sold me a watch at that time you asked or not, Mr. Towle. When he did sell, it was usually more 'an one . . . You guys go ahead an' look an' if you find what yer lookin' for, you can have it. Best chance'd be in that ol' bureau over there, but, heck, it could be anywheres, or nowhere."

Sidladjzek produced a fifth of whiskey and poured himself a drink in a cracked and coffee-stained cup. He half-laughed to himself as Tom and Max began to rummage around.

"It's been reported the watch may have had a broken band. Would that narrow it down any, Sid?" Max asked.

"I wouldn't know, Mr. Towle. The bands and the watches all get switched around, you know how it is."

After they had searched for more than an hour, Sidladjzek poured Max a cup of whiskey.

"He says there's more in the freezer," Max told Tom.

After another hour they gave up.

"If you get a line on the watch—a Hamilton with a band that's probably broken—let me know, Sid. I'll make it worth your while."

"You bet I will, Mr. Towle. You bet I will."

As they left, the dog went after them again. Sidladjzek grabbed his shotgun and fired a shot into the air. The dog shut up and ran under the porch with its tail between its legs.

"Goddamned dog . . . See you later, Mr. Towle."

Frightened and shaken by the shot, Tom cautiously stood up from a crouch after ducking behind his fender. He leaned against the Buick and shakily put a cigarette in his mouth.

"I thought I was over the war, Max . . . I guess not."

Max lit another cigar as they left. He glanced back at the house.

"I doubted we'd find it, Tom. They probably got rid of it once it got too hot. Well, we know where it isn't."

"Had to try," replied McManus, his eyes rigidly focused on the road as they drove away. As he flicked ashes in the ashtray, his hand shook.

CHAPTER TEN

When the trial resumed, Darrel took the stand for a veritable replay of his earlier testimony, the distinguishing feature being that this time it was told before the jury in open court.

"The evening you said you last had sexual relations with Nancy," asked Cook, "the Friday before the murder, you said you had some mixed drinks. How many mixed drinks did you have?"

"I had two."

"And if I were to ask you how many mixed drinks you've had in your entire lifetime, what would you say?"

"Five."

After reviewing Darrel's testimony for the jury's benefit, Cook paused for a moment. He turned and went to the defense table, where he picked up a Bible. He turned and faced Darrel.

"Do you believe," asked Cook, holding up the Bible, "that the Almighty God is as much present in this courtroom now as the people you see here?"

"Yes, sir, I do."

"Then I want you to tell the Almighty God and this jury whether or not you ever, in any way, harmed Nancy?"

"No, sir, I did not."

Darrel's repeated testimony in open court was reflected in more than one hundred pages of the transcript, but it did not end at this point. Dr. Kelley had to return to California, and through an agreement between the State and the defense he was allowed to complete his testimony before Darrel finished.

"Darrel was reared in a protected environment, an excellent home," began Kelley, "but he never got around much. As such, he is naive and unsophisticated—timid in new situations. He learned to overcome this and, if not pressed, will react in quite normal fashion. When pressed, however, he tends to withdraw and will attempt to escape from it. His withdrawal at the time of his interrogation could well be an example of this. That is why there was a quality of unreality in his mind about events the night of his interrogation. This behavior has been true all through his adult life. He has never been in fights, never been hostile. When he gets mad he goes out and does something else; he internalizes it, runs away from it rather than assaults it.

"When I examined him he was still depressed but seemed in a recovery phase. He talked about what had happened during his interrogation by Mr. Reid in the same way as persons who have just come out of a mental hospital talk about the experiences they had before they went in. There was an enduring quality of unreality in his mind about those events."

"But how do you account for the fact," asked Cook, "that so many witnesses believed he appeared normal?"

"As I said, this type of mental reaction is characterized by withdrawal—an inability to do anything except what you are told, a break with reality. These people don't let their anger out; they act as though they are the living dead. In combat such people will do exactly what they are told. They don't get excited or emotional. They will stand wherever you put them. They answer your questions; they will fill out questionnaires; they do whatever you tell them to do. They are extraordinarily suggestible. One of the most difficult problems we had in the army was getting across to our medics that these men are sick and have to be evacuated, because they look so peaceful and calm that nobody is worried about them."

"How do you explain that so many people thought he looked normal at work the morning of the murder?" asked Cook.

"Had he killed his wife that morning, he would have reacted as he genuinely did when he found her dead body. I don't think he is a person with the type of personality that would allow him to sustain a morning of activity after an act of this type and not make it very apparent that something was radically wrong with him."

When Dr. Kelley was asked what type of persons should not be given polygraph tests he listed the following: "people suffering from physical diseases, heart and lung disorders, any type of neurological disease, and the major psychoses; someone who is mentally deficient with some type of neuroses; and finally, a psychopathic personality." A psychopathic personality. The type of person that Wesley Peery was. The type of person the Lincoln Police Department said had passed their polygraph test. The man they questioned and released the day after the murder.

"Can you tell us what some of the questions were, Doctor," said Cook, "that you asked Mr. Parker when you tested him on your polygraph?" And so, another roundabout way of entering the results of Kelley's lie detector exam was attempted.

"I asked him whether he strangled his wife, if he killed his wife. I asked him where he threw the watch, if he threw the watch out the window or into the toilet or out in the yard. I asked him if he had sexual relations with his wife on the fourteenth, the day of the murder; if he had undressed his wife and took off her pants; if he took off her shoes. I asked if he had strangled her in any way, if he went to the basement on that day, if he hit Nancy, if he gagged her mouth. I asked him if he lied when he gave the confession. All of these questions interspersed with others such as: Is this Lincoln? Is your name Darrel Parker? Do you smoke? Is this February? What we term non-relevant questions, in order to get a baseline."

Cook, anticipating Scheele's readiness to object, ceased his questioning of Dr. Kelley.

"You stated, I believe, that you are a member of some polygraph organization?" asked Elmer Scheele abruptly when he began his cross-examination that, this time around, would be much more cautious.

"I belong to the American Academy of Polygraph Examiners, Mr. Inbau's society. He is the president."

"And who is the vice president?"

"John Reid."

"And we know by now that they've written this textbook entitled *Lie Detection and Criminal Interrogation*. You testified the other day, Doctor, that you use that textbook in teaching some of your courses?"

"We use *parts* of it, the polygraph part, but we don't think much of the interrogation part."

"You consider yourself a criminologist, don't you?" continued Scheele, quickly passing over Kelley's response.

"I don't really know what a criminologist is. If you deal in criminology in any form they seem to want to make a 'criminologist' out of you."

"Did Mr. Parker tell you at the time of your examination that his wife was having sexual relations with him as often as he desired?"

"He told me he was completely satisfied sexually."

"You said you found, in your examination of February 24, that Mr. Parker had a spotty amnesia?"

"Yes, he couldn't remember certain things. I tested him every way known to modern medicine, and that showed me he was telling the truth."

"But if you assume Mr. Reid made no threats to this young man, if you assume Mr. Reid did not accuse him of looking like a criminal, and if you assume that Mr. Reid in no way abused or threatened this young man, then do you want the jury to believe that your opinion remains unaltered?" Scheele asked smugly.

"I get to assume that Mr. Reid stroked his head, looked him in the eyes, held his chin up, and touched his body? That was in the evidence."

"That was in the evidence, yes," said Scheele. "Mr. Reid has so testified."

"Then I can draw my conclusion from that. My conclusion would remain unchanged. You just don't do that in a proper interrogation."

Scheele paused, momentarily thrown off track by yet another rebuke from Kelley. "This matter of hypnosis . . . you say you don't feel Mr. Reid has the power of hypnosis?"

"By 'hypnotic power' I don't mean the capacity to hypnotize in the literal sense; I mean the ability to look a person in the eye, to intimidate him, and then wither him down. Any person can 'hypnotize' a person in that way."

"Well, what is wrong with that?"

"It produces a hypnotic effect. It's spellbinding. The mere touching of a person, looking in his eyes, and keeping his chin up are techniques from hypnosis."

"Will a person confess to a crime while under such a spell?"

"They certainly can; I have hundreds of cases of this. Under hypnosis you can get a person to confess to anything."

"Does Reid and Inbau's book recommend—"

"No," interrupted Kelley angrily, "their book doesn't recommend that you rub someone's head, lift their chin, or stroke their hair. That's not advocated in the book. That's why I couldn't believe he did it."

"Your testimony is that, in your opinion . . . that Mr. Parker was legally insane at the time he signed this confession?"

"That is my opinion."

"And is it also your opinion that Mr. Parker is not a psychopath?"

"That's right."

Kenneth Cook rose by the defense table. He looked at the wall clock and addressed Polk.

"Your Honor, Dr. Kelley is under subpoena in California for tomorrow. If he is kept here after lunch he won't be able to catch his flight and return on time."

"That's all," said Scheele, only too happy to be rid of Kelley. Dr. Kelley was dismissed to leave the courtroom. That afternoon he was on a plane to California.

After Dr. Kelley's departure, Darrel returned to the stand to finish his cross-examination by Scheele. It would be the fourth repetition of the same information—where he was born, a description of his family, his size and weight, when he met Nancy, his high school years, his college life, his marriage, his employment, the organizations he'd joined, what apartments he and Nancy had lived in, an excruciatingly long description of the events the day of the murder, the interrogations, how he had given the confession, how he had signed the confession, how he had initialed the corrections in the confession. Like Scheele's previous questioning, it seemed deliberately designed to drive the jurors into a state of numbed inattention.

"You testified that when you awoke at the police station on the morning of December 22, you realized you had signed a confession the night before?" asked Scheele.

"I realized the seriousness of what had happened, yes."

"Did you know you had furnished details surrounding the manner in which the crime was committed?"

"I didn't realize there were any details until Mr. Cook brought the confession to me weeks later. I didn't realize that I had said *any* of those things."

"One thing troubles me, if Mr. Reid treated you in the way you now say, why in the world didn't you say something to me?" Scheele pled innocently.

"I was too scared."

"But you weren't scared of me, were you?"

"No, sir. Not then."

"Then why didn't you tell me? I just can't understand that."

Darrel was on the verge of tears. His head dropped to his hand. Kenneth Cook quickly spoke up on Darrel's behalf: "You're the one who introduced him to Reid!"

"Let him answer the question," shouted Scheele as he quickly turned toward Darrel. "Why didn't you tell me if he really did those things and treated you in that manner?"

"He did, sir," Darrel said, finally breaking down in tears. "He did."

Scheele pressed on, ignoring Darrel's emotional breakdown. "And these corrections in spelling, correcting typographical errors, they were done by you without any suggestion from anyone else, weren't they?"

Darrel paused until he regained his composure. He sat up straight in the witness chair and looked Scheele unsteadily in the eyes. "If you say they were, I would have to take your word. I don't know."

Another hundred pages of transcript had been taken. The tedium of the proceedings orchestrated by Scheele had begun to have its full effect at just the time the defense witnesses were to begin their testimony.

The *Journal*'s by now standard abbreviated report of the day's events was printed that evening: "Tears came to Parker's eyes when

Scheele questioned him about details of the confession. He began sobbing when asked repeatedly if he remembered signing it and if he had known he admitted the slaying."

George Gohde, the police officer in charge of the records section of the police department, was an impromptu witness called by Towle concerning the subpoenaing of police records.

"Did you receive a subpoena yesterday, George, to bring all the records the police department had in the Parker murder case?"

"Yes, sir," answered Gohde.

"And I told you to come back with them, didn't I?"

"Yes, sir."

"But you didn't bring those records, did you?"

"No, sir."

"Mr. Masters told you not to bring the records, didn't he?"

"I can't answer that question."

"Well, Mr. Masters told you in the hall in my presence just a little while ago that you wouldn't bring those records without a court order, didn't he?"

"Yes, sir."

Dorothy Miille, the park secretary, ruefully testified that Darrel and Nancy were always kind and considerate toward each other and that on the day of the murder he seemed to be his normal self at work—"as calm and courteous as ever." Glenn Francisco, a workmate of Parker's, said that Darrel was "awful good to the men. They all liked him." Glenn Suiker, Darrel's immediate superior, who had been to Darrel and Nancy's house more than once, said he found them always to be "kind and affectionate toward one another." Leon Snyder said, "Darrel was the perfect boss. All the men liked him. When we visited their home, they were both kind and affectionate toward each other . . . The morning of the murder he was no different than any other morning." Warren Andrews, one of Darrel's closest friends who worked on the tree gang at the park department, "had never seen them quarrel . . . They always got along well together . . . and on the morning of December 14, he appeared no different than he had any other morning."

Bob Lundberg and Jim Whipkey, both radio station employees, testified that the morning news and weather, which Darrel and Nancy had listened to at breakfast, "comes on at 6:52 and is over at 6:58." Kenneth McCaw of the chamber of commerce said he met with Darrel at 10:30 the morning of the murder. "We looked for decorations for the statehouse Christmas tree. There was nothing out of the ordinary or unusual about Darrel's behavior." Peter Trucano, Darrel's minister from Henderson, told of Darrel's regular attendance at the Wesley Chapel Church as a child and his activities with the choir: "He often sang solos in our service. We loved to hear him sing. He was a fine Christian boy who was praised by everyone that knew him." James Ager said that he and his wife and the Parkers "exchanged visits to each other's homes frequently. The two of them were always affectionate towards each other and always appeared to be very much in love with each other . . . He got along very well with his men at work and had all of their respect."

When Towle asked him how Darrel reacted after finding Nancy murdered, Ager said, "He was almost incoherent and crying; well, hysterical would be the best description—overcome with grief."

"Mr. Ager," asked Towle, returning once again to the man he felt had killed Nancy Parker, "during the fall of 1955, did you have employed an ex-convict by the name of Wesley Peery?"

"Yes."

"How long did he work for the park department?"

"Approximately three weeks."

"And he was later discharged by you?"

"Yes."

Before a lunch recess, Elmer Scheele reticently addressed the court: "Your Honor, Mr. Gohde has given me a list of people who saw a car parked on Sumner Street on December 14. Mr. Gohde has gone through the reports and has a list of nine people who contacted the police department. And here is that list, Mr. Towle."

Bonnie TeSelle, a young housewife who was one of the nine people to have seen the car, was on her way to work at the Elgin watch factory in the northern part of the city when she drove by the Parker home the morning of the murder.

"As you approached the Parker home," asked Max Towle, "did you observe a parked automobile?"

"Yes, it was facing northwest, looking toward the Parker home."

"Was there anyone in it?"

"Yes, there was a man in it."

"And what color was the car?"

"It was dark. I would say it was black."

"You told me you thought it was a 1949 Ford? I'm going to show you a picture," said Towle, handing Mrs. TeSelle the picture Rank had taken of Peery's car. "I don't expect you to say that it is the car you saw that morning, but does it look like the same type of car?"

"Yes, it does."

"You are of the opinion that it was a Ford automobile?" asked Elmer Scheele dubiously in his cross-examination.

"No, I am sure it was a Ford."

"And you're sure of the color?"

"I'm almost positive it was black."

"Where are you employed, Mr. Saathoff?" asked Max Towle.

"The Lancaster County Motor Vehicle Department."

"I asked you a couple of days ago to look up a registration on a 1949 black Ford Tudor automobile, did I not?"

"Yes, it was registered to Marzetta Carter and Wesley Peery."

"Mr. Smith," asked Max Towle of the imposing hulk of a man that sat in the witness chair, "are you the same man who played football here at Nebraska and now plays for the Cleveland Browns?"

"Yes."

"In October of 1955 did you own a Ford automobile?"

"Yes, it was a 1949 Ford Tudor."

"And did it have any insignias on the front or back of the car?"

"Yes, there were three decals—a fraternity sticker on the front, along with a campus parking sticker, and a football decal on the back window."

"You are actually relying on the fact that the pictures here are photographs of the same make and model of car that you had?" began Scheele skeptically.

"I am positive that is my car. The fact that the right front blinker light was busted out by me before I left town proves it."

S. J. Miller, the retired and wizened farmer from Milford who now owned the car, was asked by Towle if he owned the black Ford in the pictures.

"Yes, that's it."

"Up until the time that I came out and photographed the car, Mr. Miller, had the police department or any law enforcement office ever talked with you or questioned you about this car?"

"No, sir."

"From whom did you buy the car?"

"Wesley Peery on the evening of January 19."

Robert Guenzel, a Lincoln attorney who also taught law part time at the university, had driven by the Parker house the morning of the murder. He said that he had seen "a dark-colored Ford parked on Sumner Street, facing east, about thirty to fifty feet east of the house. It was between twenty minutes till eight and a quarter of eight."

"And did some thought occur to you as you looked at the car?" Towle asked, probing for the information he knew led to the identification of the car he had photographed.

"It occurred to me that it was a university student's car."

"Was the car you saw occupied or empty?" asked Elmer Scheele in cross-examination in what was perhaps one of the most revealing, yet overlooked questions of the trial.

"I could see no one in it."

"And tell the jury whether it is common to see parked cars in that area?"

"It is not unusual to see parked cars in that area."

Two tire experts called by the defense came to the same conclusion regarding the rare X-patterned tires on Peery's car. "In the pictures," testified James Van Horn, a service station operator who dealt in Goodyear tires, "you can see distinctly the inside center diamonds, they made a very clear print in the snow. The side of the tire has four little ribs and a break, four little ribs and a break; that can be

clearly seen in the side of the snow along with the center diamonds
. . . The tires were discontinued in 1950. I am firmly convinced in
my mind that the tire in this picture made this mark. The tracings
are all there."

"There would be very few of these tires in Lincoln or any other
place?" asked Towle.

"That's right."

"Mr. Van Horn, have you ever appeared in court before to identify tire treads?" asked Scheele skeptically.

"No, sir."

"Have you ever received any special training that would prepare
you for rendering such an opinion other than your general day-to-
day experience?"

"No, sir. None other than my training as an adjuster for checking
tire characteristics."

"I know you've given an opinion, but you can't say that that
opinion was given with a degree of certainty, can you, in all
honesty?"

"It is my opinion that it is."

"Do you know the procedure or techniques used by a laboratory
expert in making tire comparisons?"

"No, I do not."

As any good prosecutor would do, Scheele continued to put
doubt in the jurors' minds about the defense witnesses, in this case
Van Horn.

Robert Pritchard, another Goodyear tire dealer, told Towle that
"due to the wear of this particular tire in the photograph, it is my
opinion it made the same track in the snow that the plaster cast was
taken from."

"But you can't say with certainty that the tire you saw on the car
is the same tire that made the prints in the snow, can you?" asked
Scheele.

"No."

Robert Nichols, superintendent of the state reformatory and an
ex–Lincoln policeman, was one of two men who gave Peery a lie
detector test the day after the murder. He was asked by Max Towle

if, on the date of December 15, he'd had a "talk" with Wesley Peery. Nichols said he had given Peery a cursory examination.

"And in your conversation with him did he tell you that he drove by the Parker home rather early in the morning the day before Mrs. Parker was killed?"

"He said he drove through the park."

"Did you ask him specifically whether he passed by this particular house?" asked Scheele when it was his turn to question.

"No, I didn't."

"Did you ask him which part of Antelope Park?"

"No."

"Mr. Henninger also questioned him, didn't he? And after the two of you were done, he was released that night?"

"Yes."

"I went to Johns Hopkins Medical School in Baltimore," offered Dr. Frank Barta, the second of three psychiatrists to testify for the defense. "Following that I went to Yale for my psychiatric residency, and after the war I returned to Omaha, where I went into private practice. I am also chairman of the Department of Psychiatry at Creighton University."

Towle asked Barta how he would describe Darrel after his examination of him on April 2, the week before the trial started.

"Mr. Parker impressed me as being an extremely passive individual, one we think of as a dependent type who likes to please other people and go along with them rather than being strongly self-willed."

In order to stress the independence of Barta's opinions on the case, Towle asked if Barta had "ever talked to Dr. Douglas Kelley of California."

"No, sir, I have never met the man."

"Your approach then, to Darrel Parker, was new, without any conference with any other psychiatrist. Your own opinion?"

"That's right."

Towle reviewed the day of the murder for Dr. Barta as well as the day of the interrogation. He then asked Barta if he could "form an opinion as to Parker's state of mind at the time of the confession."

"I can be reasonably certain that he was in a state of hyper-suggestibility, a trancelike condition intermingled with the remorse he undoubtedly was still feeling toward his wife. He was in what we call a fugue-like state.

"For example, you can stand behind someone and ask them to close their eyes and then keep telling them they're falling backwards. After a while a large percentage of them will actually start falling backwards. They are suggestible you understand, but not hypnotized. They are particularly this way if they have been weakened by a constantly applied stimulus, such as being interrogated or weakened by hunger or fear.

"The closest analogy I can make is that he was in a state that some of our prisoners of war were in when they made false confessions to the Reds during the Korean War—a thing we now call brainwashing. We have heard quite a bit about it in the last year or two."

"Does such brainwashing depend upon any length of time?"

"It depends on several things. The time element, the stress of stimuli, and the kind of personality of the person involved. I don't think you can say it depends on any one particular factor. There are some people who can withstand these things longer than others.

"Darrel Parker, I would say, is the most suggestible type. The most susceptible to this kind of condition, being a passive, introverted type of person."

"Doctor, from the pictures you've been shown and the type of crime suggested by the presence of seminal fluid upon Nancy Parker and the quilt that she was lying on, can you give us an opinion as to the type of person who committed this type of crime?"

"One could go into great length with that. Quite simply, it is a person who has an actual mental aberration in regard to sexual attitudes—a person who has developed pathological and abnormal attitudes toward sex and his reaction to it. It could be someone who might find pleasure in having relations with a person who couldn't resist or couldn't fight back. But even someone who wasn't a psychiatrist would have to assume that this was a sexual crime committed by a sexual psychopath, just from viewing the photographs."

"Do you have an opinion as to whether a person could murder his wife, appear normal for five hours, and upon discovering the body go into a state of genuine shock and hysteria?"

"I can't conceive of anyone that could do that. Someone who saw him in the succeeding hours would have noticed that he was in a daze of some kind. I don't think it's possible that such a person could exist."

Scheele, in an attempt to discredit the entire field of psychiatry, stated to Barta that "psychiatry is not considered an exact science, is it?"

"That depends on what you mean by 'an exact science,' Mr. Scheele. Behavior is never absolutely determined. All anyone can say is that we determine the probabilities of behavior."

"But you can't tell this jury with any degree of certainty that the person who killed Nancy Parker was a sexual psychopath?"

"It is a very strong probability from the information I have seen."

Asked if Parker was in a psychotic state on the day of the interrogation, Barta replied, "We would speak of it as a condition in which he was not responsible for his actions, but I would assume it didn't last very long. After all, it would have been produced by this particular kind of questioning at the time of the interrogation. I would assume that after a night's sleep, for example, by the next morning, it would be reasonably cleared up. People of his type don't normally show their feelings, so if he were in a trancelike state you wouldn't notice much difference. He is not the kind of person who normally shows his emotions."

Asked whether Parker had any "repressed inward hostility," Barta replied, "Every introverted person of his type has uncharitable feelings toward themselves, but usually not toward anyone else. He did, however, really seem to be afraid of this Mr. Reid—he became visibly disturbed when I asked him about Reid."

Virgil Falloon had covered the trial from the start. Up to this time there had been no feedback from anyone he'd written about, but after his reporting during the trial that concerned Peery's car and Peery's questioning by Nichols and Henninger, Falloon received a brief typed message in the mail. It said simply:

VIRGIL FALLOON

YOU BETTER LAY OFF PEERY AND THE HOLE PARKER

CASE IF YOU DON'T WANT TO COME UP MISSING

THIS GOES FOR THAT TOWLE GANG TO

WATCH YUOR STEP WE MEAN IT

It was the only threatening letter anyone received during the trial. Towle and Falloon laughed it off, assuming it came from Peery's crowd. Tom McManus, on the other hand, took the threat seriously and bought himself a .38 Colt Special from a retired policeman he knew. Being threatened by someone like Peery or his friends he took seriously.

J. Whitney Kelley was the final psychiatric witness for the defense. Like Dr. Barta, he was from Omaha, and like both of the other defense psychiatrists, he had outstanding credentials. He was unrelated to and, like Dr. Barta, had never spoken to Dr. Douglas Kelley. He obtained his medical degree at Creighton University and completed his psychiatric specialty work at Bellevue Hospital in New York. During the war he was responsible for testing to determine the qualifications for air force pilots—"We had to try and determine aggressive tendencies because we wanted aggressive men to be our fighter pilots."

Kenneth Cook began with the same question asked of the other two doctors, "How would you class Mr. Parker's emotional character at the time of the interrogation?"

"People who have some inferiority feelings, like Mr. Parker, are more likely to be unstable under stress than those who are aggressive. I would describe him as having been in a semi-amnesic fugue state. In other words, not true hypnosis, but a state in which a person is repeating things that are suggested to them, with an inability to recall a good portion of what they've said. That is what we call a flat affect, they do not display a change of emotion."

"If you take into account the presence of semen, as testified, and from the examination of the pictures of Nancy Parker, and the violence and method of the crime they portray, what is your opinion as to the type of crime this was and the type of person who committed it?"

"This crime could only have been committed by a sexual psychopath—a person with a deep-seated neurosis, which has its beginning in the early raising of the child. Generally, it is started in the first seven years of life and is found in an individual whose home life is unstable, with a broken family or other traumatic factors that produce instability in the development of the child. A sexual psychopath is one whose aberrant behavior is along sexual lines, and there are many, many different kinds of them. Some of them are the result of involvement with people of their same sex or incest, others involve sexual pleasures from violence, and finally there are those that take advantage of people who do not give their consent, in other words, rape."

"Is Darrel Parker, in your opinion, a sexual psychopath?"

"I would classify him as being the type of person least likely to become a sexual psychopath. His background simply does not fit the definition."

Kelley was asked if anyone could commit such a crime and then go to work and act normal. His answer was almost identical to Dr. Douglas Kelley's.

"I don't think anyone can do that. That would be the kind of person I have never met. I don't think it could be done."

"Have you ever testified in a murder trial before, Doctor?" asked Elmer Scheele acerbically as he looked dramatically toward the jurors' box—sounding as though he were still questioning one of the tire experts.

"No, I haven't."

Turning toward Kelley for further effect, Scheele asked, "Have you ever seen the play *Sadie Thompson*?"

"I beg your pardon."

"The play, *Sadie Thompson*, which was based on an actual case?"

"No, I haven't."

"Isn't there disagreement among psychiatrists as to just what a sexual psychopath is?"

"A sexual psychopath is pretty clearly defined. It is an individual whose sex drives are extremely aberrant from normal."

"Are you unwilling to admit that anyone except a sexual psychopath could have committed this crime under the circumstances?"

"That's right."

"But there are exceptions to every rule; isn't that right?"

"Of course. Anything is possible in medicine, or life."

Just as he had done with Dr. Barta, Scheele asked if Dr. Kelley thought Parker was psychotic the night of the interrogation.

"Psychosis is something that is long-lasting, a medical term, whereas insanity is a legal term that encompasses an interpretation of what is right and wrong. The night he signed the confession he was semi-amnesic and was not responsible 'for his behavior. He didn't know the difference between right and wrong."

"And in forming that opinion, you are assuming to be true what you just said?"

Dr. Kelley moved uncomfortably in his seat, wondering how to respond to what he'd just heard—it seemed to him as though Scheele was implying he might be intentionally lying on the stand.

"Of course," Kelley finally said.

Thus began the most bizarre exchange of the trial.

"Let me ask this," began Scheele. "Suppose your opinion is based on the hypothesis that we have factors A, B, C, and D. Now suppose you take away factor D. Would that cause you to change your opinion?"

"What is factor D?" asked Kelley, sitting erect in the witness chair as he slowly drew his feet beneath him.

"Now, if Your Honor please," interjected Kenneth Cook, holding his arms out at his side, "we don't know what factor A is, we don't know what factor B is, we don't know what factor C is, and we don't know what factor D is! The question is silly! It's preposterous. Objection."

Polk responded immediately. A pensive look appeared on his face as he spoke. "I think the doctor understands the question, Mr. Cook, and he has said that he couldn't answer the question until he knows what to delete and he would want to know what D is."

Dr. Kelley and Cook both looked at Polk in dismay.

"I was just about to give him D," Scheele interjected without missing a beat. "Let's assume that factor D is that Mr. Parker was accorded the treatment by Mr. Reid that you have assumed he was given and that details were suggested to him by Mr. Reid and that he received the treatment just in the manner as outlined in that hypothetical question. Now, if I take away factor D from that hypothetical question, would your opinion be any different?"

"Then you would have an impossible situation because you would also have to assume that various other factors in his confession were different than they were. I don't think you can do that."

"All right," continued Scheele on his tortured course. "You started out with the assumption that this man was innocent; that is the very first thing you assumed, wasn't it?"

"In the hypothetical question, yes."

"And you also assume his version of events on the day of December 21 to be one hundred percent true; is that right?"

"In the question, yes."

"Now, if we take away factor A and factor D, would that change your opinion, sir?"

"Your Honor," objected Kenneth Cook, "this is so ridiculous that the doctor couldn't possibly answer."

"Overruled."

"If you're going to present a hypothetical question," replied Kelley, "I would prefer you to present the question. This is so mixed up I can't follow it."

"You understand what I mean by factor D?" asked Scheele.

"Frankly, I don't have a clue what you mean."

"Factor A is, you have assumed Mr. Parker's innocence. Let's take out those two factors. Would that change your opinion?"

"Listen," said Dr. Kelley, "when I went to examine the boy, I went to Lincoln with the idea that he was guilty because everything I had read in the newspapers pointed towards that. I had to completely change my opinion after I talked to him."

"I move to strike that answer as being not responsive," said Scheele.

"The question is," began Scheele again, "with reference to the hypothetical question you were asked, in which you assumed Mr. Parker's innocence to be true—what I am now referring to as factor A. If you now remove from the question that hypothetical question, that assumption, plus the one we have been talking about as factor D, would that cause you, sir, to change your opinion?"

"No," said Dr. Kelley, apparently the only person in the courtroom who could follow Scheele's question, "because you still leave
me with the assumption that he was telling the truth."

"Is that another factor here?" asked Scheele.

"It is a very important factor."

"Well, then, let's take that out. Then would you change your
opinion?"

"Then you haven't got much left."

"This is absurd," objected Cook.

"I think the question is all right," said Polk. "He may answer it."

"You're left with nothing to answer."

"Well, would that cause you to change your opinion if you left
out those factors?"

"I wouldn't have an opinion if I didn't have those factors upon
which to base it."

Kenneth Cook and Max Towle looked at the jurors. Most of
those who weren't nodding off were stupefied by the exchange.
They would remember little of what had been said by Dr. J. Whitney
Kelley. Scheele's cumulatively tiresome, confusing, and drawn-out
cross-examination was having the desired effect.

"You do have an opinion on the complete question?" asked
Scheele.

"Oh, sure."

"If you have an opinion, after those things are deleted, you would
change your opinion?"

"If I hadn't read the newspapers and if I hadn't come down to
Lincoln to examine him, that's right, yes."

"I believe that's all," said Scheele as he moved quickly and, in his
mind, triumphantly to the prosecution table.

"We planned a surprise birthday party for him on November 2; he
was going to be twenty-four," said Evelyn Setzer, a friend of Darrel
and Nancy's from Iowa State. "We visited them at their new house
in Lincoln and helped Nancy prepare the party. Darrel had gone
to a meeting, and we made the plans and preparations while he
was gone. Nancy baked a cake, and all of us set the table and hung
decorations. When he came home the lights were out, and when he

came in the door Nancy turned the lights on and surprised him. He was very, very surprised, and he went right over to Nancy and kissed her."

"Did you have an opportunity to talk with Nancy about her married life?" asked Cook.

"Yes, I went to work with her that morning, and on our way I mentioned the fact that their new home was so nice and how happy she seemed, and she said, 'Yes, we're very happy.'"

"While you were there, Mrs. Setzer," continued Cook, "during this visit, was there any evidence of disunity or lack of harmony between these two young people?"

"None at all. They were very affectionate."

Mary Robbins, the neighbor of Lynn Parker's, testified that she had been present at the Parkers' farmhouse on the morning of December 21, 1955, when Darrel stopped on his way to Lincoln.

"Did you have an opportunity to observe Darrel—how he looked and acted that morning?" asked Cook.

"Well, I guess I realized that he wouldn't be looking normal after what he had been through, but I was certainly surprised by what I saw. He was terribly fatigued. It showed in his face, which was pale, and there were dark circles under his eyes. He just seemed so tired, almost to the point of exhaustion. I have observed a lot of patients. I knew what I was looking at."

"No cross-examination," said Scheele.

"It is my opinion that it could not have been less than thirty minutes," said Lewis Harris, owner of the largest scientific laboratory in Lincoln. That was his estimate of the time that Nancy Parker's stomach contents had to digest after breakfast.

"Is that opinion a definite one?" asked Max Towle.

"Yes. And that is based, although I haven't kept a record, on my analysis of twenty-five or more human stomachs over the years."

"Those initials R.B.H. seem to ring some kind of bell. Can you tell us what your initials stand for, Mr. Gradwohl?" asked Kenneth Cook.

"I was born on the day Rutherford B. Hayes was inaugurated president of the United States, and my parents named me after him."

"Your postgraduate work, what field did it cover?"

"It covered largely bacteriology and pathology. In other words, criminal medicine. I was interested in developing courses that would teach legal medicine, such as the courses at Harvard and the University of California at Berkeley.

"I first made an investigation of what I would call the slipshod methods in vogue in many parts of the country in regard to official medical-legal investigations. I then made a study of the coroner's system in England, and I eventually put it into effect here by organizing a scientific police laboratory in the city of St. Louis. After several years in that position I called a conference of the various authorities I knew, and we formed the American Academy of Forensic Sciences, of which I was made the first president. That society has become a very forceful agent in the development of legal medicine in this country."

"Is there a difference between criminal pathology and hospital pathology?"

"The problems of hospital pathology have little or nothing to do with court work and have nothing to do with medico-legal investigation. In autopsies, for instance, when legal situations arise, these people have no experience and are very likely to overlook some very important facts."

Gradwohl explained his experience by stating that he had personally conducted more than five thousand autopsies and five hundred rape cases. When Scheele took the floor, he was ready to ask another of his questions that would be more beneficial to the defense than the prosecution.

"The defendant in this case is accused of having strangled his wife prior to 7:15 A.M., on December 14, 1955. Her body was found at about 12:07 of the same day. And at about 1:30 P.M. of the same day Dr. Tanner made a superficial examination of her and found rigor mortis of the legs only. Based upon Dr. Tanner's testimony, do you have an opinion as to the time of death?" asked Scheele.

"My opinion is that the time of death was a short period, possibly three to four hours before she was found."

Called as a rebuttal witness by the prosecution, Dr. Don Fitzgerald took the stand and answered Scheele with a brief recital of his credentials.

"I am a clinical psychologist at the state mental hospital in Lincoln. I have been in practice since 1942 after receiving my master of arts degree."

"Dr. Fitzgerald, your testing of Mr. Parker was drawn short when he called his attorney to see if he should take your tests, is that right?" asked Scheele.

"Yes. However, I did give him one test before he talked with his attorney."

"When your testing was interrupted by Mr. Towle, did you then report the results of your findings to Dr. Stein and Dr. Farrell?"

"Yes. I also said there was an unusually high number of responses that indicated Mr. Parker was attempting to place himself in an unusually good light with regard to his past history of social behavior."

"You're not an M.D. are you, Mr. Fitzgerald?" asked Max Towle cynically in cross-examination.

"That is correct."

"And you're not a psychiatrist?"

"Correct."

"And if I am not mistaken, before you took the witness stand today, you and Dr. Farrell and Dr. Stein all gathered down at the county attorney's office before you came up here. Isn't that correct?"

"We did discuss certain aspects of the case, yes."

"Yes, and at some point during your examination, after Darrel said he wanted to call his attorney, you and I had a little confrontation. He told you he had called me. When I asked you to call me you got irritated and told Darrel, 'If your lawyer wants to see me, he can find me out at the state hospital.'"

"I was a little bit irritated under the circumstances, I shall grant; yes, sir. Under the circumstances I thought I was justified in doing so."

"Finally, from the examination you did make, the one examination, you learned nothing?"

"No, sir. The least one could say is that Mr. Parker was attempting, in responding to these test items, to give an undue impression of conscientiousness and good social behavior. That is the least."

Chester Farrell, another graduate of Creighton University in Omaha, had worked at the Hastings outlet of the Nebraska State Hospital and served as a staff member of the federal prison system. At the time of the trial he served as a professor of psychiatry at Creighton in Omaha.

When he examined Darrel Parker in March, Farrell said that Parker "gave his history quite well—his work, school, his family, and his jobs. When I started to discuss with him certain aspects of his marriage he immediately informed me that he could not answer those questions because he'd been so instructed by his attorney."

"Following that examination, were you able to evaluate his personality make-up?" asked Scheele of his second psychiatric rebuttal witness.

"I felt I could arrive at an opinion, yes. In my opinion he showed no evidence of a frank psychosis; his background indicated he was a man who had a goal to shoot at; and he knew what he wanted to do and had been pretty successful in accomplishing that. I checked his blood pressure and pulse and checked him over superficially neurologically and looked at his eyes with an ophthalmoscope."

"Did that examination reveal anything?"

"His blood pressure was elevated, and his pulse rate was rapid."

"Did you find any indication of psychosis or prior reactive depression?"

"No, sir."

"Dr. Farrell," continued Scheele, "in your opinion could a sensitive, intelligent, hardworking adult who is tender-minded and rarely loses his temper and who has some feelings of insecurity and reacts inwardly and who has adapted well but has to work at it, could he possess any repressed inward hostility?"

"I think so; yes, sir."

"Do you feel that Darrel Parker did at the time you examined him?"

"He expressed it by his cold, clammy hands and by his elevated pulse rate and blood pressure. I think he was definitely under tension."

"If his wife rejected his suggestion to have sexual intercourse the night of December 13, and again the following morning, would that have any psychiatric significance?"

"I would think that it might heighten his aggressiveness."

"Can such a person be hypnotized against his will?"

"No, sir."

"If a person had killed his wife and then gone to work, his normal routine, would it be possible for him to refrain from exhibiting an outward show of emotion?"

"I think he could."

Scheele had persisted, even if only superficially, to counter the defense testimony. If the defense had three psychiatric witnesses, then so would he.

Robert Stein, a University of Nebraska graduate and a practicing psychiatrist in Lincoln, was the doctor who examined Darrel on Sunday, March 25, two weeks before the trial began.

He completed the questioning as the last of the prosecution's psychiatric rebuttal troika.

"I told Mr. Parker that he was not obligated to answer any questions, that I just wanted to get his personal history, and he voluntarily said, 'I'll give you the history then.' He gave this history clearly and was very cooperative. He briefly discussed a difficulty he had in the third grade, at which time there were some problems with his reading. In college, he said he was just one of the guys. He told me about coming to Lincoln, and when I asked him questions regarding the day of the murder, he said he refused to answer. At about that time Mr. McManus came in the room and was very agitated. He asked what was going on and told Darrel he was not to be talking to me."

"Dr. Stein, what is a personality mask?" asked Scheele.

"The word *personality* is derived from the Greek word *persona*, which means a mask an actor puts on to fool the spectator. If masked, one could say that emotions felt on the inside are not visible, not knowable, to another person on the outside."

"If you assume his immaturity, his dependency on his parents in early life, then after his marriage could he have transferred that dependency to his wife?"

"He made the statement to me—and I will quote him—he said that his wife was an 'outgoing, pleasant, cheerful person, just the type of person I need.' So I feel he very definitely received emotional support and was dependent upon his wife."

"Doctor, could a person set the stage to make it appear that someone else had done it, then be able to go about his normal routine for four hours without showing any outward signs of emotion?"

"That is very possible. I have known cases in particular that follow the type of personality that Mr. Parker has had, because he has always been a person that held his feelings within."

"Is there disagreement among psychiatrists as to what is a sexual psychopath?"

"I think there is a universal disagreement as to the exact definition and description of a sexual psychopath. If there were three or four psychiatrists present I think you would get a different answer or different definition from each of them."

Stein's rebuttal testimony ran for fifty-four pages. One question alone by Scheele ran to eight pages and resulted in the answer, "I have [an opinion]. Darrel Parker could have gone about his normal routine chores without showing any outward sign of emotion for that length of time."

"Doctor," began Max Towle deliberately, "while we are on the subject of sexual relations, let me ask you this question: if a man, if Darrel Parker, was in bed with his wife in the early morning hours and if he had sex on his mind from the preceding night and they lay in bed for four or five minutes close to each other in just their pajamas, and then his wife got up and undressed in his presence and dressed in his presence while he still had his pajamas on, and then after that he put on his work clothes and then they went through their morning routine and ate breakfast, and then he got ready to go to work, now . . . at which time would he be most likely to suggest sexual relations—he or any other man, Doctor?"

"Well, I think the average person would have suggested it before he got dressed."

"That's right. Let me ask you another question. You said there is universal disagreement among psychiatrists, your own crowd, as to just what a sexual deviant or a sexual psychopath is, is that right?"

"That's right."

"Yet wouldn't it make a difference to you, Doctor, whether a fellow had a clean record all his life as being a religious, church-going person or whether he had a record as a rapist, a degenerate, and a lifelong convict? Wouldn't that make a bit of a difference to you?"

"Objection."

"Sustained."

"You said something here a minute ago about a lie detector test, if I'm not mistaken, that it had no value in connection with psychiatric examinations; is that correct?"

"No. I said that the American Psychiatric Association had gone on record stating that the polygraph was not scientifically accurate enough to be admissible in court."

"Would it make any difference to you, Doctor, if you knew Mr. Scheele had enough confidence in the lie detector machine that he asked John Reid to bring his lie detector all the way from Chicago down here to Lincoln for the sole purpose of examining Darrel Parker and now he refuses to give us the results of that test?"

"I object," cried Scheele.

"Sustained."

"The day that you went out to the penitentiary, that Sunday morning, could Darrel have been upset because his parents were waiting right outside the room, waiting to see him and had been there for more than two hours?"

"I didn't know his parents were there, and I didn't know that he knew his parents were there."

"Doctor, do you think it is a common thing for a man to kill his wife because sex is being rationed?"

"I don't know. I don't know if I can answer that."

"That's all," said an exasperated Towle.

"Some men do kill their wives!" shouted Elmer Scheele from his chair at the prosecution table.

"Yes, that's true," blurted Stein in agreement.

"Good Lord," bellowed Towle to the gallery. "Some women kill their husbands!"

The courtroom erupted in laughter.

T. O. Haas, a local tire dealer, testified for the prosecution concerning the tire tracks left in the snow: "I couldn't say that this particular tire made that particular track." Captain Harold Smith, of the highway patrol, likewise said it was "not possible to say which tire made the tire tracks shown in the exhibits."

Scheele called on several of the police officers who had worked the case. He called on firemen who had been at the Parker home the day of the murder to describe Darrel's state of mind just after the murder. But he had no witnesses to counter the defense's character witnesses. No one other than Opal Closner had stood up to say that Darrel and Nancy Parker's marriage had been in turmoil. Scheele may have placed doubt in the jurors' minds about the tires, about Darrel Parker's state of mind, and about his actions the day of the murder, but one thing was certain, there were nine witnesses on record who had seen the black Ford parked outside the Parker home on the morning of the murder. The car had been there, and the car had been empty.

CHAPTER ELEVEN

Every trial has a moment when the testimony is decisively revealing. Often its importance is not immediately apparent, its impact totally unexpected, its emotional and factual significance overshadowed by other witnesses called to the stand for just such an effect. John Reid's testimony, however, once it was over, would leave little doubt as to its importance, at least to the defense team. Yet Reid's testimony did not come at the dramatic end point of the trial, as it so often does in literature and film, where it would be fresh in the jurors' minds. It came before the trial was half over, only to be followed by another thousand pages of testimony.

Reid, for his part, was sure his earlier testimony during the "trial within a trial" had sat well with the jurors. He'd watched them closely as he answered Scheele's and Cook's questions and was confident that, despite Dr. Douglas Kelley's opinions to the contrary, his version of the interrogation had been accepted. He'd done this repeatedly in his career. He was practiced. He was sure of himself. This was just repetition. Something he'd done hundreds of times. He was already thinking about his next trial. He was ready to go back to Chicago.

When John Reid was called for cross-examination, Max was ready for him. Tom McManus and Max had done just as Douglas Kelley recommended. Their preparation had been painstaking. They had gone over *Lie Detection and Criminal Interrogation* in detail, chapter by chapter, line by line. Towle wanted to ensure that the true nature of the "technique," as Reid called it in his book, was laid bare for all to see, contrasted with the glossed-over version of the interrogation that had been presented during the "trial within a trial" and his testimony in open court under Scheele. Reid, on the other hand, was even more relaxed, more at ease, than he had been earlier. Any additional testimony on his part, he was sure, would be merely perfunctory, the period at the end of the sentence. He continued to sit with Inbau, continued to make light of the proceedings. He was sure that he would be called to quickly repeat his earlier testimony and that would be that.

As Reid strode to the stand, confident and self-aware, he expected to be questioned again by Kenneth Cook, expected the same softball questions and the same result. He sat casually in the witness chair and studiously raised a hand to his chin. When the moment for questioning finally came, however, Max Towle rose from the defense table and advanced on him, wasting no time with preliminaries. Max came out of the starting gate just like one of his thundering Thoroughbreds.

"Mr. Reid, about these corrections in exhibit 66—the confession—you instructed Miss Wheeler to make those mistakes on purpose, didn't you!" began Towle.

"Yes, I think I did," replied Reid slowly in a calm but soft voice, a voice that was almost inaudible beyond the witness stand. Reid had been somewhat thrown off by the fact that Towle would question him, but any surprise he may have had did not register on his face. He was not worried in the least.

"Sure you did! Come on . . . why hesitate about it? You told her to do the same thing in this case as you have done in all your other cases—make mistakes in the confession on purpose so you could then trip up the man being questioned into correcting them!"

"To prove the voluntariness of the statement," replied Reid, his tone solemnly hushed, his voice barely audible in the jury box, let alone in the courtroom.

"That's right. You told Miss Wheeler to make those mistakes, because she wouldn't misspell *March*. She wouldn't make that many mistakes in a year if she tried. You told her to make mistakes to trick this young man into correcting them so you could then tell the jury that he realized what he was doing!"

"I told her to make some mistakes," said Reid.

"Yes. And you want to tell this jury that you started talking to this young man at a quarter of twelve on the day of the interrogation—talked to him until 3:00 or 4:00 constantly and steadily that afternoon; and then you started again talking to him at 6:30 and talked to him until 8:00; and then you talked to him until 10:00; and all that time you were talking in the same tone of voice you have been talking in right now?"

"That's right. Yes, sir."

"You kept your voice down real low and real quiet like you're doing now," cooed Max, directly in front of Reid. "You just carried on a little social gathering with this young man; is that right?"

"Pretty much so, yes."

"You didn't raise your voice at any time?" said Towle in a near whisper.

"No, sir. We speak very softly."

"What did the police tell you about this crime after you arrived in Lincoln?" asked Towle, abruptly changing the subject.

"They gave me a rundown, a briefing on the whole case . . . That Nancy Parker was murdered and she died on December 14, 1955, and was found in her home on Sumner Street. And that a wristwatch was stolen. That's substantially the whole story."

"That's the whole story . . . Did they tell you Darrel Parker lived on a farm all his life, was an Iowa country boy who had come to the big city?"

"I was only interested in the story of the woman."

"You wished him good luck, didn't you?"

"After the confession was signed, yes, I wished him good luck." Reid smiled and looked over the gallery, then into the jury box.

"Now, Mr. Reid, let's be honest about this."

"I am honest, sir."

Max moved quickly to Reid's side, raised his foot to the riser of the witness box, and banged his knee forcefully into Reid's. Reid jerked bolt upright in his chair and recoiled, putting each of his hands on the arms of the witness chair. Max put his face within a foot of Reid's. Reid pulled his head away.

"Weren't you this close to him, so your knees touched like this?" Max yelled and then banged knees with Reid again. Reid's tone of voice momentarily raised and then quickly lowered.

"That's . . . that's right."

"Within a foot like that, glaring right in his eyes, and saying, 'Look at me, look at me, look at me!' " Towle yelled.

"I didn't do it that way, sir," stammered Reid quietly.

"How did you do it then?"

"I put my hand on his shoulder," demonstrated Reid, holding his arm out in front of him, "and I said, 'Darrel . . .' "

"Looked him right in the eyes?"

"That's right. That's right. I said, 'Darrel, let's get this whole thing straightened out.' "

Reid's hushed voice had finally become too much for some of the jurors. Several of them had been whispering among themselves and shaking their heads as Reid testified. Heads shook again and cupped ears turned toward Reid. Finally one exasperated juror put his hands to his mouth and half-yelled at Reid.

"We can't hear you, Mr. Reid. Will you please speak up!"

"All right. All right," Reid answered loudly. "But I want the jury to understand. I'll talk louder, but I wasn't talking any louder than that when I talked to Darrel Parker. I put my hand on his shoulder and urged him to tell me the truth about his wife's death. And sometime during the course of that talk he dropped his head, and I put my hand under his chin and I said, 'Darrel, look at me.' "

"So you did touch him?"

"Yes, I did."

"It was only a matter of degree then as to the force you used in lifting his head up?"

"I didn't use force, sir."

"You had to use enough force to lift his head, didn't you!"

"That's right. He was very pliable."

Max had been walking toward the jury box, away from Reid, when he heard the word *pliable*. He immediately wheeled around.

"What did you just say?"

"Flexible," Reid said, hurriedly changing his words.

"When did he get that way, 'flexible'?"

"He was that way pretty much during the whole talk with me."

"You stroked his hair?"

"Yes."

"You heard Darrel say that when you stroked his head and brushed your hand through his hair that it made him feel like you were petting some kind of animal. Why did you do that?"

"I wanted to get a friendly attitude and atmosphere with him."

"You wanted to make him think you were his friend, is that it?"

"Yes, sir. I wasn't his enemy."

"Oh, you turned out to be a pretty good friend, didn't you! So . . . how many times did you stroke his head and brush your hands through his hair?"

"A number of times, several times."

"I see. Did you pull his hair?"

"No, absolutely not."

"But it became more or less a persuasive way, didn't it?"

"No. Friendly."

"You want to impress upon the person being interrogated that you are the master of the situation, don't you, Mr. Reid? Not only in this case, but in all the cases you work on?"

"I am interested only in the truth."

Towle turned from Reid to the busily typing court reporter. "Read him the question!"

"No, I don't want to be the master of the situation!" cried Reid.

"You say you don't want to convey the idea that looking intently at a person and having your eyes within a foot of theirs and talking persuasively, that is not trying to be master of the situation?"

"I am appealing for the truth. Only the truth."

"I assume you told him you are a former policeman and a lie detector interrogator from Chicago?"

"No, I didn't tell him anything like that."

"Why didn't you?"

"I didn't want to scare him."

"You finally did, though, didn't you?"

"I don't think so."

"How long did you visit with him before you tied him up on that machine of yours?"

"About fifteen minutes."

"And what did you talk about those first fifteen minutes?"

"As I said, he immediately started to cry regarding his wife's decease, and I wanted to take a little time with him there until he gained his composure and was able to go on from there."

"When did you strap that machine around him, then?"

"I put the machine around him soon after he came in the room. I put a blood pressure cuff around his right arm and then a pneumograph tube around his chest."

"Oh, so you hooked it up right away . . . Is this tube around his arm painful?"

"When you pump it up. You don't have it on long enough to have any pain."

"But you connect it and squeeze it, it is painful, isn't it?"

"No, not until a certain time. Some people can take it for fifteen or twenty minutes. I've had some people take it for nearly half an hour."

"How long did you 'visit' with him before you started telling him his wife was running around with other men?"

"I didn't."

"You didn't tell him, 'Your wife is running around with other men and everybody is getting it but you'? You didn't tell him that?" asked Towle.

"No, sir."

"Did you tell him in the Catholic Church it was a sin for women to refuse their husbands?"

"Yes . . . yes. Sometime during the course of my conversation."

"During this interrogation did you ever have a tape recording outfit there?"

"No, sir."

"Was there a window in the room, or a two-way glass where somebody could see in and witness what was going on?"

"No, sir."

"No, and at three o'clock or so, when you came out, could Darrel have left and gone home if he wanted to?"

"Oh, sure. There was nobody holding him there."

"Did you tell him that or give him the impression he could leave?"

"No."

"No . . . and at some point you told him it was important for the state to find out what became of the watch, didn't you?"

"No. I said it was very important that we get the watch."

This was the first in what would become a bizarre series of statements by Reid in which he would first make a denial of Towle's question and then make an outright admission in his very next sentence—a contradiction of which he seemed to be totally unaware.

"You told a different story here yesterday about this bowline knot than what you're telling us today?"

"I said yesterday that the bowline knot—that Darrel made the correction on it."

"That's right, he did do that, but at whose direction?"

"At Mr. Masters' suggestion."

"That's right. You heard Miss Wheeler testify earlier that Mr. Masters suggested that Darrel make the change?"

"You have the statement there, sir. Whatever you say it was, that is what I said yesterday. Because that was my recollection of it at the time I testified, and I testified honestly as to what I recalled at that time. But when I heard Mr. Masters make the statement after I testified, then I was sure he was right because it recalled and refreshed my recollection."

"Refreshed your recollection . . . What I am trying to get at is, if you were wrong yesterday, couldn't you be wrong about some things today?"

"We can all be wrong about some things. But I am not wrong about that now."

"So it's your practice then, if a fellow doesn't fall into this trap and catch these misspellings, that you tell him about it and point them out to him?"

"That isn't a trap."

"I know what it is!"

"The idea—the errors are—the purposeful errors in the statement is to prove that the statement was read by the man. I didn't tell Miss Wheeler to make a specified number of mistakes."

"But you told her to make mistakes. That's right, isn't it?"

"That's right."

"Mr. Reid, this whole business is just kind of a big game with you isn't it? You get great satisfaction maneuvering a person around into an advantageous position for you, where you can overpower his resistance until he succumbs; isn't that true?"

"No, sir, that is not true."

At just the time when it seemed to Reid that the cross-examination was nearly at an end, Max Towle turned his back and deliberately ambled over to the defense table. Lying before Tom McManus on the defense table was a small gray book profusely festooned with white page markers. Reid and Inbau's book. Max extended his arm and McManus softly placed the book in his hand. Max returned to the witness chair and held the book up for Reid to see. Slowly turning a ring on his right hand, Reid no longer affected an air of unbridled self-confidence.

"Do you recognize the book I have in my hand, Mr. Reid?" Max asked, as he eased closer to Reid's side.

"Yes, sir, I do."

There was a frozen moment. Reid looked at Scheele as if for support, then to Inbau, Carroll, and Masters. The prosecutorial conspirators looked as though they were actors in a play who have suddenly forgotten their lines.

"It's the book written by you and Mr. Inbau over there. And in this book, you advocate the following to your pupils and to the police departments that you sell this book to."

Max inserted his finger into the first of fifteen markers. He slowly opened the book and put the first marker in his jacket pocket. He paused briefly as the courtroom hushed. Reid looked again in the direction of the prosecution table.

"I read from page 185," began Towle. "'During this period the interrogator's task is somewhat akin to that of a hunter stalking his game. Each must patiently maneuver himself or his quarry into a position from which the desired objective may be attained' . . . Is that in the book?"

"That's in the book. You're reading it right from the book!"

"'And in the same manner that the hunter may lose his game by a noisy dash through the brush, so can the interrogator fail in his efforts by not exercising the proper degree of patience.' That's in there, too, isn't it?"

"That's right."

"It *is* a game with you, though, isn't it?"

"It's no game at all; it's a profession with me."

"Oh, I think it is . . . I think it is. You say you visited with Darrel for fifteen or twenty minutes before you hooked him up to your machine?"

"I didn't say that."

Max ignored Reid, turned to face the jury, and read aloud: "On page 11, 'The greeting which the examiner extends should be cordial but firm. The subject should be requested to sit down in the chair and the examiner should immediately hook up the polygraph and at the same time inquire, "Have you ever been on a lie detector before?"' Is that what you advocate?"

"Yes, I do. That's exactly the way I did it." Reid thus admitted something he'd earlier said was done fifteen minutes after Darrel had entered the room.

"I also asked you whether or not you tried to conceal the fact that you were an officer of the law . . . On page 148 you say, 'Avoid creating the impression that you are an investigator seeking a confession.'"

"That's right! I didn't want to scare him, but I didn't conceal from him who I was. If he would've asked, I would have told him. I just wanted him to know that I was interested in the truth, and I got that across to him. I didn't bring it out to the jury because I didn't want to cause a mistrial, because lie detectors aren't admissible in evidence."

"I see. You said earlier that you didn't suggest to him anything about the misconduct of his wife?"

"I did not."

"But in your book you advocate that very thing!"

Towle prepared to read another excerpt from the book as Scheele fumbled frantically through his own copy of the book, hurriedly thrust upon him by Inbau. "What page, Mr. Towle?"

"Page 163. 'In the interrogation of an accused wife-killer the interrogator proceeded to condemn the wife's relatives who were known to have meddled in the offender's marital affairs. The interrogator remarked that probably the relatives themselves should have been shot. The subject's wife was alleged to be a provocative, unreasonable, and unbearable creature, who would either drive a man insane or to commit the very crime he was accused of. The interrogator then stated that the subject's wife was "just like most other women." The subject was also told that many married men avoid similar difficulties by becoming drunkards, cheats, and deserters, but unfortunately the subject tried to do what was right by sticking it out, and it got the better of him in the end. This, of course, rendered the subject's offense less reprehensible in his own mind.'

"Do you advocate that practice?"

"In that case, the woman who was killed had a bad reputation." This practice was labeled in Reid's "technique" as a "Blame the Victim" approach to interrogation, done in order to get a confession by implying the victim deserved it.

"Are you advocating that a man kill his wife because she has a bad reputation?"

"It could be a reason, yes."

"But you didn't find anything like that here, did you?"

"No."

"You say you stroked his hair. You also advocate a tap on the stomach, too, don't you?"

"No, sir, I do not."

"You probably know right where it is in this book!"

"I do not advocate tapping anybody in the stomach. No, sir. You will not find it in there!"

"Page 156." Towle removed another marker and calmly began, "'When interrogating a subject it is advisable to remind the subject that he 'doesn't feel very good inside,' that this 'peculiar feeling' is the result of a troubled conscience. While making this statement it is well for the interrogator to touch or tap the subject's abdomen.'"

"That is a misleading statement."

"How hard a tap do you give them?" continued Towle, with anger rising in his voice.

"None at all . . . There is no hard tap, sir. It is an indication of where the man feels the discomfiture because of his all knotted up—"

"'In addition,'" Towle read on, "'it is advisable for the interrogator to obtain as much information on the suspect as possible to create a psychological advantage in favor of the interrogator!' You wanted to show this young man that you had an advantage over him?"

"Absolutely not."

"Mr. Reid, are you trying to tell us that you don't possess a strong personality, a strong force of persuasion?"

"I try to persuade people to tell me the truth, yes."

"Do you remember telling Darrel, 'Now, boy, why don't you blame your wife? Why don't you put the blame on her? I'll help you build a defense so you won't be tried in the newspapers!' Do you remember saying that?"

"No, sir, I do not."

"How many times do you think you accused him of killing his wife?"

"I didn't accuse him of killing his wife. I was interested in having him tell me the truth."

"You mean you thought by just talking to him, stroking his head, grabbing his chin, and tapping his stomach that he would come out and say, 'I killed my wife'!"

"No, sir. I didn't visit, and he didn't all of a sudden tell me anything!"

"So, you want the jury to believe that you didn't accuse him of killing his wife?"

"I said, 'You're not telling me the truth.' I said, 'You did kill your wife.'"

"Well, how many times did you tell him that?"

"Two or three times, several times, but I was interested strictly in the truth!"

"But you wanted the truth your way, didn't you?"

"There is only one way with the truth." Reid, who by now had slumped somewhat in the witness chair, looked toward the jury as if there was solace to be found there.

"Page 69: 'However, an extensive interrogation based upon constant accusations of guilt may adversely affect the accuracy of the test, especially if the test follows. This is particularly true if the interrogation is accompanied by physical abuse, or threats of physical harm administered in an effort to obtain a confession.'

"Why do you refer to physical abuse or threatening behavior?"

"I don't know. I've never engaged in it!"

"Why do you mention it in your book, then?"

"That is a very common defense that attorneys like to use—the third degree."

Towle had been speaking in an angry tone of voice. As he asked the next question, he casually approached Reid and spoke calmly and quietly.

"Does a sudden accusation have anything to do with the results of a lie detector test or confession?"

"Sudden accusation? How do you mean?"

Towle quickly moved closer to Reid until he was right beside him. Reid reflexively recoiled, by this time unsure of what Towle would do next. Max put his face within a foot of Reid's and suddenly yelled, "Look at me! Look at me! You know you killed your wife, you've been lying to me! Look at me!"

Reid jerked stiffly upright and leaned as far back in his chair as he was able. He brought his hand up across his face and then, just as quickly, dropped his arm to his lap and hesitated before answering.

"You wouldn't do that on a lie detector test . . . You'd never do it in that respect!" Reid said loudly. His face reddened, and he looked quickly away from Towle.

"Page 178," Towle continued. "'The first approach, consisting of an implication or accusation of guilt, possesses the desirable element of surprise, and by pursuing this course the interrogator may successfully "shock" his subject into a confession in the event he is the guilty person.' That's fine and dandy, Mr. Reid, but what if the subject is an innocent man?"

"That's not right. No, sir."

" 'If the subject is innocent,' " Towle continued reading from the book, " 'he may become so confused and excited as a result of the guilt accusation that you won't be able to ascertain the subject's innocence.'

"That's in there, isn't it?"

"That's in there," replied Reid, "but it is advocating *not* to do that. You're reading it out of context!"

"You're a great believer in perseverance and persistence, aren't you Mr. Reid? You advocate that in your book?" Max stood calmly with his finger marking yet another page.

"I do." Reid, now totally unhinged and unsure what was coming next, once again looked nervously at Scheele. Max opened the book.

" 'Another prime requisite'—page 186—'for a successful interrogation is persistency. In this respect the following rule of thumb is helpful: Never conclude an interrogation at the time when you feel ready to give up, but continue a little while longer. The authors have observed many instances where the subject's resistance broke just at the time the interrogator himself was about ready to abandon his efforts.' "

"Patience and persistence. *Patience* is a good word," responded Reid quietly.

"Page 149: 'The interrogator should sit close to the subject, and between the two there should be no table, desk, or other piece of furniture. The presence of an obstruction or distance from the subject seems to afford the subject a certain degree of confidence not otherwise attainable.' " Towle looked at Reid. Max asked no question but dropped the book to his side and waited as Reid grasped for a rejoinder.

"When interrogating, we want to be close to the man."

"I see. They can hear you better if you're within a foot of their face, is that it?"

"We talk very softly, sir. Very softly."

"What is the object of not having the table there?"

"So that we can properly appeal to the man without having anything between us."

"You recognize that unless you found something that corroborated this confession—like Nancy Parker's missing watch—that it was weakened, just like you say in your book?"

"The confession does not lose its force—any of its force! The confession will stand on its own!"

"I like your book, Mr. Reid . . . I read it clear through."

"I like it, too," said Reid, drained and leaning on one elbow.

"When was it exactly that you talked with Darrel about the watch? Where he'd 'put the watch'?"

"It was before Miss Wheeler came in . . . Between 8:00 and 10:00."

"And why were you so anxious to find the watch?" asked Towle.

"I was interested in getting all the evidence we could that would help the case."

"But Mr. Reid, in your book that's the very thing you point out, that unless you get something to corroborate this confession, it loses some of its force?"

"That's up to the court to decide. I did not say the confession loses all of its force! I say in the book that the confession will stand on its own!"

Towle removes the final marker from the book. "'A confession that is unsubstantiated by other evidence is far less effective at the trial than one which has been investigated and subjected to verification or supporting evidence.' You were interested very much in locating this watch, weren't you?"

"I was interested in locating the watch, yes. But Darrel misled me."

"You mean this young farm boy was trying to mislead an experienced Chicago policeman and interrogator?"

"This young farmer boy is as intelligent as I am."

"Oh, I don't know about that, Mr. Reid . . . So, did you say, 'Darrel, you misled me. The watch is not in the car'?"

"I didn't say that. I said, 'Darrel, you have misled us. The watch is not in the trunk of the car.' I said, 'It is most important, Darrel, that we find where the watch is.' And he said, 'Important for whom?' And I said, 'Well you're right. It is important to the State.'"

"This all came about because this poor boy didn't know where the watch was and couldn't tell you. That's a fact, isn't it?"

Reid did not respond. Towle waited. Reid had fallen silent and did not reply. The court reporter wrote, "No reply."

"That's all, Your Honor," Towle said at last, slamming Reid's book shut and dropping the last book mark into his coat pocket. Polk banged the gavel down and called for a recess.

At the defense table Towle sat down heavily next to McManus.

"If two people tell different versions of the same story, Tom, and one of them is caught lying, then what does that tell you about the other person's version?"

As the courtroom cleared, Scheele huddled at the prosecution table with Fahrnbruch. After a few moments the pair proceeded up the aisle through the gallery. Virgil Falloon stood as they neared him. Scheele slowed, sure that Falloon wanted to interview him. Falloon smiled, reached out, and slapped Scheele on the shoulder.

"Elmer, it's obvious as hell that man of yours is lying through his teeth."

Scheele immediately wheeled and headed for the exit. He spoke to Fahrnbruch at the door. Fahrnbruch looked back at Falloon. Falloon said that Scheele would have nothing to do with him from that day forward.

CHAPTER TWELVE

Gene Masters, with a look of grim resolve on his face, ambled across the creaking oak floor to the witness chair for the last time. He would be the final witness of the trial. On the stand he told Scheele that Parker had "showed no emotion when I saw him December 21 and did not appear to be depressed, or to have any signs of having been struck by anyone."

"Mr. Masters," asked Scheele, "is it true that during the course of this investigation Wesley Peery was brought to the police station for questioning?"

"That's right. On the evening of December 15."

"You questioned him yourself?"

"Part of the time. Lieutenant Henninger and Robert Nichols also questioned him."

"And while he was there was his automobile carefully checked?"

"It was."

"After that interrogation by you and the others, was the information that Mr. Peery gave you checked out?"

"Yes."

"And following that what was done with Mr. Peery?"

"He was released to go home."

"What was done with his automobile?"

"It was turned over to him."

Kenneth Cook approached Masters with a copy of the confession in his hand. He revisited his earlier question about errors in the confession.

"When Mr. Reid recited the following part of Mr. Parker's confession, 'and then I got another piece of brown cord and wrapped it around, too. I didn't tie it,' did Mr. Parker say that wasn't true?" asked Cook, reading from the confession.

"No, sir," replied Masters.

"It wasn't true, though, was it?"

"No."

"'And then I took her sweatshirt off, tore it off.' Did Mr. Parker say anything about that not being correct?"

"No."

"It wasn't correct, either, was it?"

"No."

"So, regardless of the change from slip knot to double bowline—at whose suggestion—it was OK'd by Mr. Parker, wasn't it?"

"It was."

"And it wasn't true, either, was it?"

"I don't know whether it was true or not. All I know is there were knots—"

"Darrel OK'd, at *someone's suggestion,* a kind of knot which, as far as the facts are concerned, didn't exist!"

"He OK'd the change."

"Which wasn't the fact?"

"According to the testimony, no."

"We are going on the testimony, aren't we Mr. Masters?"

"Yes."

Scheele calculatingly and soberly eyed the jurors. They reflected the same torpor that had been exhibited earlier in the trial when the psychiatric evidence and the discussion of knots was given. Yet another discussion of the rope and twine only added to their confusion, and Scheele duly noted the vapid stares. He smiled to himself and leaned back in his chair, confident that he had done his job and done it well.

Towle watched the jurors also. There were at least two jurors—Mrs. Watson, the woman from the motor vehicle department, and Clyde Blackledge, the white-haired man who sat behind her—who were alert and who had remained so throughout the trial, paying close attention to all of the testimony. Although Towle knew that just one juror could make the difference, he also knew that most of the jury had been persuaded by the prosecution long ago.

"You were there, weren't you, Mr. Masters, when this confession, exhibit 66, was signed?" pressed Cook.

"That's right."

"You were there, and Chief Carroll, Captain Beave, Miss Wheeler, and Mr. Scheele, and, of course, John Reid. Six people, most of them officers of the law. Did anyone, anyone at all, suggest to Mr. Parker that before he signed this statement that he should consult with his attorney?"

"No, sir."

"No. Did anyone suggest to him or tell him that what he was about to sign would be used against him?"

"No. That wasn't told to him."

"He was alone with all of you law officers . . . What kind of officer would you call an ex-policeman from Chicago, Mr. Reid?"

"I would call him a criminologist, like he said he was."

"And would you say he had considerable experience in the very thing that was going on? . . . That is the reason Mr. Scheele got him, wasn't it?"

"That is correct."

"Yet, in the face of all that, with all of you there, this young man about to sign an instrument of grave import wasn't asked if he wanted to contact me, was he?"

"No."

"And he wasn't asked if he wanted to telephone anyone?"

"No, sir."

"Mr. Masters, you have known Wesley Peery for a long time before this case, haven't you?" asked Towle, as he took over for Cook and continued the cross-examination of Masters.

"Yes, sir."

"Over what period of time would you say you've known him?"

"I have known him for twenty years or more."

"Did you know him socially or professionally?"

The gallery erupted in laughter. Polk jumped at the eruption and banged the gavel down repeatedly.

"Professionally," said Masters, sitting up as he tugged on his tie and awkwardly crossed his legs.

"He was released from the Nebraska penitentiary last October, and before that he served a term in the Washington State Penitentiary?"

"Yes, sir."

"And before that, another term in the Nebraska State Penitentiary?"

"Yes."

"And since you questioned him, he has been convicted of rape up in Sarpy County?"

"He has."

"And in between that time he broke into your house and stole a gun, didn't he?"

"That's what he's being charged with, yes."

"He stole your revolver. Walked right up the street a few doors and held up one of your neighbors, robbed them at the point of a gun—used your gun?"

"That's our contention," Masters answered curtly, his eyes focused squarely on the back of the courtroom. Once again the gallery tittered.

"And he's now in jail awaiting sentence on this rape charge?"

"That's right."

"And that is the kind of man you folks released the evening of December 15?"

"Yes."

Towle turned toward the judge. He held his arms out at his side as he pled one last time to have Peery testify.

"Your Honor, I ask again that we be allowed to bring Wesley Peery before this court to let him explain himself concerning the murder of Nancy Parker."

"I object," said Scheele, not bothering to get up.

"Sustained," replied Polk. Towle hesitated for a long moment. He finally spoke, quietly yet firmly.

"Then the defense will have to rest, Your Honor. But I would first like to make the same motion that we made at the start of the trial."

Before he heard the motion, Polk removed the jury.

Towle then addressed the judge. "Comes now the defendant and moves the court for a directed verdict, for the reason that the evidence is insufficient to sustain a verdict of guilty."

Polk overruled Towle and quickly returned the jury. Polk then quietly addressed the weary group of twelve: "Ladies and gentlemen, this concludes the taking of the testimony and the evidence in the case. The next stage in the order of the trial is the argument of counsel and the instructions of the court. We will adjourn until nine o'clock Monday morning, and you will observe the instructions that have been given you about not discussing the case, nor should you form or express an opinion until [the case] is finally submitted to you on Monday morning, April 30."

By late Sunday evening Max had completed the preparation of his closing arguments. Dressed in his robe and slippers he went out on his front porch, a Scotch in one hand and a cigar in the other. The neighborhood was deserted and a light but steady rain fell, cleansing the street, as he sat pensively in a wicker rocking chair next to the porch railing. He looked out on the glistening pavement, inhaled the sweet humid air, and placed his glass on the center of the porch rail. He took a long drag on his cigar, exhaled slowly, and looked up into the streetlight where the rain passed straight down in the dim glow. He picked up the Scotch, placed his arm on the railing, and closed his eyes. His lips moved slowly as he talked to himself in silence.

At the prison, thunder vibrated the entire complex and echoed throughout the cellblocks. Flashes of lightning danced wildly upon the ceiling, and rain ran down the windowpanes like the tributaries of some miniature river system. In the hospital room the lights were out. Darrel lay on his back with his hands clasped tightly on his chest. His eyes were open wide as he watched the flashes, shadows, and rain ghosts dance on the ceiling.

A hard drizzle fell, along with the temperature, on Monday morning. The *Star* reported that the farmers were happy at the rain that had "brought much needed moisture to the parched topsoil in the state but much more would be needed to reach the subsoil."

At the courthouse there were many more reporters in the court-room than there had been during the trial. They spilled over into the gallery, much to the disgruntlement of the people who had faithfully followed the trial from the start—many of whom were now relegated to the ranks of the standing, or to those who had to wait in the hallway. There was even one of the new mobile, but just barely so, TV cameras set up just outside the courtroom doors. Polk instructed the jury that the attorneys for each side could make their final arguments for up to six hours each.

Elmer Scheele began his closing remarks: "Ladies and gentlemen of the jury, are you going to let them get away with it?" bellowed Scheele. He would spend the next two hours addressing the jury.

I don't think you are . . . Max Towle, who I've known for years, has conducted one of the shrewdest jobs of defense I've ever seen—a typical defense where they drag out a red herring to confuse you, mix you up so you don't know what you're doing. Mr. Towle had the same tactics used against him when he was county attorney, and he knows how to use them now against us.

The pictures of the murder scene that were shown to you depict a crime of hatred, of suppressed inner reactions—a compulsion—toward the person on whom Mr. Parker depended and who had frustrated his need. Nancy was a good, clean, wholesome woman with a splendid future ahead of her [Scheele was holding aloft one of the crime scene photos of Nancy's nude and bound body]. And this is what happened to her.

I must honestly say that I feel that Darrel Parker has had a particularly fair and impartial trial. We've done everything humanly possible to protect his constitutional rights.

A stranger did not kill Nancy Parker, because a stranger would not have known that the station wagon she drove was used by her and not by her husband, or that he had in fact already left for work. And a stranger would not have been admitted to the house because of her fear from the burglary. A stranger would not have known there was rope in the broom closet, and a stranger would not have known where the handkerchiefs were. There was no evidence that Nancy had been raped. There were no signs of a jimmied door or window, no sign of a struggle, and no tracks in the snow around the house. Would a stranger have known that she was not going to depart for work at her normal time?

No, she was not killed by a stranger. And I have more confidence in the jury system than to think that when you weigh the evidence you've heard that you're going to let them get away with it. Darrel Parker has admitted he committed this crime, and the evidence shows that he did it. He came voluntarily to Lincoln, and he knew he was under suspicion when he did so . . .

The defense claimed that Mr. Reid hit Parker, pulled his hair, poked him, and hit him in the chin. Well, they finally toned that down and conveniently said that John Reid used hypnosis to get his answers. Mr. Reid, ladies and gentlemen, is a man of integrity. He could not afford with his reputation to do the things he is accused of in this case. No, he could not. We just don't believe in third-degree tactics in Lancaster County!

In addition, I don't think anyone outside of Darrel and Nancy Parker knew the true facts of their marital life, and now no one will ever know because Nancy is dead. Darrel Parker, when he confessed . . . it was just like any man who had gotten something off his chest. After he'd confessed verbally he signed the written confession over and over, voluntarily. And he signed it in front of witnesses. Mr. Reid did not "bully" him, did not "force" him to sign. He signed of his own free will and accord . . .

Now, Mr. Towle has been critical of us for bringing Mr. Reid in from out of town. I should like to remind Mr. Towle once again that when he was county attorney he did the same thing. He brought Dr. Douglas Kelley here all the way from California, didn't he? He brought Mr. Gradwohl all the way from St. Louis!

So, don't be confused, ladies and gentlemen. Don't be stampeded by these attempts to mix you up. We're depending only on the facts and the evidence . . . the facts and the evidence . . .

In closing I would like to mention one last thing. The Morrisons, Nancy's parents—to have to listen to all of the gruesome details of their daughter's murder would have been most inhumane. And while they were here in court, they were not asked their opinion on the case. Well, I'm telling you now, I know what that opinion is.

"Objection," shouted Towle.

"Overruled," came the, by now, automatic judgment of Polk.

Towle grew red in the face. He grabbed a pencil and wrote furiously on his legal pad.

The jurors sat as if they were statues. Most of them were done with this trial. They knew how they were going to vote, and they were tired. It had become an ordeal for them, an ordeal that would end only with a verdict.

"This case is exceptional," began Kenneth Cook in his closing remarks, "very exceptional, in that there isn't any evidence, not one shred of hard evidence, to show that Darrel Parker committed this crime."

And what did he tell John Reid and Detective Masters? Why there wasn't one word of corroboration from them or anyone else. There were no witnesses to any of these conversations. We only have their word against Darrel's. If any of you jurors think, even slightly, that this confession was not freely and voluntarily given—*even if you think it is true*—it is your responsibility to throw it out . . .

"Remember, John Reid admitted touching, violating, Darrel's person during that interrogation. At that point, if not before, the 'confession' became involuntary. Once he laid a hand on Darrel Parker, John Reid became the author of exhibit 66—the 'confession'—not Darrel Parker. If we allow that kind of behavior from our legal officials, if we condone actions of that kind, we won't have the kind of legal system we want and deserve in this country.

"Now, we have presented evidence throughout this trial to show you the good character, the good reputation, and the Christian activities of Darrel Parker in his church and community. We have tried as much as possible to open up to you the very soul of Darrel. You have heard that his entire life has been one of devotion, hard work, and self-discipline. He has told you himself, with God as his witness, that he did not harm his wife—that he loved her and she loved him.

"All of the things said in the confession about what supposedly happened that morning, were said to have taken place between breakfast—which ended a little after seven—and seven fifteen when

Darrel went to work. Now, I don't think anyone can look at all of those things he was accused of doing in that time period and believe they could have been done in ten minutes. Why, I doubt if they could have been done in twice the time . . .

"I think we have shown beyond a shadow of a doubt that Darrel Parker was somehow made to confess to his wife's murder; was coerced to admit something he was totally incapable of doing and, in fact, had not done. I ask you now, each and every one of you, to remember what all of the defense psychiatrists testified to, that Darrel Parker was the least likely person to have committed such a crime."

Cook would go on for another hour and twenty-five minutes. While he spoke, Max Towle studied the impassive jurors. He was certain they would not be able to muster a majority in their favor. He was certain that their best hope, their only hope, was to have firmly convinced a few of those in the minority.

Max Towle began:

I want to remind you again that without this coerced and false confession that there is no physical evidence, nor any witness, that can link Darrel Parker to the crime. Mr. Scheele, Mr. Reid, and the Lincoln police have made a horrible and tragic mistake with these charges . . . Public opinion and the newspapers demanded that they catch someone and catch them in a hurry. And they did that. They went right out and caught someone.

What kind of a kangaroo court situation is this? It's just like Mr. Reid told Darrel during the interrogation, "You'd better confess now or they'll try you in the papers." You notice that the newspapers haven't reported on certain evidence that proved a sexual assault had happened. Why was that? We can talk about murder, but we can't talk about the motive! It's obvious what the motive was in this case. It's obvious what brought the killer to 3200 Sumner. It was an assault. A brutal sexual assault. A brutal and deadly rape . . .

After taking the Parker case I remember asking Darrel for the truth if I was going to defend him. He looked me straight in the eye and said with conviction, "I didn't do it, Mr. Towle." This young man was honest with me, and he's been honest in this courtroom with all that he's had to say—and that was a most prodigious amount! Yet, when all is said and done, I doubt if most of us could have held up under such repetitive and relentless questioning and the kind of tactics that were used against him . . .

How might someone have known things about the Parker house that morning, as Mr. Scheele asked? I'll tell you why. First, a person might have known Nancy Parker was home and the station wagon was her car if he had been watching the house that morning from a half block away. He would have seen Darrel Parker leave the house, jump-start his car, and drive away, and he would have known that Nancy was alone. Second, a stranger might have gained entry to the house if he had used some type of force, or a show of force—like a gun. If that was the case she would have opened the door, there would have been no sign of forced entry. There wouldn't have been a need for it. And, finally, once entrance had been gained to the home it would not have been difficult to force Nancy Parker to show him where the rope was that he bound her with. It would not have been difficult to force a fearful Nancy Parker to do his bidding.

This leads me to Wesley Peery's car, the black Ford. How long must that car have been outside the Parker residence to have been seen by nine different witnesses between 7:00 A.M. and 7:40 A.M.— and how much later? It was seen empty. When did it leave? Who or what was he watching if not the Parker house? No one seems to know the answers to those questions, and no one seems to want to find out . . . No one seems to want to find out.

Dr. Kelley and others stated that the police should have kept the investigation going, should not have stopped when they got this so-called confession. But they did stop. And that is the problem with a false confession. The investigation stops; all evidence to the contrary is ignored—just as all the evidence that pointed toward Wesley Peery was ignored . . .

Wesley Peery is a lifelong criminal in this community, and he was at the scene of the crime the day the murder of Nancy Parker took place. He was working for the park department just weeks before, and he worked on the crew that put up the security fence around the Parker home after the break-in on November 13. Why on earth hasn't he been requestioned about this crime? I'll tell you why, because Mr.

Reid got this coerced confession, this false confession, from Darrel Parker, and the police and Mr. Scheele believed it. They didn't want to follow where the real evidence led them. They didn't want to consider that perhaps they were wrong, didn't want to consider that perhaps they'd made a colossal and horrible mistake.

Remember, Dr. Douglas Kelley gave us the whys and wherefores of what went on in that little windowless room out there at highway patrol headquarters with John Reid. Remember Dr. Kelley's words, "Everybody can be broken, it's only a matter of time."

We need to understand that "everybody" includes you and me. At the start of the trial I remember saying to all of you, "If Darrel Parker was like you and me, he would've gotten right up and walked out of that room with John Reid." Well, I'm not so sure about that anymore. After what I heard Dr. Kelley and the other psychiatrists say, I'm not so sure at all! John Reid used his experience in such things, used his power, to hold sway over Darrel and manipulate him—and who knows what else—until he said what Reid wanted him to say.

Max looked grimly at the Parkers sitting behind the defense table. He turned and put his right hand on a corner of the defense table and looked squarely into the jury box.

"So, when you cast your vote, I want you to remember that under the same conditions Darrel Parker might have been you or me . . . or maybe your son. Can we honestly say whether we could have held up? And if you think you're strong willed, if you think you could have withstood such an interrogation, could you have done so if you'd been drugged?" Max stared at each juror and took his seat.

"There are four verdicts that can be found," Judge Polk mechanically instructed the jury. "Guilty of first-degree murder, guilty of second-degree murder, guilty of manslaughter, or innocent of all charges." He dismissed the two alternate jurors and instructed the rest of the jurors that in the event of a first-degree murder conviction that they would have to recommend the punishment, either death or life in prison. The penalty for second-degree murder was an automatic sentence of ten years to life. Manslaughter carried a penalty of one year to ten years. With that, Polk dismissed court and directed the bailiff to take the jurors to the jury room. It was 5:16 in the afternoon of May 1. May Day.

The jurors did little more than choose a foreman before they were taken on foot in a heavy mist to the Lincoln Hotel for supper. They were escorted en masse by Claude van Landingham and Fera Jenkins, the two bailiffs. After eating supper the jurors returned on foot to the courthouse and immediately asked for all of the exhibits. All ninety-eight exhibits were delivered to them, and they remained in deliberation until 10:40, when they retired for the evening without having arrived at a verdict.

In the morning *Star,* Virgil Falloon reported that the three weeks of testimony and argument had come down to two basic "show-down" questions for the jury: "Did Darrel Parker strangle his wife at their home last December as charged by the State and as Parker confessed a week later?; or, was it a 'false confession,' that had been browbeaten by the Chicago criminologist out of a bewildered, grief-stricken, and emotionally immature young man, as the defense contended?"

The *Evening Journal* quoted Scheele as saying in his closing remarks that

> Parker told Masters orally that he had tied Nancy's hands behind her back "so if any spark of life was left she could not struggle to get free."
>
> "There's the clincher if you need one," said Scheele.
>
> Scheele said the evidence clearly showed that Nancy had not been raped, and that there were no signs of a struggle anywhere in the house. "Keep your feet on the ground," Scheele told the jury. "Don't be stampeded by attempts to confuse you and get your attention away from the facts. Just because a man has gone to church and has a good reputation does not mean that kind of person under certain circumstances and stresses could not commit a crime like the slaying of Nancy Parker."

Wednesday morning the jurors resumed their discussion, and it was not long before the atmosphere became audibly heated. Virgil Falloon, one of the few newsmen who stayed in the courtroom the night before and who was present early Wednesday morning, met Claude van Landingham in the men's washroom.

"So, it's getting pretty hot in there, huh, Claude? . . . Can you tell who's leading it?"

"Now, Virg, you know I can't tell you that."

"Well, if they're arguing then it's not the sure thing some predicted."

"I can say that much. It's not a sure thing, no."

Back in the courtroom, Falloon sat with several other newsmen who had set up a vigil, waiting for the decision. By Wednesday evening the jury requested more detailed information of the various charges. Polk met with the attorneys before denying the request. At 10:00 P.M. the jury again retired for the evening. After their departure Kenneth Cook addressed the gathered newsmen: "The judge has denied any clarification of the definitions of first-degree murder, second-degree murder, or manslaughter. They must go forward with the information they learned during the trial."

It was also learned from Cook, reported Falloon, "that the jurors had asked for clarification of the terms: good character and good conduct." Parker had to be present for the court's consideration of those requests, and he was brought from the prison and appeared before the judge dressed in a drab gray flannel suit. He looked, according to Falloon, "haggard." Accompanying him were his father and Reverend Trucano. Trucano told reporters that he had a quiet "spiritual visit" with Darrel Tuesday night and Darrel had told him, "If there are a thousand witnesses against me, I will always know in my heart that I am innocent."

Reverend Trucano said that during their conversation he had found Darrel "anxious and low in spirits from the agony of waiting to hear his fate." However, he had been "greatly comforted by our presence and assurances."

Outside the courtroom, the hallway crowd had begun to slowly swell in numbers compared to the day before. It was apparent that the spectators sensed a verdict was near. At lunchtime several ladies in the courtroom brought out elaborately prepared meals, some even had corn on the cob. The reporters' ranks continued to grow as well, and some of them had formed an impromptu betting pool as to just when the verdict would be in. The jurors forged ahead with their only breaks, aside from meals, coming in the form of midmorning and midafternoon coffee. Their deliberations, as would be later reported by Falloon, had become even more heated and more vocal as the day wore on.

In the Thursday morning *Star* the Parker trial shared the headlines with the report of a tragic B-47 crash near the Lincoln Air Force Base. Four airmen had been killed in the second crash within a month. The two ill-fated bombers had become the latest casualties in a string of similar B-47 accidents across the country.

When van Landingham went to the jurors with their afternoon coffee, he overheard an argument in full swing before he opened the door. In spite of the noise he knocked and quickly opened the door. "No, we aren't going over the same goddamned—" yelled the jury foreman as van Landingham stuck his head in the door. Van Landingham immediately asked if they would need the hotel rooms another night. The foreman took the coffee from him and said brusquely, "No, we'll have a verdict by 5:00!" before kicking the door shut.

The jury announced their final verdict at 4:32 and signaled van Landingham that they were ready to return to the courtroom. At 5:10 Darrel was led back to the defense table and seated once again next to Kenneth Cook. Darrel crossed his hands nervously on the table, then just as quickly raised his hands to his chin. His fingers trembled, and the color had left his face. Kenneth Cook noticed and put his hand gently on Darrel's arm. "When the verdict's in, Darrel, I want you to know that it's going to be very hard to get it changed." Darrel nodded without looking at Cook. He interpreted that as Cook meaning it would be an acquittal. He was momentarily buoyed. Cook's intent could not have been more different.

"Have you reached your decision, Mr. Foreman?" asked Judge Polk.

George Walters stood up. The hardness in his face and the harshness in his voice left no doubt as to the verdict. "Yes, we have, Your Honor. We find the defendant guilty of second-degree murder."

Darrel slumped in his chair and sobbed uncontrollably.

"I don't understand," he cried. "How can I be found guilty of something I didn't do! How can I go to jail when someone is out there who did this! . . . I don't understand. I don't understand." He covered his face with his hands and continued to sob unmercifully. His mother and father moved to his side and wept openly with him. For Mrs. Parker it was the first breakdown of the trial, her only outburst of emotion.

On the other side of the room Scheele rose triumphantly from his chair and vigorously shook hands with Fahrnbruch, Chief Carroll, and Gene Masters. Towle eyed them bitterly as he loaded his briefcase. "I hope the sons-a-bitches are happy," said Towle to McManus. The courtroom cleared in minutes. The exodus was led by the newsmen rushing to see who would be first into the hallway and the awaiting phones and cameras.

Kenneth and Edgar Cook moved into the hallway, where reporters asked questions beneath blinding TV lights.

"We know Darrel is innocent," said Ken. "There is no doubt. The jury's verdict doesn't change that belief in the least. We will of course be filing an appeal immediately in order to get Darrel out of jail. And we know that somehow, some way, eventually the real killer will be found."

After Cook ended his comments, the reporters turned en masse toward Scheele. "I consider that it is a just and proper verdict. It has been a difficult case for the jurors because of the large amount of highly technical medical and scientific testimony. The results, however, confirm my deep faith in our jury system."

"We gave him a good defense, Tom," Towle said quietly, still at the defense table. "A hell of a defense. We won all the battles . . . all of them! It was that goddamned confession that did it. They had nothing else, nothing at all, except maybe Elmer's ability to continually obfuscate and drag out the testimony of the witnesses until the jurors' eyes fucking glazed over."

In the jury box, two women remained seated, wiping away tears. One of them was Mrs. Watson, the juror Towle and McManus had referred to and watched throughout the trial. She got up slowly, and after exiting the jury box, instead of leaving, hesitantly approached the defense table. She looked at the Parker family as they embraced and, finally, turned to Max Towle.

"I'm sorry, Mr. Towle . . . but they made me do it . . . They made me change my vote. There were three of us who believed he was innocent . . . who believed Dr. Kelley and the other two defense psychiatrists. But they wouldn't let up, and one by one the others changed their vote. I was the last. I tried to stand up to them . . . It was the foreman who led it. He yelled and screamed at me, swore and pounded the table and screamed some more. After it was over, after he got what he was after, he wanted everyone to sign a statement saying that we wouldn't reveal what had gone on during deliberations . . . I'm sorry . . . I know he's . . . I just couldn't stand up to them."

Towle and McManus stood in stunned silence. The woman took another look at the Parkers and fled in tears.

"And it only takes one, Tom," said Max, looking after her. He sat down heavily, dropped his muscular hands to his lap, and slowly shook his head. Except for Tom McManus and Max Towle, the courtroom was empty and, for the first time in more than three weeks, eerily silent.

At the back entrance to the courthouse, Sheriff Karnopp led Darrel through the cold mist to his waiting car for the short ride to the penitentiary. When Darrel walked beneath the overhanging limbs of an aging Chinese elm, a gust of wind whipped the limbs and great drops of water fell on his shoulders. He did not look up this time. There was nothing left in him. His foot caught a crack on the pavement and he stumbled forward, nearly falling. Karnopp reached out to steady him. In the car Darrel rested his head in his hand and tried vainly to stop weeping. Sheriff Karnopp tightened his lips and looked straight ahead, saying nothing. Slowly the car pulled out of the courthouse driveway. It entered the southbound rush hour traffic on Ninth Street and headed toward Darrel's home for the next thirteen years.

CHAPTER THIRTEEN

19615. A number. That's what Darrel Parker became. After Sheriff Karnopp delivered him to the prison, the first thing they gave him was the number. One he "must never forget," and one that he never would forget. After the number came the clothes, the uniform—white pants, white shirt, white socks, white underclothes. The only things they gave him that weren't white were his black belt and black shoes.

The first thing that hit him inside the walls other than the shadowy dimness was the overpowering smell. The clothes smelled. The hallways smelled. And the cells smelled. The pervasive odor seemed to come from a sickening combination of mildew, urine, pine disinfectant, and old paint. The only thing similar he'd experienced was the permeating smell of animal waste and cleansers inside the Lincoln Zoo, the building that sat behind the park department office in Antelope Park.

The first morning he was awakened at 6:00. When he got up Darrel groggily gazed out his cell window and found that it looked directly to the northeast, squarely at the stark red brick facade of highway patrol headquarters, the place where it had all begun. He could see Colonel Sand's office directly above the main entrance.

In the mess hall his cell mate, Fred Overton, led Darrel into line for his first breakfast. "Eat fast, Darrel, they only give us twenty minutes, and then it's nothing until lunchtime." He watched wide-eyed as a gray fried egg slid across his plate on a sheen of bacon grease.

If you wanted to eat, you didn't talk. Lines. Rows.

Doors—barred doors, metal doors, remotely operated doors. The clanging and banging of doors went on continuously.

He recognized the most difficult barrier he would have to conquer, and it wasn't the doors. The one that would confront him every day of every month of every year. Time. His time was already spent for him in the form of a sentence; yet the problem was how he could reclaim some of it, how he could fill it with something of meaning, however slight. His life from this day forward would be defined by a grotesque distortion of time.

MURDER HOME CLEARED; YULE WREATH REMAINS was the cryptic headline above a small article in the Monday, May 7 *Star*. Virgil Falloon wrote:

> The furniture and household goods belonging to Darrel and the late Nancy Parker were being moved Friday from the forester's home in Antelope Park. The items were being stored with a Lincoln mover until arrangements could be made by the two families for their disposal.
>
> The residence has remained under lock and key during the trial. Even the Yuletide wreath, a reminder that the tragic death occurred just eleven days before Christmas, was still on the door five months later. A pile of dried needles has collected on the threshold.
>
> Park Department Superintendent James Ager said the city-owned house "is being readied for future occupancy, but plans are not definite as yet."

In spite of what those plans may have been, no one would ever live in the tragedy-stricken house again.

By Saturday the "pact of silence" made by the jury, which Mrs. Watson had referred to, was broken. Virgil Falloon had found two jurors who were all too willing to talk, and they told him that the high point of disagreement came Thursday afternoon when two jurors, whom they would not name, steadfastly held out for acquittal on eleven consecutive ballots. This was in stark contrast to other jurors in the majority who would later say that there had been no disagreement about the verdict, only about the length of sentence.

The day after the trial Reverend Trucano wrote Detective Masters a scathing letter. Trucano, a Mason, had noticed during the trial that Masters wore a Masonic ring. In the letter Trucano shamed Masters, saying that he could not believe a man who was a Mason could get on the witness stand, swear on the Bible to tell the truth, and then lie as Masters had done—Masters' statement that Darrel had "gone to the kitchen and gotten a paring knife that he used to cut Nancy's sweatshirt" was not mentioned anywhere in the confession and was deemed by Cook and Towle to have been a fabrication by Masters to fill one of the many voids in the confession that were discovered after the authorities had gotten the lab report from the FBI. Trucano told Falloon that he knew nothing would happen as a result of the letter but said he felt considerably better having written it.

In Monday's "The People Speak" column of the *Star*, Mrs. W. A. Johnson wrote under the assigned title THE PARKER JURY. Her brief comments recognized the verdict as just and reasoned. In her opinion it was "the logical conclusion" to the events of the last three weeks—"I would like to shake the hands of the jurors of the Parker murder case for their clear-headed decision in the trial."

The next day a small column appeared at the bottom of the front page of the *Evening Journal*—PEERY FILES APPEAL IN RAPE SENTENCE. Within weeks Peery would win that appeal. The rape charge would be thrown out, and he would end up serving time only for the theft of Masters' gun. In less than one year he would be released, slipping through the system yet again, but until then he would be in the same penitentiary as Darrel Parker.

On Friday, May 11, the Parker attorneys filed a motion for a new trial. In the motion, forty-two irregularities were cited by the defense as having prevented a fair and impartial verdict. In the first affidavit Towle stated that Elmer Scheele was guilty of gross misconduct when he referred to the undisclosed opinions of the Morrisons. The appeal argued that Scheele's statements left the clear impression with the jurors that the Morrisons felt Darrel Parker was guilty.

In support of another affidavit Towle noted that Scheele told the jury in his final arguments that "even though you may not want to believe these police officers, you have to believe Audrey Wheeler, the official court reporter of Judge Polk." Wheeler had been "a very important witness for the State by testifying about the taking of the 'confession' and the circumstances surrounding it. Her testimony supported the State's position," said Towle, and created "a halo about her head, which undoubtedly prejudiced this jury."

Chief among the complaints cited by Towle was the error by the court in not ruling that the confession was taken involuntarily after the defense had shown that Parker's mental capacity had been diminished and the statement made under duress. Finally, Towle said an error was made in failing to exclude the testimony of Carroll and Masters concerning their oral discussions with Parker after Reid's confession had been taken, which violated the best evidence rule.

On Monday morning, May 14, Virgil Falloon was having his morning coffee while reading the *Star* in the city room. He glanced over the editorial page—which also carried the paper's "The People Speak" column—and noticed the title OUR JURY SYSTEM. He quickly scanned the letter:

> To the editor of the *Lincoln Star:* Is our present jury system fair? Shouldn't there be some mental yardstick whereby the qualifications and IQ of potential jurors could be measured? I refer in particular to the Parker murder trial in which so much scientific and medical testimony was given. It seems appalling that many people hold the idea that psychiatrists are not to be taken seriously and that their testimony and observations should be disregarded.
>
> READER

Falloon immediately went to the editor of the column and asked if he could see the entire letter. The letter was much longer—two pages—than what had been printed. When he read the name of the person who'd sent the letter, it looked familiar. When he checked it against the list of jurors in the Parker trial, he found that it was the same juror, Mrs. Watson, who had approached Tom McManus and Max Towle after the trial.

Falloon telephoned Mrs. Watson at work and asked if he might talk with her—off the record if she preferred. She agreed. When they met, she told Falloon that she had been quite upset with the *Star* for running only part of her letter. Falloon explained that he had no control over such decisions, that that was not his department. He asked for her reaction to the verdict.

She told Falloon that according to the testimony she believed Parker had been intimidated, coerced, and frightened by John Reid, and that those tactics are what led to the "confession" if, in fact, he had not been drugged. The testimony, as she heard it, indicated that Reid was the one lying about the interrogation, not Darrel Parker. The psychiatrists for the defense had much more impressive credentials than those who testified for the State, and the fact that they had all arrived at the same conclusions about Parker independently was what convinced her of their arguments. She did not feel it was proper for the State's psychiatric witnesses to meet together before testifying so that their stories would all be the same. She again expressed deep regret at having caved in to the "tyrants" on the jury, particularly the foreman. She hadn't been able to sleep through the night since the trial and intimated that it was something that would forever haunt her if Mr. Parker remained in prison. Although others on the jury had belittled the testimony of the defense psychiatrists and gave it little or no weight in their deliberations, in her mind the psychiatric testimony was the most important, it was what the trial hinged on.

On Saturday, June 2, it was announced that Judge Polk had overruled the defense motion for a new trial. He sentenced Darrel Parker to life imprisonment, as the jury had recommended.

Tom McManus began writing the appeal to the state supreme court the following week. The appeal, which would be ninety-three pages long, contained ten propositions of law. The most important, as would be shown in the coming years, was the following, as spelled out in Proposition 1 of the appeal:

> Before a confession may be received in evidence, it must be shown that it was freely, voluntarily, and intelligently made; the admission of confessions obtained from an accused who is inexperienced and immature and while illegally held without benefit of counsel or friends, without being advised of his constitutional rights, while mentally incompetent or confused, and after intense questioning with a lie detector, and when such questioning employed psychological

techniques calculated to insidiously break down his powers of resistance and perception, and while in a state of shock and without food for many hours, violated due process of law as required by the Fourteenth Amendment of the Constitution of the United States and the due process and self-incriminatory clauses of the Constitution of the State of Nebraska.

The appeal was turned down.

The supper bell rang. Into the noisy din of the mess hall with twenty minutes to eat what Overton called "shit on a shingle." No more meals in the room. The second bell. Out—"In line!"

When his head hit the pillow those first nights, Darrel was light-headed, a feeling that came in part because so much had been shorn away. For entire days it felt to him as though he had been swimming in molasses, moving in slow motion.

His thoughts ran away from him—*Whatever I was, whatever I might have been, I will never be again. I am not of this place. I am not one of them. Yet I am here, and I am one of them.*

An aging trusty told him late in the afternoon of his first day: "Parker, you'll never make it in here unless you can learn to take it one day at a time." The old man had held his index finger up for emphasis and repeated the line, "One day at a time."

From then on he would consider nothing else, Darrel told himself that night. Not tomorrow. Nor next week, nor next month, nor next year. Today. Only today. He rolled onto his side and closed his eyes tightly. As he would do on countless nights at the end of countless days, he cried. Until he was asleep.

Darrel's first assigned job was as clerk for Chaplain Richard Canfield. They soon developed a strong bond, and it didn't take long for Canfield to become a believer in Darrel and a champion of the cause to prove his innocence.

In the spring of 1957, when Canfield learned that Peery would soon be released, he masterminded a scheme to set up a meeting between Peery and Parker with the idea that Peery could somehow be made to implicate himself, either intentionally or inadvertently, in the death of Nancy. The plan was to maneuver Peery into a position where such an admission could be recorded. Canfield's main hope was that Peery's ego would lead him to brag about his deed to Darrel.

Canfield knew the sound engineer at the *Back to the Bible* broadcast, which was headquartered in Lincoln at the old *Lincoln Star* building. He was confident that a concealed recording device could be fabricated and then placed on Darrel to record the conversation with Peery.

When Max Towle received a call from Canfield explaining the plan to induce Peery to say something incriminating, Towle quickly demurred. Canfield told Max that the meeting would be held without the knowledge of the warden. Upon hearing that, Max informed Canfield that Darrel's attorneys couldn't be part of such a plan. However, if any information was uncovered that could be independently verified and could free Darrel, it might be worth trying. He left it open for Canfield to proceed on his own. The meeting was set up, and Darrel was fitted with a primitive hidden microphone by the sound engineer.

According to Virgil Falloon, who later heard the tape made of the meeting, "You could only catch a word here or there between the prison doors banging open and shut every few seconds. Canfield had the sound engineer try to filter out the clanging doors, but he was unsuccessful. Peery wouldn't incriminate himself, and I think the tape proved worthless because Canfield never mentioned it again."

Towle did, however, make a trip to the penitentiary to meet with Peery before his release. Peery had high hopes of making an appeal bond and had asked to meet with Towle. When they met, Peery tried to bait Max with the fact that he had information on the Parker murder that he would reveal if Towle could help him get the bond. When Max refused, Peery baited him by instructing him to ask Darrel if there was something missing from the house that had originally gone unnoticed.

That set off a round of frenzied activity by Towle and McManus. McManus went to the courthouse and itemized everything in Nancy's purse. He took the inventory to Darrel along with a list of all the other items in evidence. Darrel couldn't remember anything that was not already on the list and could not remember anything else in the house that might have been missing. But then something that had been missing could hardly have been on the list of items in evidence. Peery didn't get the bond and gave Towle no more information.

Peery was released from the penitentiary on April 23, 1957, having served less than one year in prison for the burglary—both the holdup and rape charges had been dropped. He quickly made his way east, staying with a sister and her husband in Columbus, Ohio. As usual, it didn't take him long to fall back into the "life." On September 27 he was arrested in Columbus for armed robbery and the rape of a young woman who was eight and a half months pregnant.

Peery had staked out the woman's home in exactly the same manner as he had the Parker home. After the husband left for work on the morning of the crime, Peery drove up the long driveway that led to the isolated house. Having seen the woman before, Peery had to know she was pregnant. Evidently that was no deterrent. When the woman answered the door, Peery said he had a package to deliver. He held up a cardboard box, and when she unlocked the door he removed a sawed-off shotgun from the box and forced his way in, just as he had done with Nancy Parker.

The young woman called her two young children and pleaded with Peery that they not be harmed. He told her to get rid of them or he would. She placed them in the bathroom. Peery then ordered the woman into the bedroom. When she hesitated, he struck her in the face and forced her onto the bed, where he bound her hands behind her back and raped her.

While Peery searched the house for valuables, the young woman made her way into the bathroom and locked herself and the children inside. Peery took a few dollars from her rifled purse and left.

In court the woman testified that Peery had worn white gloves but took them off during the rape. After the assault, she said he carefully wiped everything off that he had touched with his bare hands. He had evidently learned by now about the incriminating nature of fingerprints and how they could be used as evidence.

Within a few days of his arrest Peery was clamoring to be returned to Nebraska and said that he had information concerning a murder in Lincoln. The reason for his sudden willingness to release information on the Parker murder was that he desperately wanted out of Ohio. Tom McManus later found out that the Columbus police, angered at the brutality and the sickening nature of Peery's rape, had given Peery quite a "working over."

When Max Towle learned of Peery's arrest he alerted the Cooks. As a result, Edgar Cook placed a call to the detective in Ohio who was in charge of Peery's case. After hearing the multitude of similarities between the Parker murder and their case, the Columbus detectives said they would share any information they gained with Cook. Peery did not confess, they said, but he told the detectives he had knowledge about the Parker murder and told them to "ask the authorities in Lincoln if there was a missing suitcase from the Parker house."

During Peery's subsequent trial on the rape charge, a psychiatrist testified who had interviewed him for the State of Ohio. Peery, he concluded, was "entirely antisocial and should never be turned loose on society again." He was convicted and sent to the Ohio State Penitentiary, the same facility where Dr. Sam Sheppard had been incarcerated. Peery's sentence was three twenty-five-year terms to be served consecutively. Theoretically, he should have spent the rest of his life in prison.

With information given him by Towle, Virgil Falloon contacted the Morrisons concerning the suitcase and was told that they had given Nancy a three-piece luggage set for her college graduation present, and "Yes, the middle-size suitcase was missing when we moved Nancy's personal items out of the house." Each bag, Falloon was told, was initialed NEM. Mrs. Morrison stated that when she and her husband visited Nancy and Darrel for Thanksgiving that Nancy had shown her father two pillows she'd bought as a Christmas present for her mother. She'd put them in the medium-sized suitcase for storage. The pillows were never found.

One of Peery's girlfriends, the same one McManus said had gotten rid of the watch before the trial, claimed that she remembered seeing a suitcase in Peery's possession immediately after the murder and it had three metal initials on it. She said she couldn't remember the exact sequence of letters, but the three letters would spell *men*. This same woman, who had been intimate with Peery on numerous occasions, said that Peery had a peculiar habit when they engaged in sex. She said Peery would never ejaculate his semen inside her. He would always remove his penis just before an orgasm and ejaculate his semen outside her body.

On January 2, 1958, on the front page of the *Lincoln Journal* was a three-column story describing the suicide of Dr. Douglas Kelley in Berkeley, California. The Berkeley Police Department reported that Dr. Kelley had committed suicide by swallowing sodium cyanide—just as Hermann Goering had done. Dr. Kelley, said the article, "insisted the young husband, Darrel Parker, was innocent of the strangulation slaying of his wife." The slaying, said Kelley, was "sexually motivated and a horrible example of vicious, sadistic assault." The same words used by the Columbus, Ohio, police to describe Peery's rape of the young pregnant woman.

That spring Max Towle received disturbing news concerning the Parker jury. Late one afternoon Towle went into Tom McManus's office and placed before McManus a note he'd just taken over the telephone from an old friend. The man told him of an acquaintance who had known the jury foreman from the Parker trial for several years. He had learned something he thought Max should know. In a conversation, the Parker trial had come up, and the friend had expressed dismay that someone with the foreman's background had been selected to sit on the jury. The foreman, he said, had a sister who had been killed by her husband years before. It didn't seem right, the source said, that someone whose sister had been killed by her husband should sit in judgment of a man being tried for the same offense.

In his first meeting with John Greenholtz, the deputy warden, Darrel was told that if he were to "act like a man while in prison, he would be treated like a man." Dubbed "Big John," Greenholtz was respected by most of the inmates, and those who didn't respect him feared him.

Greenholtz had talked with Canfield about Parker several times with Canfield expressing his high opinion of Darrel. After seeing how diligently Parker went about his work, Greenholtz eventually put Darrel in charge of maintaining the prison grounds and operating the greenhouse. When Darrel first visited the greenhouse he found it in a state of neglect and disrepair. Finding the greenhouse smelling of dead flowers and dry soil and littered with broken pots and rotten stands, Darrel went to work and methodically transformed it back into a place of new growth and moist fertile soil that once again produced rich sweet fragrances from the multicolored bedding plants he grew for the prison grounds.

"It took me three or four years to mentally heal from what I had been through, and I never would have been able to recover had it not been for my job. I will always be indebted to John for giving me that opportunity. He never said so in so many words, but I think deep down he believed in my innocence. He treated me like a favored employee, not a prisoner."

Returning to physical work strained his muscles, made them taut, and allowed him in time to begin sleeping through the night. Able to work outside, he eventually managed to lose all the weight he'd gained during the trial. The color returned to his face, and the black circles disappeared from his eyes.

As the scope of his work grew, so did Darrel's respect and trustworthiness in the eyes of Greenholtz and the other prison administrators. Greenholtz eventually gave Darrel a room in the greenhouse as his cell. There were no bars, no guards, and no clanking doors. No one else in the prison shared such a privilege.

"The only thing bad about my job was that occasionally, while working on the grounds, I would see Elmer Scheele walking up the sidewalk to the prison entrance. He must have been there working on cases—prosecuting someone else. He never recognized me, never looked at any of us. Likewise, Chief Carroll would appear from time to time accompanied by Masters. It was tough to take."

A small cocker spaniel, Penny, a gift from Greenholtz, became Darrel's constant companion. He would leave a small pail in the prison kitchen to be filled by the cooks with steak bones for the dog. At night when the guards made their rounds, they often found that Penny had climbed onto Darrel's bed and was asleep next to her master, her head resting on his pillow.

Virtually everyone he came in contact with in the prison eventually came to feel that Darrel was not guilty of the crime he'd been convicted of. As a further example of that trust, Greenholtz often allowed Darrel to go back and forth between the prison and the prison farm, which was located south of the penitentiary. He drove the tractor used for grounds maintenance and would go right down Highway 2 alone and unguarded. That practice eventually had to be abandoned, however, when someone on the outside learned "that a murderer was being allowed outside the prison unsupervised."

When Darrel was notified by the court that the furniture had been removed from his house and was going to be auctioned off, he wrote Tom McManus and listed the items he would like to have bought back—the bookshelves he'd made, Nancy's Alpha Gamma Delta pledge paddle, and two glass mugs from their fraternity and sorority houses. At the end of the letter he said, "Tom, I trust everything else is moving along as satisfactorily as possible. My life rests with you and Max."

A few weeks later McManus visited Darrel, not to report on the furniture sale, or the appeals, but just to talk. At first they groped between awkward pauses for something to say.

"It stinks in here, Tom, but my work saves me. If I didn't have that my routines wouldn't help."

"Routines?" asked McManus.

"Like how I eat. When I eat. How I place my silverware. When I go to the bathroom—at a certain time, a certain can. Anything that'll make you think about what you're doing at the moment, make you forget the rest—how much time is left ahead of you. On Sunday when there's no work, you slow down. You take your time at everything you do. If you need a drink, you take a long drink. If you have to walk somewhere, you take the long way, not the short way. I ask for overtime, as much as I can get—in the greenhouse, outside—it doesn't make any difference where, as long as I'm busy."

After several more fits and starts, the conversation ended. The two would communicate several more times by mail, but they would never meet again face to face. In 1959, after McManus notified Darrel of Kenneth Cook's death, Darrel wrote him back. At the end of the two-page letter—the maximum allowed prisoners—he said, "It would be good to see you again, Tom. Sometimes I wonder where it will all end. After a while a person feels numb to what goes on in here, but I guess we have to continue to hope."

In 1966 the United States Supreme Court announced its landmark ruling on a series of four related cases. Ernesto A. Miranda, the first petitioner, was the man whose name would be forever linked with the sixty-four-page decision.

"The constitutional issue we decide today," said the Court, "is the admissibility of statements obtained from a defendant questioned while in custody or otherwise deprived of his freedom of action in any significant way . . . They share salient features—incommunicado interrogation of individuals in a police-dominated atmosphere, resulting in self-incriminating statements without full warnings of constitutional rights."

The Court cited the Wickersham Report made to Congress in the 1930s: "Not only does the use of the third degree involve a flagrant violation of law by the officers of the law, but it involves also the dangers of false confession, and it tends to make police and prosecutors less zealous in the search for objective evidence.

"A valuable source of information about present police practices may be found in various police manuals and texts which document procedures employed with success in the past, and which recommend various other effective tactics. These texts are used by law enforcement agencies themselves as guides."

A footnote for that quote reads: "The methods described in Inbau & Reid's *Criminal Interrogation and Confessions* are a revision and enlargement of material presented in three prior editions of a predecessor text, *Lie Detection and Criminal Interrogation* (third edition, 1953). The authors and their associates are officers of the Chicago Police Scientific Crime Detection Laboratory and have had extensive experience in writing, lecturing and speaking to law enforcement authorities over a twenty-year period. They say the techniques portrayed in their manuals reflect their experiences and are the most effective psychological stratagems to employ during interrogations."

"The officers," the Court continued, quoting Reid and Inbau, "are told by the manuals that the 'principal psychological factor contributing to a successful interrogation is privacy—being alone with the person under interrogation' . . . The officers are instructed to minimize the moral seriousness of the offense, to cast blame on the victim or on society. These tactics are designed to put the subject in a psychological state where his story is but an elaboration of what the police purport to know already—that he is guilty."

Reid and Inbau's book is referred to seven more times in the ruling, including the quote that Towle used during the Parker trial— "To obtain a confession the interrogator must patiently maneuver himself or his quarry into a position from which the desired objective may be attained."

"The constitutional issue we decide in each of these cases," concluded the Court, "is the admissibility of statements obtained from a defendant questioned while in custody or otherwise deprived of his freedom of action in any significant way. In each case, the defendant was questioned by police officers, detectives, or others in a room in which he was cut off from the outside world."

Another interrogator's methods were cited, yet they sound as if they could just as easily have come from John Reid: "Where emotional appeals and tricks are employed to no avail, he [the interrogator] must rely on an oppressive atmosphere of dogged persistence. He must interrogate steadily and without relent, leaving the subject no prospect of surcease. He must dominate his subject and overwhelm him with his inexorable will to obtain the truth . . . In a serious case, the interrogation may continue for days, with the required intervals for food and sleep, but with no respite from the atmosphere of domination."

"In the cases before us today," the Court proclaimed, "we concern ourselves primarily with this interrogation atmosphere and the evils it can bring . . . It is obvious that such an interrogation environment is created for no purpose other than to subjugate the individual to the will of his examiner."

Summarizing the majority opinion the Court said:

> . . . when an individual is taken into custody or otherwise deprived of his freedom by the authorities in any significant way and is subjected to questioning, the privilege against self-incrimination is jeopardized.

Procedural safeguards must be employed to protect the privilege and unless other fully effective means are adopted to notify the person of his right of silence and to assure that the exercise of the right will be scrupulously honored, the following measures are required:

He must be warned prior to any questioning that he has the right to remain silent, that anything he says can be used against him in a court of law, that he has the right to the presence of an attorney, and that if he cannot afford an attorney, one will be appointed for him prior to any questioning if he so desires . . . But unless and until such warnings and waivers are demonstrated by the prosecution at trial, no evidence obtained as a result of interrogation can be used against him.

This decision, in effect, negated the entire Parker trial, since the only evidence against Darrel Parker was in the form of the illegally obtained confession, as defined by the Miranda ruling. Even though Masters had stated that Darrel Parker had not been asked if he wanted an attorney, had not been asked if he wanted to call his family, and had not been told that what he might say could be used against him, an appeal would not be easy.

The Court concluded its ruling by quoting Justice Brandeis:

Decency, security, and liberty alike demand that government officials shall be subjected to the same rules of conduct that are commands to the citizen. In a government of laws, existence will be imperiled if it fails to observe the law scrupulously. Our government is the potent, the omnipresent teacher. For good or for ill, it teaches the whole people by its example. Crime is contagious. If the government becomes a lawbreaker, it breeds contempt for law, it invites every man to become a law unto himself; it invites anarchy. To declare that in the administration of the criminal law the end justifies the means would bring terrible retribution.

Justices Harlan, Stewart, and White dissented. Harlan, writing for the minority, said, "I believe the decision of the Court represents poor constitutional law and entails harmful consequences for the country at large." He continued with a unique rationale for his opposition, which might just as readily have been a description of

John Reid: "Those who use third-degree tactics and deny them in court are equally able and destined to lie as skillfully about warnings and waivers."

After the Miranda decision, there was no one left from the original defense team to carry on a new appeal for Darrel Parker. Kenneth Cook had died, Max Towle was in ill health, and Tom McManus had become a municipal court judge in Lincoln, renowned nationally for his pioneering work in the reform of drunk-driving laws.

Since the court record had been established, all that awaited was for someone to connect it with Miranda. Over the next three years an Omaha attorney, Richard Bruckner, took Darrel Parker's appeal step by step through the court system. The state supreme court upheld the original conviction.

"I always knew that if I was going to get out it would be outside of Nebraska through the federal courts," Darrel said. "When Dick told me about the Miranda ruling I'd like to say I was excited, but I wasn't. After what I had been through it was hard to believe I could ever get a reversal of my conviction through the legal system. I was resigned to my fate. I had given up hope." A case was put together that centered on the U.S. Supreme Court's Miranda decision. Rejected by the Nebraska Supreme Court, Darrel appealed to the Eighth Circuit Court of Appeals.

The Eighth Circuit Court strongly ruled in Parker's favor and listed the reasons for holding the confession involuntary:

> . . . the fact that Parker had not received any warning with regard to his constitutional rights; that he was summoned to Highway Patrol Headquarters without indicating he was a suspect so as to put the defendant off guard and minimize the possibility that he would consult with an attorney; that Mr. Reid, who conducted the interrogation, is an experienced criminal investigator obtained from Chicago and is coauthor of works on criminal interrogation and confessions. His publications and tactics are discussed in considerable detail by Chief Justice Warren in Miranda. The use of some of the tactics advocated in the book are admitted by Reid. The interrogation took place in a small room without windows with only Reid and the defendant

present. Reid had defendant sit at a table facing him with their knees touching each other. Reid admitted patting the defendant on the shoulder and stroking defendant's hair a number of times. He insisted defendant constantly look him in the eye and lifted up the defendant's chin to accomplish this objective. Defendant was subjected to a lie detector test and was told that the machine revealed he was lying. Defendant was accused a number of times of murdering his wife. Such activity clearly goes beyond approved standards.

The court went on to note that Darrel had been under great strain when he drove from Des Moines to Lincoln "by reason of the death of his wife" and had not been fed all day. They also pointed out that the confession contained "statements known by Parker to be wrong."

Finally, and most importantly, the court noted: "The prosecution conceded in oral argument and we concur in such view that the record, absent the confession, would not support the conviction . . . We hold as a matter of law that when the totality of the circumstances are considered . . . a determination is required that the confessions received in evidence were coerced and involuntary, and that the defendant's constitutional rights were violated by the reception of the confessions in evidence and the submission thereof to the jury. The judgment appealed from is reversed."

The court stated that since there was no evidence other than the confession, Parker should be retried or released within ninety days. It all seemed so simple. Too simple.

The State appealed to the U.S. Supreme Court. The Court, in spite of Miranda, ruled that there should be another hearing to decide whether or not the confession had been voluntary—even though the Eighth Circuit had already ruled otherwise.

Darrel Parker, aware of the outcome of the original hearing on the voluntariness of the confession—the "trial within a trial"—had to decide whether to go through with the hearing and fight for a new trial or to accept a negotiated release that had suddenly been offered by the State of Nebraska. "My God, we already had one hearing during the trial on the voluntariness of the 'confession,' and we knew the results of that. I felt certain I'd remain in prison. When you approach forty, when you've wrongfully spent nearly half your life in prison, you begin to see things a little differently."

The State had again made his legal position uncertain. They told his attorney that if the case was tried again it could take as long as two years, and during that time Darrel would have to remain in prison. If anything, his previous experiences had proven to him that, regardless of the Eighth Circuit's opinion, he would suffer at the hands of the justice system if he returned to court. His decision, which seemed to him the right one at the time, would once again alter all that followed.

In his mind, the choice between remaining in prison and being released under terms of a parole was a simple one. He wanted out. Those who believed him guilty in the past would continue to do so he felt, regardless of the outcome of a new trial, and those few who believed he was innocent would not change their opinions either. His release was negotiated. His parole was granted by the pardon board, whose chairman at the time was John Greenholtz.

In the fall of 1970, after more than thirteen years in prison, Darrel Parker was released by the State, on the condition that he would not pursue further litigation. He was free, but he was not exonerated. His release would go down in the records as a parole. At the time he was not concerned about whether he had been exonerated, paroled, or anything else. All he cared about was getting out. All he cared about was returning to life.

CHAPTER FOURTEEN

Numb. Detached. Alone. Darrel walked out of the penitentiary just as he had entered. The windows on either side of the prison entrance foyer gave the slanting rays of the midmorning fall sun a misty religious quality. Darrel made the solitary walk from the checkout room to the front door with Penny at his side. Richard Bruckner waited alone for Darrel outside the entrance. Also waiting was Virgil Falloon.

When he stepped out of the front doors onto the landing and looked across the road at highway patrol headquarters, he did not look anything like the young man who had entered. His face was gaunt, his hair was receding and thinning, and the youthful sparkle had left his eyes. He moved slowly down the steps—the acquired reaction to the pace on the inside remained with him. He stopped beside Falloon and calmly and quietly answered his questions. No, he wouldn't be staying in Lincoln; no, he had no immediate plans; no, he had no idea what he would do once he returned to Iowa. On the inside he had thought about being released only in reference to when. He had given little thought as to what he would do if he was in fact released. One day at a time . . .

None of Darrel's family was present. His mother was bedridden, and his father had remained home to care for her. When it was finally time to leave, Darrel told Falloon good-bye and got in his attorney's car. Bruckner pulled slowly out of the prison parking lot as Darrel took one last look at the dreary institution through the car's rear window. He had brought color to the prison's grim facade, but he had never convinced them to plant more trees. It looked the same as it had in 1955. Dull, grimy, and forbidding. Like a prison. *Parker,* he told himself, *say good-bye to hell.*

Darrel turned and looked straight ahead. He did not lean back against the seat but perched like a stiff bird on the seat edge, his left hand resting on his knee and his right forearm on the armrest. Penny lay at his feet.

The city had changed. The city park and recreation departments were now combined, and the new head of the Department of Parks and Recreation was James Ager. A new young graduate had been hired as the city forester—"there is never a dull moment on this job." His assistant was Warren Andrews. The old county court-house had been torn down, and a new block-long white granite city-county building, referred to locally as the "wedding cake," had taken its place. The deadly B-47s had been decommissioned and the Lincoln Air Force Base closed.

But Darrel didn't want to go through Lincoln, didn't want to see the capitol building, didn't want to see any of it. He said the only thing he wanted to see was the Iowa border. The entire state of Nebraska had become, in his eyes, the repository of all his ill feelings toward John Reid, Joe Carroll, Gene Masters, and Elmer Scheele. The trial, after all, had been the "State of Nebraska versus Darrel F. Parker."

When he got home there was no celebration. No one was waiting at the door. The house was silent and dark. The shades were drawn. The only light on was in the living room, where his father sat quietly reading the newspaper next to a dim table lamp. When he saw his mother, asleep in her bed, it was a shock that momentarily took Darrel outside of himself. At the time he'd left, she ran the house in the same way his father ran the farm. She was ordered and method-ical. Everything was spartan. Everything had its place. No more. His father seemed war weary as well. He'd had to sell one of his farms in order to pay off Darrel's legal fees, and he was no longer physi-cally able to farm himself, so he rented out his remaining acreage. Darrel sadly recognized that he wasn't the only one who had been beaten down by it all.

Later that evening Darrel and his father quietly prepared supper. Mrs. Robbins had stopped by earlier in the day and put on a pot roast for them. To Darrel even the food had the smell of freedom about it. His father carved the roast and mashed the potatoes while Darrel set the table—aligning the handles of the silverware along the end of the napkins, the glasses directly in line with the knives, the rim of the plates straight with the ends of the napkins. Routine was hard to break.

During the meal Darrel and his father spoke little. They talked about the farm, about his mother, and about what Darrel might do for a job.

After supper, after washing the dishes, Darrel stepped outside on the back porch and deeply inhaled the crisp October air. He walked cautiously through the yard and approached the garage, dimly lit by a lone night-light. Hanging at an angle beneath the gable was his old basketball hoop. He studied it. The birds had picked the netting clean for nest material, and the rim was brown with rust. He turned back toward the house, and then suddenly he moved, quicker than he had for a long time, to his left while at the same time bringing his right arm up over his shoulder in a long slow arc. *"Parker shoots a hook shot at the buzzer. It's . . . good!"*

Inside, in his old room that overlooked the front yard, he found his bed turned down. He hung his shirt on the chair beside his bed, just as he had done in prison, making sure that it was centered on the chairback with both sleeves hanging at the same angle. He started to fold his pants along the creases as he looked around the room at his old trophies, his graduation picture, and a small picture of his first girlfriend from high school. A serene look came over his face, and he let the pants drop loosely in a pile on the floor. He was about to lie down when he looked at the window. He got up and opened it. The breeze lightly moved the drapes.

His head, still spinning from the day's events, did not rest on his pillow that night so much as it seemed to float down upon it. His eyes closed, and he slowly inhaled the cool, fresh, and free air of the country. He slept well that night.

Darrel wasted no time after his release. Within a week of arriving home he had gotten a job helping an old family friend who was a house painter. The newfound routine was a godsend because, just like life on the inside, work left him with much less spare time to deal with, much less time to think about how much of his life had passed him by.

The evening after he received his first paycheck, he went to a movie in Red Oak. He arrived early and bought popcorn, Jujyfruits, a Snickers bar, and a Nehi grape soda. He took a seat near the back where he could watch all the people—a sight which he thought alone was worth the price of admission. Before the lights went down he marveled at the current fashions, the women's hairstyles, and the sweet smells of perfume and cologne that lingered in the air after couples passed on their way down the aisle. He wondered if anyone in the theater really appreciated what it was like to breathe such fresh and sweetly scented air.

When the movie started, the high school kids who sat in front of him laughed at a joke among themselves. Darrel caught himself laughing along with them. It was his first belly laugh in over thirteen years, and after the kids quit laughing, Darrel kept on. From that evening forward he knew that he would make it, knew that even though it would always be there, he wouldn't be held captive by the past.

The following spring Darrel's old university professor Harold McNabb offered him a job assisting with a Dutch elm disease project at Iowa State. McNabb still harbored guilt feelings about having steered one of his top students into a job that, in effect, had ruined his life. He felt a special obligation to help Darrel in any way he could and had made it a point to include him in the research.

Darrel moved to Ames and began his new job. Through a local minister who knew Reverend Canfield, Darrel was introduced to a woman visiting in Ames, Eleanore Jeanne Vandling of Wilkes-Barre, Pennsylvania. A former art student at the Pratt Institute in New York City, Ele was outgoing and immediately attracted to Darrel because of his "kindness, gentleness, and stable personality." After returning to Wilkes-Barre, Ele became pen pals with Darrel. By the end of summer Eleanore returned to Ames, where she became an overnight sensation by preparing a gourmet four-course meal for Darrel, Professor McNabb, and several other professors from Darrel's undergraduate days. The meal served as a send-off for Darrel. McNabb had recommended him for a job with a tree company in Bettendorf, one of the Quad Cities on the Mississippi River between Iowa and Illinois, and Darrel had been accepted. Maybe this time it would go right. The next week Darrel was to depart Ames for Bettendorf and start his new job in an area that would be his home for the next forty years.

From the first night he arrived in Bettendorf, Darrel maintained his correspondence with Eleanore in Pennsylvania. He wrote her several times a week and anxiously looked forward to her replies. A pretense he often used as an excuse to call was to get one of her recipes. Several more visits cemented the bond between them, and by the early spring of 1971 Darrel proposed.

"I had never experienced the true friendship of a man until Darrel came along and gave me the kind of emotional stability that had never existed for me before." On May Day of 1971 they were wed.

During the trial and in its aftermath, Darrel's cause had been championed in Iowa by a United Press International reporter in Des Moines—John McCormick. McCormick's sympathetic coverage of the Parker case in turn influenced the *Des Moines Register*'s supportive editorial reporting. By the time Darrel and Ele moved to Bettendorf, McCormick had become an editorial writer for the *Quad-City Times*. He also happened to be chairman of the Scott County Conservation Board, and with his assistance Darrel made a gradual transition back into a management position in forestry. After working as the first forester for Scott County, Darrel applied for the position of supervisor of parks in Moline, Illinois—one of the Quad Cities that sits on the Illinois side of the Mississippi—and was accepted. A strange irony associated with the job, which didn't seem to bother Darrel or his new wife, was that the city of Moline provided them with a subsidized home, similar to the house on Sumner in Antelope Park. They lived in the home for five and a half years and, according to Ele, enjoyed some of their happiest times together there.

"I felt fulfilled in my work. Proud of my advancements and achievements. It felt like I had earned something back."

In 1970 Wesley Peery was transferred from the Ohio State Penitentiary to the Chillicothe Correctional Institution. Five years later, the man "who should never be released in society again" was set free. Like a runaway dog he returned once again to Lincoln in the spring of 1975.

Put on a supervised work release program, Peery got a job at one of Lincoln's largest motels doing maintenance work. Continually tardy and absent, he was released after ninety days. He was hired next at Nebraska Wesleyan, a small Methodist university on the northeast side of Lincoln. As with his job at the park department in 1955, he'd gotten the position after being recommended by a friend who already worked at Wesleyan. Shortly after he'd begun work, Peery began planning a robbery along with the man who recommended him for the job.

The object of the robbery was a coin shop in Havelock, a small town that had been absorbed by Lincoln, a little more than a mile northeast of the Wesleyan campus. The two men, accompanied by Peery's girlfriend, snuck off the job early one morning and drove to the Mitzner Coin Shop. Next to the Joyo Theater on Havelock Avenue, the shop was very small—no more than ten feet wide. Mrs. Mitzner, who was tending the shop for her husband, was taken by Peery to a bathroom in the back while his cohorts hurriedly began ransacking the store.

Peery bound Mrs. Mitzner on the toilet, in what was by now his trademark fashion, with her hands behind her back and her feet tied together. He also gagged her and tied a rag around her mouth. Peery returned to the front of the store where he helped loot the display counters of coins and watches. Unaware of the true value of the merchandise, especially the coins, the group left many of the most valuable pieces on the shelves.

Peery toted the loot, which had been loaded into plastic garbage bags, outside to the car. Just before leaving, Peery suddenly ordered the other two to wait in the car, and he walked back into the store alone. He went straight to the bathroom, where he took out a small pistol and shot Mrs. Mitzner between the eyes. He pulled down the gag and shot her once more through the roof of her mouth. Then he moved to her side and shot her once through the temple. As the blood slowly drained from her body, Peery strolled out the front of the store and calmly got into the waiting car. He and his associates returned unnoticed to Wesleyan, where they uneventfully finished the work day. Peery, evidently, was a person who *could* kill someone and then go to work and act normal. But then, Wesley Peery was a psychopath.

One of the most bizarre aspects of the Mitzner case, as it related to Wesley Peery and the Parker murder case, went totally unnoticed and was never reported in the press. Photographs of Nancy Parker and Marianne Mitzner, when placed side by side, appear to be pictures of either the same woman or identical twin sisters. Two women killed twenty years apart by the same man were, for all intents and purposes, the same person.

A photograph of Peery's mother, taken at age seventy-eight, shows her still wearing the same hairstyle she'd worn when she was younger—cropped short, no lower than her neckline. The same hairstyle worn by Nancy Parker and Marianne Mitzner. She wore the same winged eyeglass frames she'd had for years—the same style frames worn by Nancy Parker and Marianne Mitzner. Her hair was dyed black, the same as Nancy Parker's and Marianne Mitzner's natural hair color. She had the same nose, the same mouth, and the same chin. At age seventy-eight, Marzetta Peery Carter Glantz still bore an uncanny resemblance to photographs taken of her forty years before and to the photographs of Nancy Parker and Marianne Mitzner.

In the Mitzner case the Lincoln police and the Lancaster County attorney did not prosecute someone else in Peery's place. Nor was an effort made to link any of the evidence from the Mitzner case to the Parker murder. The Parker case had long since been forgotten. Peery was convicted of the Mitzner murder and sentenced to die in the electric chair. He was returned to the Nebraska State Penitentiary for the last time. Peery had received the death penalty, and as far as the authorities were concerned, that was the end of it. No one would revisit the fact that one woman had been horribly raped and another murdered because Peery had been released after the Parker murder.

In the spring of 1978 Marjorie Marlette, Scheele's old friend and the *Journal* reporter who wrote the homage to "the men who wouldn't quit" after Darrel Parker had been arrested, visited Peery in the pen. The lead sentence of her article read, "The laugh lines around Wesley Peery's eyes are still there and still crinkling."

"It's my usual way of life," Peery answered, when Marlette asked him why he was so cheerful. "The only thing that would change it is if something happened to my mother." Peery's purported love and devotion toward his mother touched Marlette. At the end of the article Peery said, "A lot of things I've done in my life have not been caught. But there's the idea you don't want to be punished for something you didn't do."

In the fall of 1978 Peery summoned the attorney who had represented him in the Mitzner murder case, Stanley Cohen. Peery informed him that he wanted to have a book written about his life of crime. Cohen and the attorney he shared an office with, Toney Redman, had numerous interviews with Peery at the penitentiary in which they took Peery's taped and written confessions. When Cohen and Redman discussed Peery's past crimes with him, he admitted to many more than he'd ever committed and, for most of the so-called crimes, gave brief descriptions of what later proved to be false events. Yet, for three of the crimes he admitted—the Parker murder, the Mitzner murder, and the rape of the pregnant woman—Peery gave lengthy and exacting detail when describing what he'd done. As Dr. Douglas Kelley had said, "A person who commits such crimes has them literally burned into the mind forever." And that is why Peery was able to remember twenty-five years later every detail of the Parker murder when he wrote this oddly lettered confession:

> I parked 49 Ford south of the ParKer house——Then walKed shuffling my feeT so I wouldn'T leave any TracKs. I came To The back door and Knocked. Nancy Parker came To The door. I had a 12 gauge shoTgun and I pointed it at her. I Told her iT was a robbery and I wanTed all her money. She backed into the KiTchen and I followed her in. She picKed her purse up from the KiTchen table and gave me the money ThaT was in her purse ($10.). I told her I would have To Tie her up, and ask her iF she had some rope. She wenT To a cabineT on the wesT side of the KiTchen and gave me a new rope. I Took her inTo The bedroom and had her lie on

The bed. I tied her arms behind her, I Then Tied her feet. AT This point I decided to rape her, so I unTied her Feet. I sTarTed to Take her blue jeens oFF and she sTarTed to FighT, so I hit her on the leFT side oF her jaw a couple of Times, ANd she quiT. I TooK her jeens and panTies oFF, and cuT The sweat shirt off with my KniFe. I then cut her bra oFF. I cut boTh articles oFF the middle of her body and spread Them apart to boTh sides oF her body. I Then raped her with her arms Tied behind her. I had a climax outside oF her body. IT was Then I reaLized I would have To KiLL her so she couLdN'T idenTiFy me, so I Tied her FeeT Again. I drew her FeeT up to her arms in back with The rope. I Then broke The band on her waTch when I jerked iT oFF her ARM. I Looped The rope Twice around her NecK buT beFore I couLd Tie iT, she sTrained so much ThaT she broke The Rope beTWeen her Feet ANd her ARms. I Tied The rope on her NecK AFTer I TighTened iT up. I Went To The Room EAsT oF The bedroom and TooK a Fuzzy Rope oFF a Box and Tied iT around her necK Too. I wenT To a dresser IN The souThwest CORNer oF The bedroom ANd TooK Two or Three hanKerchieFs ANd STuFFed Them in her mouTh. I Then searched The whole house For ANy ARTicLes ThaT I couLd sell. There were 2 1/2 booKs of S+H Green sTamps ThaT I Found in a puLL out desk in The NorTheasT room. I Found a suiTcase in the ATic. It was brown in color, ANd They had three brass initials on Top by The Lock. I Later TooK These iniTials oFF wiTh a screw driver and Threw Them AWAy. AFTer I broughT The suiTcase From the ATic, I wenT To The bedroom To see iF she was sTill Tied Tight. I don'T ThinK she was dead aT This Time but I Knew she wouLd be beFore she WAs Found. I TooK everyThing ThaT I had ANd LeFT The house by The bacK door. I had puT The shoTgun in The suiTcase. I leFT The house by The bacK door and ReTRAced my sTeps back To my cAR. I Knew I wouLd have To have an ALibi, so I wenT sTraight To a LocKsmiTh shop and Had Them puT a lock on my Trunk on the 49 Ford I owned. I was there The resT of The morning.

When asked if there was anything else Peery could identify that would show he had knowledge of the crime, Peery said that Nancy

Parker had freckles on her chest and lower right rib cage. Darrel Parker would later confirm the existence of these marks, which he said were birthmarks.

Peery said that when the police questioned him the evening of December 15 he had Nancy's suitcase in the trunk, along with the shotgun, pillows, and green stamps. His alibi was the locksmith, and he had indeed had a new lock put on the trunk. Before he was questioned he said he put his trunk key in his shoe and told the police that he'd left the new key at home. Contrary to Masters' testimony in court, they didn't check the trunk when they brought him in for questioning.

The paper that Masters had picked up off the floor in the bedroom on the day of the crime was the wrapper off the new roll of clothesline rope that was in the broom closet. Peery said he "used a new rope out of the pantry that still had the wrapper on it."

There were no footprints in the snow between his car and the Parker house because "I shuffled my feet, making a continuous path when I crossed the ditch and when I retraced my steps to the car." Although he said he "decided" to rape her, it was surely his intention from the start to rape Nancy Parker. The fact that he had gotten the twine off the Christmas package explained the source of that twine—two-ply twine that matched the twine around Nancy Parker's neck. That is something that should easily have been ascertained during the original investigation. The three-ply twine that was confessed to by Darrel was on the roll of twine found on the basement steps. The photos taken the day of the murder by Everett Rudisil clearly show the two packages Darrel wrapped leaning against the dining room wall. The smaller of the two packages has three lengths of twine wrapped around it; the other has only one. The one with only one length has dimples in the wrapping paper at the edges of the box where the other two lengths of twine had been.

The fact that Peery said Nancy Parker broke the clothesline rope was the only explanation ever given as to why the rope had frayed ends, as FBI Agent Duckett had testified. Peery had also drawn a sketch of the Parkers' house for his attorney. It was accurate in every detail, showing the location of all the rooms and pieces of furniture.

Notable was the fact that the drawing was not oriented from the front entrance on the west side of the house as most people would draw a house plan, but from the south entrance, the one he had entered the day of the murder. All of Peery's lettering and symbols were parallel with that door. He took the medium-sized suitcase in the attic—"It had two pillows in it that I took with the rest of the stuff"—and left.

Nothing ever came of Peery's book on his life of crime. He still "over-stressed his importance." In 1982 the state of Nebraska spent forty thousand dollars for a heart bypass operation on him. In the fall of 1986 witnesses were named for what was to be the state's first execution since the 1959 execution of Charles Starkweather, the young trash collector who many called America's first headline serial killer. This time the offender to be put to death was Wesley Peery. A day before the scheduled execution, it was suddenly postponed. Peery's reprieve came from U.S. District Judge Warren Urbom, whose decision insured that Peery would never be executed. In July of 1988 Peery died of a heart attack.

On August 13, 1988, just before Peery's confessions were made public, an article appeared in the *Star* describing some of the stolen goods from the Mitzner robbery that had been found nearly a year after the crime stashed in one of the buildings on the Wesleyan campus. The evidence had been held by the police for thirteen years while appeals continued.

Following Peery's death it was announced that Ken Mitzner, the husband of Marianne, could reclaim the stolen articles valued at several thousand dollars. Mitzner declined. Rather than take the items back, Mitzner declared that he would donate all of the valuables to the police department's youth services program. He viewed the money as "Judas money, blood money," and was motivated to make the donation, he said, because he "genuinely appreciated the fine police work involved in solving the crime."

On August 28, 1988, *60 Minutes* ran a segment entitled "True Confessions." Harry Reasoner introduced the piece by describing a woman who had confessed to a murder following an interrogation that began with a lie detector test.

"When a jury considers a confession," Reasoner said, "it also considers whether the confession was made freely or under coercion. That's always a hard one for a jury to decide. After all, what goes on during a police interrogation usually goes on behind closed doors. Usually, but not in this case.

"Remember, the lie detector examiner you'll see is supposed to be impartial. At the very least, he shouldn't be stroking the hair of the accused and coaxing her to confess."

A videotape made by the lie detector examiner was shown. As the interrogator questioned the woman he slowly stroked her hair and suggested her complicity in the crime. Reasoner noted that the videotape lasted three hours and at no time was a lawyer present to represent the woman. She had been arrested and held for two days and three nights, without ever seeing an attorney. This interrogation occurred twenty-two years after the Miranda ruling.

The polygraph operator was caught on tape lying to the woman, using false information that had been supplied by the police. Reasoner asked a psychiatrist, Dr. Richard Pesikoff, to describe what was happening to the woman as she was being interrogated.

"Is that tape evidence of anything?" asked Reasoner.

"It shows somebody whose ability to resist is overwhelmed, and who crosses the line between a voluntary and involuntary statement, so that what comes out is a creation and not a confession."

Dr. Pesikoff did not know Dr. Douglas Kelley, nor Dr. J. Whitney Kelley, nor Dr. Frank Barta. And he knew nothing of the Parker case.

After more questioning the woman began to have delusions that perhaps she did commit the murder.

"She's having false thoughts," concluded Pesikoff, "and one of those thoughts is, 'Maybe I did kill them,' and that's as good a thought in this delusional state as any other thought that she's going to come up with from now on."

The accused woman asked to see pictures of the crime scene.

"Those pictures represent a life buoy," the doctor noted. "They will tell her whether she really dreamed this or not, and that will tell her what's real and what's not real, which is a condensed description of what people mean when they're going crazy. Either they know what's really happening in this world or they don't."

"Are we watching Kelly go crazy?" asked Reasoner.

"It's at the point where Kelly can no longer distinguish what's real from what's not real."

"At that point," said Reasoner, "getting accurate information from her about a past event would be chancy?"

"Impossible. It's impossible. She starts to create material for a confession which comes then more under the title of brainwashing than confession."

After the interrogation the police obtained a signed confession from the accused woman. When the case arrived in court, the judge immediately threw out the entire confession and chastised the authorities. Explaining his decision, he said, "If they had used a cattle prod on her, it would have been more humane. I certainly think the confessions were coerced."

When Darrel Parker was notified of the Peery confessions by Richard Bruckner, he conferred with Eleanore to decide what their response should be—ignore the publicity and continue with their new life in the Quad Cities or pursue the matter legally, accept the publicity, and find out if the confession would be enough to exonerate him of Nancy's murder.

"Dick told us we would get a great sum of money for all those lost years—a sure thing! We were on cloud nine.

"Yet all I ever wanted," said Darrel, "when I learned of that confession, was just a piece of paper that said I was innocent. That was all."

They decided to face the revelations that would come with Peery's confessions and pursue whatever legal actions they could that might clear Darrel's name. Preparations were made by Bruckner for a presentation at the next board of pardons hearing in Lincoln in December.

An omen of what lay ahead soon became apparent. When accounts of Peery's confession began to appear in the papers, rather than being presented as a final affirmation of Parker's innocence they were treated as merely another chapter in the "ongoing mystery of the Parker murder case." One article, typical at the time, appeared after Darrel had talked at length with a seemingly sympathetic reporter from the *Chicago Tribune*. The reporter told Darrel, "In all my years of journalism, this is the most interesting story I've ever covered." The title of his article when it finally went to print was DID HE KILL HER?

Two days before Parker's hearing in December, Chief Carroll and Eugene Masters, both retired and in their early eighties, demanded and got an interview with the *Lincoln Star*. The motivation for the interview became quite clear. Carroll declared at the outset, "I don't just think he was guilty, I know he was guilty!"

Masters said that details in Parker's confession could only be known by the murderer. He cited the sweatshirt that had been cut away, the knot that Darrel had tied—the double bowline that wasn't a double bowline—and the state chemist's testimony that "the time of death had come fifteen minutes after breakfast." The final distortion of the record came when Carroll said that Parker was not questioned for several hours, as the newspaper had reported. Carroll had personally gone to the state patrol, he said, to check their logs, and "I found that Reid had questioned Parker only from 6:45 P.M. until 8:00 P.M. on the day of the interrogation." The Masters and Carroll interview was printed in the paper on December 13, 1988. Darrel's hearing the next day would be thirty-three years to the day after Nancy Parker had been killed.

The Nebraska board of pardons turned down Darrel Parker's request for a pardon hearing. State attorney general Robert Spire, a Republican who would later become Democratic Senator Bob Kerrey's campaign manager, stated that the board would consider Parker's request for a pardon "only if there had been a clear miscarriage of justice."

"Bitterness began to slowly creep back into my life. It was as if life had played a cruel joke on me that just kept repeating, over and over.

"Next were the two attorneys from Lincoln who had gotten Peery's confessions—one of them, Toney Redman, was a distant cousin of mine, and that was another odd twist. They wanted this book written that contrasted my life with that of Wesley Peery. They came to our house with lofty promises that never materialized."

After rejection at the hands of the board of pardons, Darrel received a bill in the mail from Richard Bruckner for "past services rendered." Darrel paid all that he could, decimating his savings that had been slowly built up over the previous twenty years.

The Lancaster County attorney at the time, Michael Heavican, called his own press conference after the pardon hearing to dispute Peery's confessions to the murder of Nancy Parker. Apparently the political and ethical fallout of having to admit wrongdoing by the county attorney's office, even thirty years after the fact, was something to be avoided at all costs. Of course lurking unspoken behind the public statements by elected and appointed officials alike was the fear that there might be monetary losses to the state's coffers if the Parker conviction was ever overturned.

"Anyone who read the newspaper at the time of the killing," said Heavican, "or who was questioned for as long as Peery was in that case could pick up on that kind of information."

Heavican, by his own statement, revealed that he had not read what the newspapers printed at the time of the murder, or he would have known how little of the evidence or actual testimony ever made it into print. Had he checked the trial transcript, he also would have found that Peery was not questioned on the lie detector about the murder at all, only as to his whereabouts on the morning of the murder.

"I really have great doubts that you could coerce anybody," said Heavican, "no matter how much sleep they said they didn't have or what frame of mind they were in."

Soon after Darrel and Eleanore returned to the Quad Cities in the wake of the pardon hearing rejection, a friend recommended a retired district court judge who had expressed an interest in the case, Judge David DeDonker. Once he agreed to take on the case, Judge DeDonker went so far as to send for the box of evidence from the original trial. Darrel knew that Toney Redman and Stan Cohen at one time had the evidence in their office. Darrel's attorney called Redman, requested the evidence, and sent Darrel to pick it up in Lincoln.

Parker explained:

Judge DeDonker felt it important to see the evidence firsthand prior to filing the civil action in federal court. I called Toney and set up a noon meeting on the weekend at his home in east Lincoln. We were invited to have lunch with him and his parents. Toney was my cousin. His home was quite unique and had just been built.

After lunch he took me to another room and showed me some of the evidence from the trial. He took out a semen sample in a small round container. He also showed me a piece of bedspread that contained a semen stain. He saw that this bothered me and asked why. I indicated that it brought back all those terrible memories I had when I found Nancy brutally murdered.

I placed the box of evidence in my trunk and we returned to the Quad Cities with the evidence. I took it to the judge and remember him looking at the piece of quilt with semen on it as I walked out of his office. I never saw the evidence again. Judge DeDonker's son returned the evidence to Toney sometime in the fall of '89.

After DeDonker reviewed the evidence, as Darrel said, he had it returned to Redman's office. It was delivered by DeDonker's son, Tom, who was returning to college in Kansas via Lincoln.

"Dad gave me the box of evidence," said Tom DeDonker, "and on the way back to school I stopped in Lincoln and left the evidence at Toney Redman's law office . . . I remember getting paid a small sum for courier service and went to the university art museum afterwards."

Judge DeDonker met with the Parkers and together it was decided that the only alternative left was to sue Lancaster County and Chief Carroll, since Carroll was the only person still alive (Masters had since died) who had been in a position of authority at the time of the interrogation and trial.

"I was young," said Darrel at a news conference to announce the suit. "I was immature, easily molded, terribly naive, and trusting. The police were experienced and they wanted to solve the murder. They wanted a confession. There had just been another murder in Omaha [the Nevins murder] and people were frightened. On top of that is the fact that my attorneys, Dr. Kelley, and myself felt that

I had been drugged by John Reid during his last interrogation and became like putty in his hands."

Darrel's inability to receive justice through the courts in 1956 led him and his supporters to feel that this time the press would surely champion his cause since Peery's confession had been exposed in the fall of 1988. Falloon, now in retirement, had taken in the recent events with some reservation. It made him wistfully recall the saying emblazoned over the doors of the old *Denver Post* building: O JUSTICE WHEN EXPELLED FROM OTHER HABITATIONS, MAKE THIS THY DWELLING PLACE. Such treatment would, indeed, have been the journalism profession's ideal. However, as the experienced Falloon suspected, such hopes would be soon proven false yet again.

If politics had dominated Parker's appeal decisions in the past, his 1989 lawsuit was not treated any differently. Judge Warren Urbom, the same judge who had postponed Peery's execution, declared in March 1990, "While the truth may never be known about Wesley Peery's role in the murder of Nancy Parker, this action is not the place to find out."

Urbom, apparently unaware of Parker's original appeals in 1956, said: "If the former chief of police and the city and county violated Parker's rights when his confession was obtained, Parker knew, or should have known, of that violation in 1955 [*sic*]. At the latest, this action accrued upon his release from prison in 1970. Parker is some twenty years too late, and I will not require the defendants to search their memories of more than thirty years to redetermine issues that have already been heard."

The suit was dismissed. The tenor of the Nebraska judiciary had changed little. A house of cards had been built in 1956 to prosecute Darrel Parker with the confession at its base. Reid's "confession" is what continued to hold it all up in 1990.

Darrel and Eleanore Parker returned, disappointed once more, to their home in the Quad Cities. After more than a year passed and he was still unable to find inner peace, Darrel did something he thought he would never do. He applied for a hearing before the board of pardons for the purpose of making his own statement before the Board and requesting a pardon—no lawyers, no lawsuit, just himself. He would settle for a pardon if he could get it, rather than using the legal process as a springboard to proving his innocence through the courts—which, given the track record, by now seemed impossible to him anyway.

A pardon was something he had never sought. "I never liked the word and couldn't accept it before because I'm an innocent man. An innocent man does not have to be forgiven because of his 'good behavior.' But time creeps up your back like the evening shadows, quietly and silently. At some point I realized it's never going to happen, and all the promises and all the hopes have evaporated."

On a hot and humid summer day, June 28, 1991, Darrel's hearing was held in Lincoln. Appearing alone, accompanied by only Eleanore, Darrel made his statement: "In 1955 events happened that changed the lives of many forever. One life was needlessly snuffed out and I confessed to a crime which I never committed. That false confession changed my life and that of my family forever. No matter what has been said or written could change what some people believed. Somehow I felt this could all be righted through the courts. That is not to be."

One of the board members asked Darrel to explain the circumstances of his confession. Darrel described Reid's tactics during the interrogation and their results. He mentioned, in passing, that Reid had been cited by the U.S. Supreme Court in its Miranda ruling—the first time that those present had been made aware of that fact. He was asked why he didn't pursue a retrial. There was the ruling by the U.S. Supreme Court in 1969, Parker said, in which the courts were to decide once again on the voluntariness of his confession:

> It had taken me thirteen years to work through the state courts and the federal courts to get the case reversed. Suddenly, the U.S. Supreme Court was saying, "Well, we're going to give the State another chance before we rule on the confession." I felt I was headed right back to the penitentiary because I just knew how this hearing—it was not a trial, it was a hearing before a judge—the same judge that ruled before would have the power to send me right back to prison, and we would have to start the process all over again.
>
> So it was proposed that if I would drop all litigation, and that's in the record somewhere, then the pardon board at that time would be

willing to look favorably on a commutation. That was in September of 1970, and about the same time the district judge entered an order finding that he felt the confession was voluntary.

That answered Judge Urbom's question as to why there was no appeal in 1970. The State and the state pardon board had cut a deal to avoid further litigation, the results of which they couldn't be sure of and would surely have lost once it got outside the state of Nebraska. They held further imprisonment over Parker's head as the inducement to accept their terms. The confession may have been ruled to have been given voluntarily at the state level, but the Miranda ruling would have disallowed the results had it gone to trial in the federal courts: "unless and until such warnings and waiver are demonstrated by the prosecution at trial, no evidence obtained as a result of interrogation can be used against him."

"I appreciate your comments," replied State Attorney General Donald Stenberg. "Let me ask one last thing. If a pardon is granted would you have any thoughts or intentions of filing any lawsuits concerning this matter?"

Darrel answered, no. Stenberg's question seemed to suggest that the state wouldn't mind granting a pardon as long as it didn't have to pay any compensation, a deal similar to the one the prosecutors made in 1970. The secretary of state, Allen Beerman, then added, "I respect that you have the right to maintain that you're innocent and I do not hold that against you."

The closest anyone came to an admission that a wrong may have been committed by the State was when the attorney general made a closing statement just before the board voted:

On the one hand I certainly don't like to be in the position or have the Board in the position of essentially questioning a jury verdict, particularly one thirty-five years ago. They heard the evidence, they saw the witnesses, everyone was alive. And I'm sure they did their duty as they saw it. We're not in a position now, with many of the witnesses dead, to redo the case. And as I said at the last meeting when we decided whether we were going to have a hearing, I would only grant a pardon in first-degree murder cases in the most extraordinary circumstances; but I think perhaps this is one. While I think the jury was convinced beyond a reasonable doubt, developments in the last thirty-five years leave some question in my mind. I cannot say, having carefully studied the record and viewing all the subsequent developments that that situation should necessarily stand. Perhaps Mr. Parker did the crime as the jury found, but I'm not entirely convinced that is clear. He had no history of violent crime or any crime before or after the event. The crime seems totally out of character based on the record before or after the crime.

"No history of violent crime," said Dr. Kelley. "These things don't just drop out of the blue."

Darrel Parker was granted a pardon by a unanimous vote, barely eighteen months after the same board had refused to even grant him a hearing. Darrel had his "piece of paper," but it didn't say he was innocent. A pardon is merely an act of forgiveness. The state had spent forty thousand dollars to preserve Wesley Peery's life for six additional years, but they didn't have to spend a dime as recompense to Darrel Parker for the thirteen years he'd spent in prison.

No one at the hearing asked why a man, if he was indeed guilty of murder and had been released from prison, would suddenly want to reopen his case and draw attention to himself. No one at the hearing asked why a man who had successfully rebuilt his ruined life would want to return to Nebraska, enter the limelight, and plead for the return of his good name if he was guilty.

"I live with him, I'm closer to him than anybody," began Eleanore in her statement to the board, "and I know instinctively that he didn't kill his wife. He's an often naive, yet trusting man . . . he still is. He believes in the goodness of people. He's a good person, and I just wish that he had the chance to be free of all of this."

A pardon was as close to an exoneration as Darrel Parker would ever get from the legal system in the state of Nebraska.

Once again he felt that it was all over, that his attempts to prove his innocence had met their end.

In March of 1991, three months before Darrel Parker's last hearing before the board of pardons, the United States Supreme Court made a five-to-four ruling regarding coerced evidence in the form of false confessions. The Court ruled that using such confessions may be "harmless error" if other trial evidence is sufficient to convict the defendant.

Ten years later, in the spring of 2001, Darrel and Eleanore were playing cards with their regular pinochle group. During a break, one of the men happened to mention a television show he'd seen on public television on the subject of DNA testing and its application in criminal cases. The friend noted that some tests had been made on evidence as old as twenty-five years. Darrel remembered the quilt that DeDonker looked at, in addition to the small container, exhibit 65—the dried semen that had been removed from Nancy Parker's body.*

The sizable semen deposit found in evidence in 1955 was, indeed, a rarity for that time period. If it would be possible to have a successful DNA test performed after so much time had elapsed, it would be due solely to the preservation of exhibit 65. With the possibility of testing that exhibit, Darrel's hopes rose from the ashes once more.

Therefore, when Darrel wanted to gain access to the evidence for a DNA test in 2001, he called his cousin, Toney Redman, to see if the evidence could once again be "checked out." Redman, according to Parker, told him that he would look into it. When he didn't hear from Redman for some time, Parker said he contacted Redman again and was told the evidence couldn't be found, that it may in fact have been destroyed. When Parker asked Redman how he had previously gotten the evidence, Parker said Redman told him that he "couldn't remember ever having the evidence." After

---

*Further testament to the existence of exhibit 65 is proven by an event that occurred in January of 1989. At that time the author met with Stan Cohen to discuss the Parker case. In the course of that conversation Cohen stated that he had the evidence to the Parker case in his possession. The author, assuming the evidence had been properly obtained, later paid for and received from Cohen a copy of the trial transcript and personally made photocopies of various photographic exhibits—each bearing its exhibit number from the trial. Cohen also mentioned at that time the existence of the round metal container that held exhibit 65, "pubic hair and dried material" as described in the transcript.

writing Redman a nasty letter, Parker said he received a reply in which Redman instructed him to never contact or write him again. Enclosed in the same letter was a bill for $275 for the evidence search.

Later in 2001, after the exchange between Redman and Parker, an inquiry was made at the Lincoln Police Department, the normal repository for such evidence—the place where it is warehoused for the courts. They had no record of having the Parker trial evidence in their evidence room. There was no check-out sheet in their registry as proof of whom the evidence had last been released to. Murder evidence is supposedly kept in perpetuity or until all interested parties are deceased. The Lancaster County District Court, the originating court for the Parker trial, had no record of the location of the Parker trial evidence. And, finally, the United States District Court in Lincoln, where Darrel's last civil suit had been filed by DeDonker, did not have possession of the evidence. Therefore, without the evidence, without the semen samples that had been in the possession of several different people from 1988 until 1990, there would be no DNA test.

What can be established in retrospect is the fact that Stan Cohen had the evidence in his possession in January of 1989. At that time Redman and Cohen shared an office and together had taken Peery's confessions. In March of 1989 Cohen and Redman jointly wrote an article about the Parker case for the *Lincoln Journal*. "Our basis for the information," they said, "is the 1,753 page transcript of Parker's trial and Peery's 1978–1980 taped confession to us."

On September 22 of 1989 the request for Parker's jury trial concerning the civil suit against Chief Carroll and Lancaster County was filed in United States District Court. On September 27 an application was filed "admitting David DeDonker to practice in this case only. Copy mailed to David DeDonker and Toney Redman." The mention of Redman refers to *pro hac vice,* a legal term for a situation where an attorney in one state sponsors or in some way vouches for another attorney to practice law for a single case in a state where he is not licensed. Therefore, Redman had at least a peripheral involvement in Parker's last legal action in Nebraska.

When Toney Redman was contacted in September of 2009 he stated that at no time did he ever have the Parker evidence in his possession.

Darrel Parker had been in prison for more than thirteen years, and it had been thirteen years since Peery's confession had been made public. With the disappearance of the evidence, Darrel Parker's lonely search for exoneration came to a painful and ignominious end.

Although all of the principals in the Parker trial, except for Darrel Parker and Virgil Falloon, have passed on, the haunting legacy of John E. Reid remains. In 2008, if one were to scan the Internet using "John E. Reid & Associates, Inc." as the key words, one would find a Web site virtually brimming with self-serving information about John E. Reid's present-day personification:

> If it doesn't say "The Reid Technique" . . . it's not John Reid & Associates!
>
> WELCOME . . . Through our training seminars you will learn the Reid Technique of Interviewing and Interrogation, widely recognized as the most effective means available to exonerate the innocent and identify the guilty.
>
> John E. Reid and Associates began developing interview and interrogation techniques in 1947. The Reid Technique of Interviewing and Interrogation is now the most widely used approach to question subjects in the world . . . John E. Reid and Associates, Inc. is the exclusive owner of all rights in the copyrighted works and trademarks, and is the sole authorized provider of the current and up-to-date seminar course.

John Reid's techniques have now been copyrighted, incorporated, and trademarked. They tout their recognition by the U.S. Supreme Court—"In June 2004 in the case of Missouri v. Seibert, the U. S. Supreme Court referenced our company and our book, *Criminal Interrogation and Confessions,* as examples of law enforcement resources that offer proper training . . . Courts throughout the country have recognized the Reid Technique as the leading interview and interrogation approach used today in both the law enforcement and business communities." They don't mention the Supreme Court's "referencing" in the Miranda Decision.

The company cites an extensive client list that includes virtually all of the major police departments in the country: San Francisco, Pittsburgh, Phoenix, Philadelphia, New York City, Miami, Los Angeles, Denver, Dallas, Chicago, and Boston, among others; they list business clients as diverse as General Motors, Burger King, IBM, Dow Chemical, American Express, AT&T, Federal Express, Ford Motors, and Kroger; and they cite governmental clients such as the CIA, Department of Defense, Department of Education, Department of Labor, FBI, Nuclear Regulatory Commission, Occupational Safety and Health Administration, Marine Corps, U.S. Navy, U.S. Army, Secret Service, IRS, and Texas Rangers. They also list several countries as clients—Japan, Mexico, Canada, Belgium.

"Our book, *Criminal Interrogation and Confessions,* is considered by the courts and practitioners to be the 'Bible' for interviewing and interrogation techniques. The book has been translated into Chinese, Japanese and Turkish."

When they list their staff's experience they say they have conducted more than seventy-five thousand interviews and inter-rogations—a mere three times the number Reid alone was touted to have conducted in 1955. "Many of the staff hold a Masters of Science Degree in the Detection of Deception."

They list the satisfaction rate of their students, noting that "95% of the respondents to a survey of 2,000 Reid students reported that using the Reid Technique helped them improve their confession rate . . . The majority of the respondents said they increased their confession rate by more than 25%."

Seminars include instructions on how to properly prepare for an interview or interrogation and how to have a "proper room environ-ment" and list factors that affect a subject's behavior. Their Behavior Symptom Analysis includes such categories as "The Baiting Technique" and how to ask "Behavior Provoking Questions."

It is assumed that John Reid himself offered much to the discus-sion and implementation of these modern-day interrogation techniques prior to their incorporation. The fact that they tout the current incarnation of Reid and Inbau's book reflects the implicit power of the earlier work in the modern-day version of John E. Reid & Associates.

Touting their "successes," the company lists testimonials from students who have participated in their seminars:

> "I have been using the Reid Technique since the training. I have been very successful using this technique. I got a confession two days after the training."

> "I have literally just returned from combat operations in Iraq . . . I used the Reid Technique on several prisoners including members of the Saddam Fedayeen with OUTSTANDING success. Hands down, the real-world application of the techniques from the basic and advanced courses you provided me and my team translated into actionable intelligence on the battlefield."

> "I saw an immediate difference in my interviews! I've gotten so many confessions! It was worth every penny."

> "After I had him in custody and read miranda [*sic*] I was able to blame the victim (I love that theme) and get a full confession in just about 20 min. . . . I was pumped up. But not as pumped up as the suspect who just confessed because just after confessing he had a heart attack in the back of my patrol car! I am not kidding!"

> "Upon completion of the three-day regular class, I was able to obtain a confession the next day using information taught in the course."

As an example of the broad acceptance of their methods, Reid & Associates list their connections to popular television in the field they no longer call lie detection interrogation but classify as the detection of deception: "The national news media oftentimes contacts John Reid & Associates as experts for our comments on stories involving detection of deception issues. On many of the news magazine shows—*60 Minutes, Dateline NBC, 48 Hours,* and *20/20*—John E. Reid & Associates has been recognized as the leader in the field of interviewing and interrogation training."

Under the title "Research Suggests False Confessions Are Extremely Rare" Reid and Associates say, "In a recent publication

(2005) one author reported the following: '. . . using national estimates of interrogations, arrests, convictions, error rates, wrongful convictions resulting from false confessions range from a low of 10 (.001% of all convictions) to a high of 840 (.04% of all convictions) per year.'

"In other words, while some critics of police interrogation practices suggest that convictions based on false confessions is a common phenomena, research would suggest that 99.6% of convictions involving confessions are true and correct."

Reid & Associates do not explain what the fate is of the people who happen to fall into that potential group of 840 who have given a false confession. But the part of the Web site that relates most directly to the Parker trial and John Reid's interrogation of Darrel Parker is the section entitled "Research Suggests False Confessions Are Extremely Rare": "False confessions are a rare phenomena, but they have occurred . . . It has been the Reid position that misrepresenting evidence, in and of itself, was not going to make a 'normal' person falsely confess, but that it is always some other element that is the triggering mechanism of the false confession, such as illegal interrogation tactics (physical abuse, threats, promises of leniency, denial of physical needs, denial of rights, etc.) and excessively long interrogations."

Thus is listed all of the methods John E. Reid employed in his interrogation of Darrel Parker.

When grade-school children are given tours of the state capitol building in Lincoln, they are delivered a wide-ranging oral history of the edifice—"the limestone came from the Bedford quarries of Bedford, Indiana; Lee Lawrie was the New York sculptor who was in charge of all the bas-reliefs, sculptures, and column capitals throughout the building; Bertram Goodhue was the architect who did not live to see his dream fulfilled and died eleven years before its completion; and when finished the capitol was listed as one of the twenty-five most beautiful buildings in the world by the American Institute of Architects."

The children are taken on a tour that includes the ornate legislative chambers, which hold the state's unusual unicameral legislature;

the observation deck below the dome, which gives a 360-degree panorama of the city and its ever-growing ocean of trees; the ten-story rotunda; and the governor's office, with its imposing fireplace that is never used. At the end of the tour the groups are taken to the supreme court chambers on the main floor at the south end of the building. Inside they are shown the intricately coffered and awe inspiring ceiling that is made up of more than eight thousand pieces of native walnut and constructed with nothing but wooden pegs— there are no nails holding it together. At the head of the chamber is the bench behind which sit the judges. Dale Fahrnbruch, the assistant county attorney at the time of Darrel's trial and the man who watched Darrel during Nancy's funeral in Des Moines, was a long-time member of the court.

The front of the bench consists of nine beautifully constructed walnut panels inlaid with seventeen different kinds of wood. Behind the bench is a high walnut-paneled wall. At the top of that wall is an inlaid inscription from the Greek philosopher Heraclitus that runs nearly the width of the room. It says simply: EYES AND EARS ARE POOR WITNESSES WHEN THE SOUL IS BARBAROUS.

EPILOGUE

Ele and I still reside in the Quad Cities. At seventy-nine,
it is somewhat ironic that I still must supplement our
income with part-time work for a law firm where I serve
as a courier and mail room manager. We both have
many health issues. Although few gave our marriage
much chance of success in the beginning, we are still
happily married after thirty-eight years. We have had to
accept the way things turned out and feel that when the
final trial comes, justice will be done.

—DARREL PARKER, 2009

It is always difficult and uncomfortable for an individual, a legal
body, or a government to admit a mistake, to admit a wrong. A
position currently in vogue suggests that previous mistakes or ille-
galities should be "left in the past," that we should "move on," or
"move forward," thereby leaving the unpleasantness and messiness
of dealing with controversial, divisive, or illegal issues behind us,
unresolved, an easy contentment being much preferred to a difficult
and often complicated resolution.

Hubris and false assuredness infuse those individuals who make
such fateful decisions. They are rarely questioned in the heat of the
moment, at the time when the first steps are taken down a wrong
path. The problem with such a convenient thesis is that when a
mistake has been made there are inevitably individuals who irreparably suffer as a result. The lasting consequence is a yawning black

hole in the center of their lives which, regardless of whether there are compensatory measures, can never be filled.

Approximately half of the states now have some form of compensation for people who have been wrongfully convicted and incarcerated. Unfortunately for many, compensation and/or exoneration never come. Such has been the case for Darrel Parker.

ACKNOWLEDGMENTS

My sources include interviews with Darrel Parker, Virgil Falloon, and Judge Thomas McManus. I also quote extensively from the trial transcript and newspaper accounts of the day. Stan Cohen provided the trial transcript and additional information and stories relating to Peery, Sidladjzek, and others. Without the transcript provided by Stan the story would have been impossible. Reid's own words are what reveal his insidious nature and that of the "Reid Technique."

To Darrel and Ele Parker, who have lived through an excruciating and seemingly endless series of disappointments in innumerable attempts to clear Darrel's name: I hope this book provides some small measure of redemption.

To the talented, dedicated, and above all, forgiving staff of Northwestern University Press: Mike Levine, Acquisitions Editor, the man who embraced Darrel's story and thus allowed it to be told; David Bishop; Serena Brommel; Henry Carrigan; Rudy Faust; Jenny Gavacs; Anne Gendler; and Marianne Jankowski. Steve Drizin, of the Center on Wrongful Convictions at the Northwestern University School of Law, who took an early interest in Darrel Parker's story and was kind enough to share his perspective on modern day wrongful convictions. Kathryn E. French. Chad Nitta, who gave numerous legal insights and clarified various legal terminology.

Virgil Falloon, who gave invaluable insights as the last person in the story, other than Darrel Parker, who is still alive. He had endless stories to tell about Max Towle, Tom McManus, Joe Carroll, Eugene Masters, John E. Reid, Douglas Kelley, Elmer Scheele, Dale Fahrnbruch, etc. As a reporter, he doggedly covered the story from start to finish and sat in the courtroom every day. Virgil, as did the defense attorneys, always believed in Darrel's innocence. Virgil's son, Bill, an editor with John Wiley and Sons, who was kind enough to give me advice, references, and inspiration at the start of the publishing process.

Joe and Marsha Buda, who kindly took a flake into their home when this all began; Senator Jerry Miller (there was always an open door, a weirdly stocked kitchen, and a comfortable bed at the farm); Don and Sherrilyn Miller; Jayne Snyder; and Karen Jones Ward; all friends who endured my presence at the start of this saga when things were personally turbulent. Susan Perlman for her interest and kind and timely recommendations. Mike Cox. And finally, the "Postmaster General," Barry Urbauer, along with his alter ego, "Richard."

The theater groups in Denver (Colorado Dramatists), Thayer County, and Lincoln who invested their time and efforts for little more than the reward that comes from telling a dramatic story onstage. The late Steve Tesich, who shared his writing experiences and whose words inspired me to continue pursuing the story in spite of endless setbacks. And two other kind gentlemen of film, William Goldman and the late Fred Zinneman.

Judge Thomas McManus, my father-in-law, was the first person to tell me of Darrel Parker's innocence. All I thought I had to do when Peery died was inform a journalist of the truth and it would somehow magically appear in print. If that was only so. Everyone connected with this story, however peripheral in nature, always seemed to have their own agenda. In the end, at some point, I just decided that someone had to tell Darrel's story from his point of view.

Judge McManus gave up his love of music for a more "practical" career in law, which nonetheless caused him endless frustration and intermittent privation. He finished his career as a respected jurist.

Dr. Jody Kleinman, an outstanding cardiologist, who kept me alive long enough to finish the book. She and her dedicated team of women do an excellent, and often thankless, job.

Finally, I thank my family: Kitty, for standing by me through all the ups and downs over the years; Jessica and Tom (and Jen and Isela, the latest additions), who likewise tolerated the time I spent pursuing a seemingly endless variety of literary incarnations; and to all those who are gone with whom I won't be able to share Darrel's story.

AFTERWORD
STEVEN A. DRIZIN

Why would any person of sound mind ever confess to a crime he or she did not commit? Can a suspect really be "persuaded," through the use of psychological interrogation techniques, to confess falsely to a murder? Even assuming that a person can be persuaded to confess falsely to a murder, can he or she be persuaded to confess falsely to perhaps the most heinous of all crimes—the murder of a loved one, a child, a parent, a spouse? *Barbarous Souls,* David Strauss's riveting account of the Darrel Parker case, should be required reading for anyone looking for answers to these questions.

Parker's confession was obtained by John E. Reid, a legendary polygrapher and interrogator from Chicago. Reid and his colleague Fred E. Inbau, a law professor at Northwestern University School of Law in Chicago (where I attended and now teach), were among the most influential police reformers of the twentieth century. In the 1920s and 1930s in the United States, police agencies were notorious for using the third degree—a range of interrogation tactics, including physical abuse and extreme psychological duress— to coerce confessions out of suspects. In lieu of the third degree, Inbau and Reid taught law enforcement officers to use more subtle and sophisticated psychological techniques, which Inbau and Reid insisted were not likely to cause an innocent person to confess. These techniques were the foundation of what later became known as the Reid Technique, which according to John E. Reid & Associates, the firm that Reid founded in 1947, is the "most widely used approach to question subjects in the world."

In 1953, Inbau recruited Reid to be his coauthor for the third edition of *Lie Detection and Criminal Interrogation,* a forerunner of *Criminal Interrogation and Confessions,* a book that is now in its fourth edition and is considered by many to be the bible of all interrogation training manuals. In the 1950s, Reid devoted much of his time to building his company, John E. Reid & Associates. In this capacity, he often served as a paid consultant, a professional polygrapher and interrogator for hire, ready to assist police departments around the country in difficult cases. This is what brought Reid to Lincoln, Nebraska. He was ostensibly hired to give Parker a polygraph, but Lincoln authorities, who gave lie detector tests to other suspects in the Nancy Parker murder investigation, could have administered the test to Parker. Reid came to Lincoln for only one purpose—to obtain a confession from Darrel Parker. And the 1953 edition of *Lie Detection and Criminal Interrogation* was his playbook.

What exactly happened during the interrogation of Darrel Parker will never be known because Reid did not electronically record the interrogation and confession, a practice which, to be fair to Reid, was not widely employed at the time in law enforcement. Reid and Inbau vehemently opposed electronic recording at the time of Parker's interrogation, and they continued to oppose recording throughout their lives, usually out of concern that recording would undermine the "key " to every successful interrogation—privacy (Fred E. Inbau, "Police Interrogation—A Practical Necessity," *J. Crim L. and Criminology* 16 [1961]: 52). Carrying on the legacy of Reid and Inbau, Buckley and Jayne voiced their opposition to recording in *Criminal Interrogation and Confessions* (2001), arguing that a mandatory recording requirement, if known by the suspect, would have a chilling effect on the suspect's willingness to talk to police. Buckley and Jayne also cited concerns that recording would invite the use of defense experts to offer opinions on the coercive effects of standard interrogation tactics, a practice they claimed would have "minimal probative value" (396–97). In fact, Reid & Associates lifted its opposition to recording only in 2005, when it became clear that recording interrogations was the wave of the future and not just a passing trend.

When police interrogations are not recorded electronically, the suspect's account of the process often differs significantly from the interrogator's. This lack of recording gives the interrogating police officer a distinct advantage when the case comes to court. Policemen are professional witnesses, practiced in the art of giving credible in-court testimony. Suspects, especially those, like Darrel Parker, with no prior experience with the criminal justice system, are much more nervous and often come off as less believable, especially during cross-examination. As a result, juries are much more likely to credit police officers' accounts over suspects' accounts when weighing the evidence. Electronic recording levels the playing field, allowing jurors an objective record of what occurred during the interrogation instead of having to choose sides between police officers and suspects.

Although there is not a recording of Reid's interrogation of Parker, there are transcripts (which I have reviewed) of Reid's and Parker's accounts from Parker's trial. They differ widely.

Parker described a highly confrontational interrogation, one in which Reid repeatedly accused him of the crime, told Parker that he had failed a polygraph test, described Nancy as sexually promiscuous with other men but frigid with Parker, and suggested to Parker that he killed her because she had refused to have sex with him. Reid's first version, given under direct examination, was a sanitized version of Parker's. He claimed that he did not touch Parker, did not raise his voice, did not accuse Parker of killing his wife, and did not slander Nancy. He insisted that all he did was urge Parker repeatedly to tell the truth. The transcripts show that Reid told an entirely different story when cross-examined by Max Towle, one of Parker's lawyers. He admitted to sitting so close to Parker that their knees were touching, to putting his hand on Darrel's shoulder, to stroking his hair, and to lifting Darrel's head up by the chin and saying, "Look at me, Darrel" when Darrel's head began to drop. He also admitted to telling Darrel that "it was a sin for women to refuse their husbands."

Reid's backtracking only escalated during the most dramatic part of the cross-examination, when Towle used the 1953 edition of Inbau and Reid's book to challenge many of the claims that Reid had made in earlier testimony. Towle got Reid to admit that he repeatedly accused Parker of killing his wife and that in his book he advocated smearing the wife's reputation as a theme in wife-killing cases. Under Towle's relentless questioning, Reid also admitted that Parker could not lead him to Nancy's watch, a key piece of evidence that was needed to corroborate his confession. In a moment of frustration, Reid testified that Parker's confession "stood on its own," a statement that directly conflicts with the book's conclusion that confessions are weakened if they lack corroboration. Finally, Towle got Reid to admit that he scripted Parker's confession by instructing the typist to insert mistakes into the final written confession so that they could be later crossed out and initialed by Parker. These actions, which are still taught by Reid & Associates, are designed to bolster a claim that the confession was voluntary and to prevent suspects from later claiming that they did not read the confession.

Despite Reid's about-face during his trial testimony, the jury still convicted Parker, rejecting Parker's defense that Nancy was raped and killed by Wesley Peery, a career criminal who was an early suspect in the case. Parker's attorneys presented several witnesses who testified that they saw a car fitting the description of Peery's 1949 black, two-door Ford parked a block away from the Parker home in the early morning hours on the date of Nancy's death. The jury also heard that Peery had been part of a work crew hired to build a security fence at the Parker home less than a month before Nancy's murder. Weighed against Parker's confession, however, such evidence did not stand a chance. Confession evidence to this day is still among the most powerful forms of evidence in a court of law, leading juries to convict innocent defendants even when DNA test results suggest that another person committed the crime.

The passage of time has only strengthened the case that Peery, and not Parker, committed the crime. Peery went on to commit a series of rapes and other crimes that bore striking similarities to the Parker murder. Over the years, Peery teased Parker's lawyers with information about the crime that only the true perpetrator could have known, information which turned out to be true. While on Nebraska's death row in the 1980s, speaking to his lawyers, Peery took credit for the Nancy Parker murder. In July 1988, before he could be executed, Peery died of a heart attack. Peery's lawyers, no longer bound by the attorney-client privilege, released Peery's confessions to the public. Included among them was a detailed written confession accurately describing his role in the Parker murder.

According to the most recent data from the Innocence Project, 254 persons have been exonerated by DNA evidence since 1989. False confessions have played a role in approximately 17 percent of those exonerations. The overwhelming majority of documented false confessions have occurred in murder cases. In 2004, my own study (with Professor Richard Leo) of 125 proven false confessions found that 81 percent of the false confessions involved murder cases, often murder-rape cases, including several in which suspects confessed to murdering or raping loved ones.

Far more is known today about the social psychology of police interrogations and false confessions than was known in 1991. Social scientists did not begin to study the psychology of false confessions in earnest until the 1980s, when the work of such giants as Saul Kassin, Richard Ofshe, Gisli Gudjonsson, and Richard Leo was published. Their work has demonstrated that the primary cause of most false confessions is the interrogator's use of coercive psychological interrogation techniques, including many of those advocated by the Reid Technique. The use of such tactics is especially dangerous with juveniles, the cognitively disabled, and other vulnerable suspects but can also lead persons with average or even high intelligence to confess to crimes they did not commit. Although Reid & Associates still insists that the Reid Technique does not contribute to false confessions, today, there is overwhelming evidence to the contrary. Darrel Parker's confession may be the first example of a Reid-induced false confession on record and if he is indeed innocent makes me wonder how many other false confessions have been obtained using these techniques and how many will be obtained in the future.

There is also a general consensus among experts about how to distinguish true confessions from false confessions. In evaluating the reliability of confessions, experts look for answers to a number of questions. Does the confession contain nonpublic information that can be independently verified, would be known by only the true perpetrator or an accomplice, and cannot likely be guessed by chance? Does the suspect's confession lead police to new evidence about the crime, including information the police did not already know? Does the suspect's narrative of the crime fit (or fail to fit) with the crime facts and existing objective evidence? Without a recording of the interrogation, it is difficult to answer these questions because it is impossible to know whether the details in the confession that only the true perpetrator could have known originated with the suspect or were suggested to the suspect by the interrogator. In case after case of proven false confessions I have studied, police officers have contaminated confessions by feeding facts to suspects. Although the Reid Technique cautions interrogators to hold this information back from a suspect, time and time again interrogators, in the heat of the moment, throw caution to the wind.

The case for Parker's innocence is also strengthened by the recent realization in Nebraska that false confessions are a real, not an imagined, problem. Nebraska is still reeling from two major false confession cases in 2006 and 2008: those of Matthew Livers and of the Beatrice Six, in which DNA exonerated six people who were wrongfully convicted of the murder and sexual assault of Helen Wilson in Beatrice, Nebraska, in 1985.

In both the Livers and Beatrice Six cases, DNA evidence ultimately proved that the confessions were false. In March 2006, Livers confessed on videotape to murdering Wayne and Sharmon Stock, his uncle and aunt, after interrogations that included many elements of the Reid Technique. The interrogation tapes also reveal tactics that even Reid trainers do not advocate—both explicit threats that Livers would receive the death penalty if he did not confess and numerous examples of police fact feeding. Charges against Livers and his cousin Nick Sampson were eventually dropped when DNA testing of items left at the crime scene linked two Wisconsin teenagers to the murders.

In 2008, DNA testing of blood, hair, and semen preserved from the Wilson crime scene excluded all six of the defendants who had been convicted of the Helen Wilson rape and murder—Joseph White, Thomas Winslow, James Dean, Kathy Gonzalez, Ada JoAnn Taylor, and Deb Shelden. Of these six, five had pled guilty to participating in the murder, and four had given detailed confessions. The DNA tests linked Bruce Smith, one of the prime early suspects in the case, to the murder and rape of Wilson. The DNA test results prompted the Nebraska Attorney General's Office to reinvestigate the Helen Wilson case. The office found numerous improprieties in the way in which the Beatrice Six had been interrogated, including evidence that facts had been fed to the suspects. Several of the Beatrice Six defendants also told investigators that they had confessed only after being threatened with the death penalty. With the support of the Nebraska Attorney General's Office, Joseph White's conviction has been vacated, and the other five defendants, all of whom served years in Nebraska prisons before being released, were officially pardoned in what the *Lincoln Journal Star*—the same newspaper whose coverage condemned Parker—has called, in a series of articles beginning May 5, 2009, "the greatest miscarriage of justice in Nebraska's modern legal history."

The state of Nebraska has yet to exonerate Darrel Parker. In 1969, Parker's conviction was reversed by the United States Court of Appeals for the Eighth Circuit. It is ironic that this was due in large part to the *Miranda* decision, in which the United States Supreme Court, in 1966, condemned Inbau and Reid's psychological techniques, stating that they were "designed to put a suspect in a psychological state where his story is but an elaboration of what the police purport to know already—that he is guilty." The United States Supreme Court, while agreeing with the court of appeals' decision to reverse Parker's conviction, decided that Parker's case should be remanded to the trial court for a new hearing on whether Parker's confession was voluntary. Rather than relitigate the admissibility of the confession, the Lancaster County attorney offered Parker a deal—plead guilty to the murder in exchange for his release from prison for time served. Fearful that his confession would be admitted in his new trial and that he could again be convicted, Darrel Parker chose to take the offer and move on with his life.

Ever since, Parker and his supporters have been seeking to clear his name through the courts and the state clemency process. Parker's initial request for a pardon hearing was denied when the few living Lincoln law enforcement officers involved in his investigation, blinded by tunnel vision, argued that Parker was guilty even in the face of overwhelming evidence that Peery was the perpetrator. After his last ditch attempt to secure an exoneration through the courts was shot down, Parker again sought a pardon in 1991. This time, however, he was willing to accept a general pardon, an act of official forgiveness, rather than an official recognition of his innocence. In an unusual move, his request for a pardon was even supported by the attorney general, who stated that he was not entirely convinced of Parker's guilt. He was granted a pardon by a unanimous vote.

In 2001, Parker learned that DNA evidence was being used in criminal cases and sought to obtain DNA testing of semen samples that were taken from the crime scene. The original rape kit was still in existence as of the early 1990s, when David Strauss began investigating the Parker case for what is now *Barbarous Souls*. By 2001, however, the rape kit had been lost or misplaced, effectively foreclosing Parker from proving that Wesley Peery committed the crime.

The release of *Barbarous Souls* should prompt the attorney general's office to do what it did in the Beatrice Six case—reopen its investigation into the Parker case, including doing a thorough search for the original rape kit from the Nancy Parker murder investigation. With or without the DNA evidence, the attorney general's office should agree to officially clear Parker of his wife's murder and to support efforts through the state legislature to compensate him for the time he spent in prison for a crime he did not commit. Only then will Darrel Parker be given the justice that he deserves.

The Parker, Beatrice Six, and Livers cases should also cause a reexamination of the interrogation techniques used by Nebraska's law enforcement officers and the relationship that these techniques, including the Reid Technique, may have in producing false confessions. In 2008, Nebraska joined ten other states (plus the District of Columbia) in requiring that law enforcement authorities electronically record custodial interrogations of suspects in cases of violent crime. This much-needed reform should enable all the actors in the criminal justice system to better evaluate whether a confession is voluntary and reliable and should help to expose and prevent the problem of police contamination.

Finally, these three cases should cause Nebraskans to question whether to abolish the death penalty given the risks of executing the innocent and the ways in which law enforcement officers use the threat of the death penalty to coerce suspects to confess.